AF714994

Media Technology in Education

Uganda and Beyond

Edited by

Martin A.M. Gansinger and Ayman Kole

Media Technology in Education: Uganda and Beyond

Edited By Martin A.M. Gansinger and Ayman Kole

This book first published 2023

Ethics International Press Ltd, UK

British Library Cataloguing in Publication Data

A catalogue record for this book is available from the British Library

Copyright © 2023 by Ethics International Press

All rights for this book reserved. No part of this book may be reproduced, stored in a retrieval system, or transmitted, in any form or by any means, electronic, mechanical photocopying, recording or otherwise, without the prior permission of the copyright owner.

Print Book ISBN: 978-1-80441-346-3
eBook ISBN: 978-1-80441-347-0

Dedicated to Ismael and Ahmed

Table of Contents

List of Tables

Foreword

Believe it or not, but there are universities that ask their faculties to not include any required reading in their curriculum. Gen Z is used to 'edutainment' and has difficulties with making sense out of an article or even holding their attention in order to go through a book. As a matter of fact, it is becoming a more common observation in personal surroundings concerning regular youths between the ages of twelve and sixteen not being able to finish a single book throughout their entire lives. For those who are actually interested in reading, the task to get their hands on a copy of old-school brainfood can become quite difficult in itself, with libraries justifying the plain absence of literature aiming at teens with the claim that "They only start to read again when they are eighteen." Strange times.

In what can be described as an overall ramification of society, media in its vast variety becomes a more important tool to be applied for educational purposes. This volume aims at providing an overview on the status quo of the challenges and opportunities of today's youth, their use and acquisition of various media formats, and the influence of media channels such as video, games, TikTok, or poetry on contemporary identity constructions.

However, to provide a glimpse into the situation at hand beyond the scope of the sugar-coated parts of the map, this book intends to establish a perspective of the corresponding realities in the global south in the form of Uganda.

The effort to examine the decentralization of public university education in Uganda is being undertaken in Chapter One. The authors put forth a structure that analyzes the process of formation of new public universities and defines the numerous institutions in detail, as well as identifying gaps to be dealt with in the future. The study used a cross sectional research design and relied on official data from reports, legal and statutory instruments, and official web portals of the respective universities.

Chapter Two evaluates instructional approaches and student performances at universities in Uganda by comparing approaches such as face-to-face and more recent concepts like blended learning and computer-based teaching, which were mainly pushed during the Covid years.

However, since learning is a social process, the factor of personal relationships between students and teachers is at least as important as the proper method, as demonstrated in Chapter Three. The contribution highlights the moderating role of academic resilience on the relationship between student satisfaction and academic burnout among graduate students in a society that puts you in an awkward position if you are in your late twenties without a job to support your family.

The cultural memory of education is the central concern of Chapter Four. Its establishment and preservation via the Year Book project and stakeholders such as the Board of Governors, Parent Teachers Association (PTA), Alumni Associations, Administrative and Teaching Staff, and Non-Teaching Staff is demonstrated using content analysis and qualitative interviews. As a result, each school displays a unique kind of digital memory emblematic of the multiple recollections and remembrances of its histories.

As a final contribution highlighting the seldomly visible perspective of Uganda, Chapter Five explores the impact of social media usage, religiosity, and self-esteem on relationship satisfaction among a sample of over four hundred youths, using a questionnaire that combines the Rosenberg Self Esteem Scale, the Beck Anxiety Inventory, Hendrick's Relationship Assessment Scale, and Huber and Huber's Centrality of Religiosity Scale.

The missing medial representation of Afro-Turks and its impact on the identity constructions of those belonging to the ethnic heritage of the

Ottoman involvement in the slave trade is being discussed in Chapter Six. Next to looking at the situation in Turkey, the contribution similarly explores the influence of Ottoman Islam on the formative characters of the Moorish Science Temple in the United States, a central inspiration for subsequent Black Muslim movements such as the Nation of Islam or the Five Percenters.

Similarly, the discourse of exile in poetry is being discussed in Chapter Seven, that uses Mahmoud Darwish's "Contrapuntal" to underline the influence of the author's distance to his Palestinian homeland. The analysis is juxtaposed with the biography of the poet's compatriot Edward Said.

The pedagogical potential of a more contemporary medium is being explored in Chapter Eight, as it provides as detailed discussion of video games as cultural artifacts and how players' morality and ethical decision-making are being challenged through techniques such as ludo narrative dissonance or limited quick time event control schemes. The contribution outlines the highly complex and creative narrative techniques of "NieR: Automata," the ethically challenging "Metal Gear" series, and the cultural critique of Japan's collectivity-oriented social system of conformity articulated in "Persona 5."

While the latter impressively reflects the struggles of Japanese youths in search for individual expression, the closing contribution, investigates Adorno's concept of pseudo individualization regarding representations of subcultural aesthetics in TikTok videos. Hence, Chapter Nine analyses five categories of stylistic aesthetics on TikTok and attests users the consumption of formulaic, commodified popular culture rather than being presented with authentic individual expression.

When putting the finishing touch on this publication, it is not without hope that the proposed youth-oriented topics might inspire the one or the other to take their eyes off the screen, put down their phone, or exchange the joystick in their hands for a copy of this volume, since the need for critical media experts who are looking at the subject from all angles is possibly more urgent right now than ever before.

Martin A. M. Gansinger and Ayman Kole, May 2023

Chapter One
Decentralization of public universities in Uganda: Process, character, and gaps

Joel Isabirye

Introduction

This chapter examines the decentralization of public university education in Uganda seeking to understand the process of formation of new universities, the intrinsic and extrinsic character of the newly established public universities, and the gaps among these universities. Established 1922 as a technical institute, Makerere University became a fully-fledged national university in 1979, and remained the only public university in Uganda until 1989. In the same year, Mbarara University of Science and Technology (MUST) was established by the Government of Uganda and this set the ball rolling for a rapid decentralization that took effect in the 2000s. Currently, Uganda has a total of ten public universities, excluding military universities, and as indicated in Table 1.

No.	University
1.	Makerere University
2.	Mbarara University of Science and Technology
3.	Kyambogo University
4.	Gulu University
5.	Lira University
6.	Soroti University
7.	Busitema University
8.	Kabale University
9.	Muni University

No.	University
10.	Uganda Management Institute

Source: Ministry of Education and Sports (MOES) Republic of Uganda

Table 1-1: *List of public universities in Uganda*

The decentralization process was intended to improve the delivery of educational services at the university level. Instead of students flocking to Kampala, the capital of Uganda, to join Makerere, they would have many options around the country. Decentralization refers to a process of taking governance and programs of service delivery from the center to the regional or local governments, spaces, and communities to enhance participation of the masses in their affairs. The aim of decentralization is to bring services closer to the people to ensure that there is regional balance in the provision of services.

Public university education is a type of educational service that is provided and financed by the state. The capital and operational costs of providing these services are met by central or regional governments, depending on the existing political arrangements in a given country. A salient feature of public university education is that it should be at least partially government funded.

A brief history of public university education in Uganda

The roots of public university education in Uganda are found in the establishment of Makerere Technical School in 1922. The school was set up to impart vocational skills to Africans in the colonial territories of East Africa. Makerere Technical School did not dispose a legal instrument that guided its establishment.[1] It rather functioned as an institution set up to meet the demands for local skilled labor by the colonial government.

[1] Joseph Oloka-Onyango, "The Legal Control of Tertiary Institutions in East Africa: The Case of Makerere University," *Africa Development/Afrique et Développement* 17, No. 4 (1992): 47–66.

In 1937, the colonial Earl De La Warr Commission that inquired into higher education in East Africa recommended the formation of the Higher College of East Africa at Makerere.[2] This represented the first step towards developing a public university in Uganda. As the process of setting up an East African university gained momentum, Martin Luther Nsibirwa, Katikkiro (Prime Minister) of the Kingdom of Buganda, allocated land for the new institution. The territory, which was under dispute by a group of private citizens claiming ownership of the land led to the murder of Nsibirwa on September 4, 1945. However, the land remained with Makerere University.

The Asquith Report of 1949 recommended the enactment of the Makerere College Act forming the Higher College of East Africa at Makerere. Makerere and its constituent colleges in Nairobi and Dar-es-Salaam became an affiliate of the University of London. In 1962, the University of East Africa Act formalized Makerere College, Royal Technical College and University College of Dar-es-Salaam as constituent colleges of the University of East Africa, which was then created in 1963, the year in which the third East African country, Kenya obtained its independence.

1970 saw the dissolution of the University of East Africa, with the Milton Obote I government enacting the Makerere University Kampala Act which parliament provisionally passed on June 29, 1970, and finally enacted on October 5, 1970. Following a protracted guerrilla bush war from 1981 to 1986, the National Resistance

Movement (NRM) came to power. It quickly embarked on revamping the education sector by setting up the Education Policy Review Commission chaired by Professor Senteza-Kajubi.

[2] Earl De La Warr, *African Affairs* 49, No. 196 (July 1950): 250–252.

Kajubi's Commission released a report in January 1989 in which it recommended cost-sharing to be introduced at Makerere and the formation of new universities. Cost-sharing represented the first phase of privatizing public university education in the country. The government made efforts to cover tuition fees of sponsored students along with some basic costs. Students were expected to take care some of their living and academic costs.

In the same year, Mbarara University of Science and Technology (MUST) was created. In 1992, the Government White Paper derived from the Kajubi report was released. It proposed creation of new public universities out of a merger of the Institute of Teachers Education Kyambogo (ITEK), the Uganda Polytechnic Kyambogo (UPK), and the upgrade of the Uganda College of Commerce (UCC) Nakawa into a university. The Kajubi Commission's report also recommended the devolution (decentralization) of education to the districts of Uganda.

Five years later, in 1997, Makerere University Business School, was formed from UCC Nakawa as a constituent college of Makerere University. In 1998, the Uganda Management Institute (UMI) was upgraded into a degree-granting institute. The passing of the Universities and other Tertiary Institutions Act 2001 signified a landmark occasion that accelerated the decentralization (devolution and de-concentration) of public universities in Uganda.

Problem statement

Decentralization of public university education in Uganda was designed to decongest Makerere University and expand the provision of higher education services in Uganda. Since this process started in 1989 and was accelerated in 2002, ten public universities are offering higher educational services to the public.

The sporadic rise in the number of new public universities has changed the landscape of higher education in Uganda, and simultaneously corresponded with mounting discontent with the services offered by these universities (Parliament of the Republic of Uganda 2016).[3] Yet before this decentralization, when there was only one public university in the country, satisfaction with the quality-of-service Makerere offered to the public was high.[4]

In attempts to address the issue of low quality of service in public universities, the focus was put on identifying the gaps in the universities and coming forth with recommendations related to how those gaps can be closed. There have been little attempts to structurally examine the process of creating new public universities and the characteristics of the universities that were created to get to the bottom of the structural challenges faced by public universities in Uganda.

Objectives of the study

1. To analyze the process of formation of new public universities in Uganda
2. To examine the character of new public universities in Uganda
3. To identify gaps at the public universities in Uganda

A review of literature

Place and function of public universities

Public universities by nomenclature are providers of education as a public good, although there are questions of whether education is to be viewed as a public good or not. Education does not fit standard definitions of public goods but because of its inherent spill-over effects

---

[3] Luija Marie Ezati Azikuru, David Onen, and Betty A. Ezati, "The Influence of Planning on the Quality of Teaching in Public Universities, *International Journal of Education and Research* 4, No.12 (December 2016): 121–132; Parliament of the Republic of Uganda, *Report of the Sectoral Committee on Education and Sports on the State of Universities in Uganda, November 2016* (Kampala: Parliament of the Republic of Uganda, 2016).

[4] John Crysostom Ssekamwa, and Sam M. E. Lugumba. *Development and administration of education in Uganda*. Kampala: Fountain Pub Limited, 2001; Mukwanason A. Hyuha, "Uganda: Higher Education Modernization Needed," *International Higher Education* 90 (2017): 21–22.

on an entire nation, there is a tendency to look at it as a public good.[5] For example, the quality of doctors and teachers produced by the education system can impact a country's health and education. The curriculum design presents a strong instrument that shapes local and national values which are not limited to democratic tolerance, patriotism, and ethics.

Guided by the conception that education is a public good, many scholars perceive the provision of public goods to be the responsibility of government, since the allocation of public goods is characterized by non-rivalry and non-excludability in consumption, which cannot be provided by a decentralized market system. According to Itaya, de Meza, and Myles,[6] private provision of public goods is generally inefficient, and government should be a sole or complementary supplier of these goods. Nonetheless, governments the world over maintain a dual service of public and private education.

There are several reasons why national and regional governments continue to establish public universities. According to the American Academy of Arts and Sciences,[7] public universities play a critical role in society. The role of public universities ranges from serving the national interest, contributing to the innovation economy, and providing quality educational opportunities and programs at an efficient cost. In some countries, beyond a practical need to have public universities, these

---

[5] Francine Menashy, "Education as a global public good: The applicability and implications of a framework, "*Globalisation, Societies and Education* 7, No. 3 (2009): 307–320; Anomaly, Jonathan. "Public goods and education." In *Philosophy and Public Policy*, ed. Andrew I. Cohen, (Lanham: Rowman & Littlefield, 2018), 105-120; Tatiana Moşteanu, and Georgiana Creţan, "Education and the Characteristics of Public Goods. Overlaps and Differences," *Theoretical & Applied Economics* 18, No. 9 (2011): 33–40.

[6] Itaya, Jun-ichi, de Meza, de Meza, and Myles, Gareth D. "Who should provide public goods?." In *Incentives, Organization, and Public Economics: Papers in Honour of Sir James Mirrlees*, eds. Peter Hammond, and Gareth D. Myles (New York: Oxford University Press, 2000), 123–150.

[7] American Academy of Arts & Sciences, *Public Research Universities: Why They Matter* (Cambridge: American Academy of Arts & Sciences, 2015).

institutions have served as instruments of national pride and confidence.[8]

The legacy value of university projects can lead nations to invest in them even when there is not determination that it can be viable as a business. Bisaso[9] has referred to the national and regional symbolic value of Makerere University although it was set up to develop human resource capacity. There are times when new public universities may be established to combat brain drain.[10]

According to the National Council for Higher Education, public universities are mostly formed to provide higher education that skills the population so that they can contribute to social transformation. Occasionally, (for example Soroti and Kabale University) they have been formed because communities have lobbied for them.[11] The formation of public universities is sometimes based on the increasing demand from students who in most parts of the world prefer to attend public colleges and universities.[12]

Public universities are attractive to students because they offer funding opportunities. In some countries, public universities have better facilities and have clearer accreditation statuses than private universities. Students' demand for public university education keeps rising as the populations of countries grow. The formation of public universities may then serve to match population growth rates. This has

---

[8] "Starting a New University? Read This First," (n.n.), sasaki.com, January 24, 2017, https://www.sasaki.com/voices/starting-a-new-university-read-this-first/.

[9] Bisaso, Ronald. "Makerere University as a flagship institution: Sustaining the quest for relevance." In *Flagship universities in Africa*, ed. Damtew Teferra (London: Palgrave Macmillan Cham, 2017), 425–466.

[10] "Starting a New University?."

[11] Ogulei, John, "New Soroti University in Illegal Eviction Scandal," *chimpreports.com*, May 23, 2017, https://chimpreports.com/new-soroti-university-in-illegal-eviction-scandal/; Kushaba, Anthony, "Museveni Endorses Take over of Kabale University," March 22, 2012, https://ugandaradionetwork.com/story/museveni-endorses-take-over-of-kabale-university.

[12] Paul N. Courant, Michael McPherson, and Alexandra M. Resch, "The public role in higher education," *National Tax Journal* 59, No. .2 (2006): 291–318.

been the case in Asia, where many public universities have sprouted owing to the rise in population.[13]

The process of forming a public university should ideally be gradual and be implemented in phases. Creating many universities overnight can have a detrimental effect not only on the project implementation, but also on the quality of service it offers. Formation and supervision of universities globally requires specific legal frameworks in respective countries. Public institutions should be governed by a body of laws derived from national constitutions, statutes, agencies, and case law.[14] Coetzee and Mbanze[15] have also argued for the strengthening of the legal framework to guide certain aspects of universities' operations.

In forming public universities, defining their character is of essence. Daniels and Spector[16] characterize the public university in terms of structure and mission. Structurally, public universities are owned by the public or governments, majorly funded by governments, and are at discretion where they are governed by state laws and regulations that shape their conduct. Their mission is to create affordability, accessibility, and community in access to education.

Defining the character of public universities is achieved through the vision and mission statements of the institutions. According to Cortés-Sánchez,[17] mission and vision statements (MS and VS) are the most frequently used strategic planning tools that were adopted in the early 1980s by the higher education sector, becoming tools in crucial practices

---

13 "Starting a New University?."

14 Fred C. Lunenburg, "The Legal Framework for Public Education," *Focus on Colleges, Universities, and Schools* 6, No. 1 (2012): 1–9.

15 Susanna Abigael Coetzee, and C. V. Mbanze, "Merging into a private university: Law regulating the transfer of academic employees in Swaziland." *Journal of Asian and African Studies* 49, No.5 (2014): 584–596.

16 Daniels, Ronald J., and Phillip Spector, "Converging Paths: Public and Private Research Universities in the 21st Century, *University Priorities and Constraints* (2016): 183–201.

17 Julián Cortés-Sánchez, Julián, "Mission and vision statements of universities worldwide: A content analysis," *Documentos De Investigación, Facultad de Administración* 152 (2017): 2463–1892.

implemented in universities worldwide. Frequently, the legal framework and statutory instruments of public universities spell out their vision and missions. The tools help to direct the affairs and business of these institutions.

The decentralization of public universities is certainly transformative but can also have different sets of outcomes. Decentralization of education can bring about a new ecology of education administration and bureaucratization, as in the case of Taiwan.[18]

Public universities in Uganda

There are differing views about the progress of the higher education sector in Uganda. Government and pro-government stakeholders list the rapid growth in the number of universities and tertiary institutions as an exemplification of a sector that has greatly transformed. Critics of government and the sector underscore what they call the deterioration of standards that require a quick fix from the state or other stakeholders.

All the major regions of the country host a public university, which represents a revolution in the education sector. Enrollment numbers have clearly increased, as reflected in the graduation output in recent years as compared to 1988, when there was only one university in the country. In that year, Makerere graduated only 1,320 students.[19] Yet in 2020, Makerere University graduated 13,509 students, while Gulu University listed 1,513 graduates. These figures represent a massive growth in enrollment and output of students who have completed university studies. On the benchmark of enrollment, significant progress has been made.

---

[18] William Yat Wai Lo, "Decentralization of higher education and its implications for educational autonomy in Taiwan," *Asia Pacific Journal of Education* 30, No.2 (2010): 127–139.

[19] Mugaga, Robert, "Makerere Graduated 13 at first graduation," *observer.ug*, January 17, 2010, https://www.observer.ug/component/content/article?id=6824:makerere-graduated-13-at-first-graduation.

The benefits accruing from enrollment have been numerous. More public universities have led to an increase in enrollment and subsequent access to higher education. Due to the growth in the number of particularly public universities, Uganda has been producing more research and has nurtured many experts in different fields.

As public universities the world over struggle with lack of funding, Court[20] applauded Makerere University for managing to raise funding to sustain itself. The critics of Uganda's public university education sector and concerned stakeholders point out several issues that hint towards problematic aspects. One of the challenges faced by public universities in Uganda is inadequate funding, with universities only being able to afford to meet thirty percent of the cost of educating a student.[21]

Lack of funds makes it difficult for universities to deliver quality education and research.[22] This circumstance, coupled with a lack of policies on research, has resulted in low levels of research output.[23] Although some studies apportion blame on government for failing to fund research, Rwothumio, Okaka, Kambaza and Kyomukama[24] suggest that staff at public universities lacks interest in conducting

---

[20] Court, David, "Financing higher education in Africa: Makerere, the quiet revolution," *Perspectives in Education* 19, No. 2 (2001): 3–22.

[21] Parliament of the Republic of Uganda, *Report of the Sectoral Committee on Education and Sports on the State of Universities in Uganda, November 2016* (Kampala: Parliament of the Republic of Uganda, 2016); Muriisa Roberts Kabeba, "Financial reforms and governance and the crisis in research in public universities in Africa: a case of Uganda," *Journal of Educational Administration and Policy Studies* 2, No. 7 (2010).

[22] Julius Omona, "Funding higher education in Uganda: modalities, challenges and opportunities in the twenty-first century," *Makerere Journal of Higher Education* 4, No.1 (2012): 11–44; S. Asiimwe, and G. M. Steyn, "Obstacles Hindering the Effective Governance of Universities in Uganda," *Journal of Social Sciences* 34, No. 1 (2013): 17–27; Hyuha, "Uganda."

[23] Amina Nakimuli, and Abanis Turyahebwa, "Institutional efficiency in selected universities in Uganda," *Journal of Education and Practice* 6, No. 10 (2015): 90–96.

[24] Joseph Rwothumio, Wilson Okaka, Stephen Kambaza, and Eugene Kyomukama,"Influence of performance appraisal in determining academic staff performance in public universities in Uganda," *International Journal of Advanced Research* 3, No. 1 (2021): 20–32.

research because they do not see how it is related to their performance. Conversely, the low levels of research output act diametral to the competitiveness of the universities in bidding for research funding when these opportunities are availed.

Ssentamu, former Vice Chancellor of Makerere, is reported to have told Parliament in Uganda that there was no need for government to keep creating new universities when it could not fund or manage the existing ones, particularly Makerere. This view was re-echoed by the Ministry of Finance and Economic Planning's recommendation that the government should stop creating new universities and instead fund existing ones. Decline in public university funding is not restricted to Uganda. Across the world, it has been noted that the education landscape has changed drastically over the last thirty years, and this calls for public universities to look for new ways of funding.[25]

Several stakeholders are quick to point out that public universities in Uganda suffer from low quality of education and poor quality of graduates.[26] It is also observed that ineffective teaching, low research output and missing publications continue to prevail, making it difficult for public universities to produce the needed human resources for national development.[27] This is partly attributed to the marketisation of public universities. Marketization/privatization, starting with Makerere, seemed to save public institutions from resource starvation until there were too many of them competing over a limited number of students. Competition regarding enrollment numbers had some of them admitting mediocre students.

---

25 Piereson, James, and Schaefer Riley, Naomi, "Reimagining the Public University," *nationalaffairs.com,* Winter 2020, https://www.nationalaffairs.com/PUBLICATIONS/DETAIL/REIMAGINING-THE-PUBLIC-UNIVERSITY.

26 Victoria Tamale Kaggwa, Denis Sekiwu, and Frances Esther Naluwemba, "Student expectations and quality of postgraduate education: the case for public universities in Uganda," *Advances in Social Sciences Research Journal* 4, No. 21 (November 2018): 25–50.

27 Rwothumio, Okaka, Kambaza, and Kyomukama,"Influence of performance."

It also led to fragmentation of courses, duplication of degrees, and elite capture, where politicians lobbied government to create new universities so that they could get mileage and jobs for people in their constituencies. The weak legal framework, which is not comprehensive and lacks financing strategies and principles of allocating public funds and accountability and operationalized quality assurance mechanisms, has been identified as a major reason for difficulties to streamline the management of public universities.

Public outcry about the low enrollment in many public universities raises the question of insufficient calculations during the planning phase. Lack of specialization between the public universities appears to have exacerbated the low enrollment of students and made it difficult for them to increase staff. However, quite early educationist Michel Lejeune, who served as the inaugural chairperson of the Uganda National Council for Higher Education (UNCHE), argued that Makerere had an advantage over other emerging public universities, because of its location in the city. This made it attractive to young students who are typically interested in studying in the capital city. Makerere also benefited from a brand name and receives the lion share of donor funding to public universities in Uganda. Perhaps, it would have been better for the decentralization process to create all new universities as constituent colleges of Makerere University.

One of the other major issues with public universities in Uganda can be found in the curriculum development. From duplication and fragmentation of courses to most of the 1,800 courses that were found by the committee not corresponding with the job market, the curriculum design is clearly inhibiting progress at these universities.[28] With many different courses available on the market, universities are having it difficult to attract students into mainstream faculties and colleges. The orientation of most of the public universities to science is

[28] Parliament of the Republic of Uganda, "Report."

affecting enrollment forcing some of them to introduce courses from the humanities.

Nakimuli and Turyahebwa[29] have observed that gender disparities remain main concerns in public university administration and in enrollment respectively. There are clearly more males than females in administrative positions and among those admitted at the universities. Similarly, Lubaale[30] has decried the lack of inclusive education in public universities in Uganda, which has affected accessibility to higher education for disabled and marginalized Ugandans.

The Ministry of Finance, Planning and Economic Development implores public universities in Uganda to diverse their sources of income if they are to meet their costs of operation. This advice coming from government indicates that it shall not in the short run be able to adjust funding levels to cover all the requirements of public universities in the country.

Methodology

The study used cross-sectional design in that it analyzed all the public universities at one point in time. Data was collected from analysis of secondary documents such as legal instruments and reports, in addition to examining the official web portals of each public university. The data was evaluated via thematic analysis by clustering thematic trends revealed by the data into meaningful categories. Effort was made to delineate the themes in relation to the objectives of the study.

---

[29] Nakimuli, and Turyahebwa, "Institutional efficiency."

[30] Grace Lubaale, "Inclusive Education Implementation in Public Universities of Uganda and Development Implications," *Research Journal of Educational Studies and Review* 6, No. 2 (2020): 29–39.

Findings

Objective 1: Analyze the process and modes of formation of Uganda's new public universities

The process of forming the universities was defined by the three steps of start-up, takeover and upgrade. Six of the public universities (Busitema, Gulu, Kyambogo, Lira, Makerere and Mbarara) were upgraded from existing tertiary institutions. Two (Soroti and Muni) were start-ups, and one (Kabale) was a takeover from private entrepreneurs who owned the university as shown below:

University	Mode of Formation (start up, takeover and upgrade)
Makerere University	Upgrade from Technical Institute
Mbarara University of Science and Technology (MUST)	Upgrade School of Midwifery at the Mbarara District Hospital
Kyambogo	Upgrade Polytechnic Kyambogo (UPK), the Institute of Teacher Education, Kyambogo (ITEK), and the Uganda National Institute of Special Education (UNISE)
Gulu University	Upgrade Gulu District Farm Institute
Busitema University	Upgrade *Busitema* Agricultural *Institute*
Lira University	Upgrade Gulu University Constituent College
Soroti University	Start Up
Muni University	Start Up
Kabale University	Takeover

Source: field data

Table 1-2: *Modes of formation of Uganda's public universities*

Legal framework

Except for Makerere University, MUST and UMI, most of the public universities in Uganda were established with the Universities and Other Tertiary Institutions Act 2001. MUST passed as a pilot test for government to venture into university education outside of Makerere. Each university was established by a statutory instrument of the act of parliament making it a national project with a valid legal mandate to offer educational services:

University	Legal Framework	Actual Date of Formation
Makerere University	Makerere University Kampala Act 1970	1970
Mbarara University of Science and Technology (MUST)	The Mbarara University of Science and Technology Statute 1989	1989
Gulu University	STATUTORY INSTRUMENTS 2003 No. 31. The Universities and Other Tertiary Institutions (Establishment of Gulu University) Instrument, 2003.	2002
Kyambogo	STATUTORY INSTRUMENTS 2003 No. 37. The Universities and Other Tertiary Institutions (Establishment of Kyambogo University) Instrument, 2003.	2003
Busitema University	STATUTORY INSTRUMENTS 2007 No. 22. The Universities and Other Tertiary Institutions (Establishment of Busitema University) Instrument, 2007	2007
Muni University	STATUTORY INSTRUMENTS 2013 No. 31. The Universities and Other Tertiary Institutions	2013

University	Legal Framework	Actual Date of Formation
	(Establishment of Muni University) Instrument, 2013	
Kabale University	STATUTORY INSTRUMENTS 2015 No. 36. The Universities and Other Tertiary Institutions (Establishment of Kabale University) Instrument, 2015.	2015
Lira University	STATUTORY INSTRUMENTS 2015 No. 35. The Universities and Other Tertiary Institutions (Establishment of Lira University) Instrument, 2015	2015
Soroti University	STATUTORY INSTRUMENTS 2015 No. 34. The Universities and Other Tertiary Institutions (Establishment of Soroti University) Instrument, 2015.	2017

Source: field data

Table 1-3: *Legal framework for establishing public universities in Uganda*

Objective 2: Examine the Character of Uganda's new public universities' objectives of formation

The objectives of formation (vision, mission, objects, and function) of each public university were examined by looking at the statutory instruments that were created when they were formed.

Vision and Mission of the University

Except for Makerere, all the other universities had vision and mission statements listed on their web portals or the statutory instruments that formed them. Kabale, Lira and Soroti universities did not have their vision and mission stated in the statutory instruments, but they were derived from their web portals. Only two public universities (Kyambogo which listed science and Gulu which noted biodiversity) explicitly stated that they were focused on science as indicated below:

University	Vision	Mission
Makerere University	Not found	Not found
Mbarara University of Science and Technology (MUST)	**Found on website:** To provide quality and relevant education at national and international levels with particular emphasis on science and technology and its application to community development	**Found on website:** To be a center of academic and professional excellence in science and technology
Kyambogo	To be a center of academic and professional excellence	To advance and promote knowledge and development of skills in science, technology, and education and in other fields, having regard to quality, equity, and the progress of society, to provide professional support and to provide a learning environment conducive for disadvantaged persons and persons having special educational needs
Gulu University	To be the leading academic institution for the promotion of rural transformation and	To expand access to higher education, conduct applied research and

University	Vision	Mission
	industrialization for sustainable development	provide quality professional training to the delivery of appropriate services directed towards social transformation and conservation of biodiversity
Busitema University	To be a center of excellence in developing practical, innovative, and motivated graduates who effectively respond to local and international communities	To enhance professionalism and innovativeness through research and community service for the transformation of society and sustainable development
Lira University	**Found on website:** To be a center of applied science and technology	**Found on website:** To provide access to quality higher education, research and to conduct professional training for the delivery of appropriate health services directed towards sustainable health, community, and environment.
Soroti University	**Found on website:** To be a center of academic excellence and professionalism	**Found on website:** To provide knowledge, skills and innovations for sustainable development and transformation

University	Vision	Mission
Muni University	To be a model academic and professional University for transformation and development	To provide quality education, generate knowledge, promote innovation and community empowerment for transformation
Kabale University	**Found on website:** To be a sustainable, vibrant university of academic excellence in the Great Lakes Region and beyond	**Found on website:** To be an efficient and effective university that excels in teaching, learning, research, innovation, and community engagement

Source: field data

Table 1-4: *Vision and mission statements of public universities in Uganda*

Objectives for Formation

Regarding the objectives for formation of the public universities, Busitema, Kabale, Lira, and Soroti universities were found to boast the very same objectives stated word for word, while there were none listed by Makerere

University. The first objective for Gulu and Muni universities were the same. The two universities (Gulu and Muni) also clearly state their orientation to science. Table 5 displays the objectives of formation for the various public universities in Uganda.

University	Objectives
Makerere University	Not found
Mbarara University of Science and Technology (MUST)	Not found

University	Objectives
Kyambogo	(a) to equitably expand access to higher education; (b) to produce highly and practically skilled manpower for service to society; (c) to reduce duplication of areas of study in institutions with close proximity and to enhance efficiency and cost effectiveness; (d) to strengthen and expand vocational studies; (e) to spearhead applied research; (f) to initiate and promote innovations in education and technology; (g) to equip technicians, engineers and teachers of technical subjects with required skills for manning the construction service, manufacturing industries and educational institutions, including universities, schools and research organizations; (h) to promote better understanding of the basic principles and methodology along with practical knowledge of construction, application, properties, operations and limitations of engineering systems, materials, processes and equipment; (i) to provide scientific and mathematical foundation to enable the recipients handle competently the technological aspects of the training; (j) to equip graduates with the analytical tools required to solve problems utilizing their scientific knowledge and appropriate technology either under the supervision of an engineer or independently; (k) to initiate, encourage and promote specific and specialized research in scientific, technical and technological fields in accordance with the needs of Uganda; (l) to promote the acquisition, adaptation and application of information technology and to solve the social, economic and educational problems of Uganda;

University	Objectives
	(m) to aim at ensuring an increased number of learners with special educational needs and to ensure that the learners receive equitable and quality education, through providing professional manpower to secure effective support of training needs; (n) to provide training for teachers and other personnel working in the field of special needs education and rehabilitation, and to cater for all kinds of persons with disabilities and special learning needs; (o) to provide a resource center for the production and dissemination of information relating to persons with disabilities and special learning needs; (p) to undertake research in disabilities and other related fields for better understanding and development of persons with disabilities and special learning needs; and (q) to initiate outreach programs to promote greater awareness among teachers, parents, leaders and the general public about persons with disabilities and special learning needs; and to promote partnership and collaboration among agencies involved in dealing with persons with disabilities.
Gulu University	(a) equitably expand higher education; (b) increase the number of basic and applied science teachers; (c) increase professionals in agriculture and environmental sciences; (d) produce engineering and technology graduates and cadres appropriate for rural industrialization; (e) produce medical personnel and health service cadres for the delivery of medical and health services in rural settings; (f) develop the appropriate human resources to match the management and administrative

University	Objectives
	demands of the decentralized system of government; (g) undertake applied research towards rural transformation; and (h) generally provide quality training in various training as need may arise.
Busitema, Kabale, Lira, and Soroti	(a) to be the standard of excellence and innovation for societal transformation; (b) to be a leader in integrating scholarship and practice; (c) to serve societal needs and to foster social and economic development; (d) to be global in perspective, organization and action; (e) to engage staff and students in creative and rewarding learning so as to enhance economic and societal development in Uganda and beyond; and (f) to assist local communities and to build their capacity for socioeconomic enhancement.
Muni University	(a) to equitably expand higher education at undergraduate and post graduate levels; (b) to increase the number of scientists in Uganda that include basic and applied science and science teachers; (c) to develop human resources appropriate for a decentralized system of governance; (d) to produce engineering, technology and medical personnel appropriate for rural industrialization and development; and (e) to undertake basic applied research geared towards rural transformation.

Source: field data

Table 1-5: *Objectives for formation for public universities in Uganda*

Functions of the university

Six universities (Busitema, Gulu, Kabale, Lira, Muni and Soroti) had the same functions stated except that Muni University did not include the last function, and where the word 'sex' was used it used the word 'gender.' Table 6 lists the respective functions of the public universities in Uganda.

University	Functions
Makerere University	Not found
Mbarara University of Science and Technology (MUST)	Not found
Kyambogo	(a) to provide instruction to all those admitted to the University and to make provision for the advancement, transmission and preservation of knowledge, and to stimulate intellectual life in Uganda; (b) to conduct pre-service training in the field of Teacher Education leading to awards of certificates, diplomas and degrees; (c) to conduct in-service education for teachers including teachers in special needs education and technical education; (d) to organize and conduct refresher courses, seminars and conferences for teachers, special needs teachers, education administrators and inspectors of schools; (e) to organize and conduct courses in teaching, special needs education, and communication skills to lecturers and tutors from all institutions in the country engaged in specialized human resource development; (f) to coordinate with all Teachers' Colleges with the objective of developing curricula and achieving high standards of education; (g) to undertake the development and organization of an education resource and service center in education and to run an orientation and

University	Functions
	mobility center for training and demonstration for purposes of special needs education; (h) to organize and conduct courses for teachers and other personnel working in the field of special needs education and rehabilitation; (i) to conduct examinations and award certificates, diplomas and degrees, and where necessary to revoke such awards; (j) to undertake the development and sustenance of research and publication in education, science, technology and technical fields; (k) to disseminate knowledge and give an opportunity of acquiring higher education to all persons, including persons with disabilities, regardless of race, political opinion, color, creed or sex; (l) to provide accessible physical facilities to the users of the University; (m) to conduct courses in science, engineering, construction, manufacturing, information technology and other practical courses; (n) to supervise its constituent colleges and institutions; (o) to do any other thing geared at the enhancement and development of technical, scientific and practical courses, education and special education and rehabilitation; and (p) to do any other thing which is incidental or connected to the foregoing.
Busitema, Gulu, Kabale, Lira, Muni, Soroti	(a) to provide instruction to all those admitted to the University and to make provision for the advancement, transmission and preservation of knowledge, and to stimulate intellectual life in Uganda; (b) to organize and conduct courses with particular emphasis on medical, agriculture, environmental and other sciences; (c) to conduct examinations and award certificates, diplomas and degrees, and where

University	Functions
	necessary to revoke such awards; (d) to undertake the development and sustenance of research and publication with particular emphasis in medical, agriculture, environment and other sciences; (e) to disseminate knowledge and give opportunity of acquiring higher education to all persons, including persons with disabilities, wishing to do so regardless of race, political opinion, colour, creed or sex; and (f) to provide accessible physical facilities to the users of the University.

Source: field data

Table 1-6: *Functions of the public universities in Uganda*

Regional character

There is proportionate distribution of universities across regions of Uganda. Three of the public universities are located in the northern region of the country, while two are located in each of central, eastern and western regions of Uganda. However, in terms of subregion, the universities are being located in only eight out Uganda's fifteen subregions, namely: Acholi, Ankole, Buganda, Bukedi, Kigezi, Lango, Teso, and West Nile (see Table 7). Bugisu, Bunyoro, Busoga, Karamoja, Rwenzori, Sebei, and Tooro subregions do not have a public university of their own, although some have campuses of the existing public universities.

Region	Subregion	University
Central	Buganda	Makerere University
Central	Buganda	Kyambogo
Eastern	Bukedi	Busitema University
Eastern	Teso	Soroti University
Northern	Acholi	Gulu University
Northern	Lango	Lira University
Northern	West Nile	Muni University
Western	Kigezi	Kabale University

Western	Ankole	Mbarara University of Science and Technology (MUST)

Source: field data

Table 1-7: *Regional and subregional distribution of public universities in Uganda*

Local and regional representation in public university administration

In five of the existing public universities (Gulu, Kabale, Lira, Muni and Soroti), the vice chancellors either came from the subregion in which the university is located or within the region it is situated, as demonstrated below:

University	Vice Chancellor	District	Subregion	Region
Makerere University	Barnabas Nawange	Busia	Bukedi	Eastern
Kyambogo	Eli Katunguka			Western
Busitema University	Paul Waako	Mayuge	Busoga	Eastern
Soroti University	Robert Ikoja-Odong	Soroti	Teso	Eastern
Gulu University	George Openjuru	Gulu	Acholi	Northern
Lira University	Jasper Ogwal Okeng		Lango	Northern
Muni University	Christine Dranzoa	Moyo	West Nile	Northern
Kabale University	Joy Kwesiga	Kabale	Kigezi	Western
Mbarara University of Science and Technology (MUST)	Celestine Obua		Lango	Eastern

Source: field data

Table 1-8: *Local and regional representation in Vice Chancellors of public universities in Uganda*

Discipline orientation of the public universities

Except for Makerere, which employs colleges as the main academic units, all the other public universities use faculties. As reflected in their academic units, all the universities were oriented towards science disciplines, with all of them having more science faculties than humanities. Two public universities (Soroti and Kabale) had only science faculties. Forty-seven faculties or colleges were found across all the public universities, with thirty-two of them listed as having a science orientation and fifteen stated to be oriented towards the humanities.

The most common faculty or college was science, which was listed three times, followed by faculty of medicine, health sciences and engineering, all listed twice. In terms of discipline, engineering appears six times, followed by five listings of agriculture:

No.	University	Faculties and Colleges	Number of Faculties and Colleges	Science	Humanities
1.	Makerere University	1.College of Agricultural and Environmental Sciences 2.College of Business and Management Sciences 3.College of Computing and Information Sciences 4.College of Education and External Studies 5.College of Engineering, Design, Art and Technology 6.College of Health Sciences 7.College of Humanities and Social Sciences 8.College of Natural Sciences 9.College of Veterinary Medicine, Animal Resources and Biosecurity 10.The School of Law	10	6	4
2.	Mbarara University of Science and Technology	1.Faculty of Applied Sciences and Technology 2.Faculty of Business and Management Sciences 3.Faculty of Computing and Informatics 4.Faculty of Interdisciplinary Studies 5.Faculty of Science 6.Faculty of Medicine	6	4	2

No.	University	Faculties and Colleges	Number of Faculties and Colleges	Science	Humanities
3.	Kyambogo University	1.Faculty of Engineering 2.Faculty of Science 3.Faculty of Arts and Social Science 4.Faculty of Education 5.Faculty of Special Needs and Rehabilitation 6.Faculty of Vocational Studies	6	3	3
4.	Gulu University	1.Faculty of Science 2.Faculty of Business and Development Studies 3.Faculty of Agriculture and Environment 4.Faculty of Education and Humanities 5.Faculty of Medicine 6.Faculty of Law	6	3	3
5.	Lira University	1.Faculty of Engineering and Technology 2.Faculty of Health Sciences 3.Institute of Management Science 4.Institute of Medicinal Plants and Biodiversity	4	3	1
6.	Soroti University	1.School of Health Sciences 2.School of Engineering and Technology	2	2	0

No.	University	Faculties and Colleges	Number of Faculties and Colleges	Science	Humanities
7.	Busitema University	1.Faculty of Engineering 2.Faculty of Science and Education 3.Faculty of Health Sciences 4.Faculty of Agriculture and Animal Sciences 5.Faculty of Natural Resources and Environment 6.Faculty of Management Sciences	6	5	1
8.	Kabale University	1.School of Medicine 2.Faculty of Agriculture and Environmental Sciences 3.Faculty of Engineering, Technology, Applied Design and Fine Art 4.Faculty of Computing, Library and Information Sciences	4	4	0
9.	Muni University	1.Faculty of Technoscience 2.Faculty of Agriculture and Environmental Science 3.Faculty of Management Science	3	2	1
10.	Uganda Management Institute	No faculties	0	0	0
		Total	47	32	15

Table 1-9: *Faculties and colleges at public universities in Uganda* Source: field data

Funding models for public universities in Uganda

All the universities had a three-part funding model: government, private students and grants, as indicated below:

No.	University	Funding Model
1.	Makerere University	Government, Private Students and Grants
2.	Mbarara University of Science and Technology	Government, Private Students and Grants
3.	Kyambogo University	Government, Private Students and Grants
4.	Gulu University	Government, Private Students and Grants
5.	Lira University	Government, Private Students and Grants
6.	Soroti University	Government, Private Students and Grants
7.	Busitema University	Government, Private Students and Grants
8.	Kabale University	Government, Private Students and Grants
9.	Muni University	Government, Private Students and Grants
10.	Uganda Management Institute	Government, Private Students and Grants

Table 1-10: *Funding models for public universities in Uganda*

Objective 3: To identify gaps at the public universities

Since their establishment, there have been serious challenges affecting the operations of the new and old public universities. A report from the Parliament of the Republic of Uganda[31] presents the most pressing problems at each university, as reflected in Table 11.

[31] Parliament of the Republic of Uganda, "Report."

University	Gaps
Makerere	• Funding Gaps (arrears, research, land issues, decaying infrastructure) • Lack of staff and facilities for dentistry • Brain drain due to poor remuneration
Mbarara University of Science and Technology (MUST)	• No accommodation and transport for students and staff at new site • Lacks equipment for training doctors and nurses and dental surgery
Kabale University	• Funding Gaps (arrears prior to acquisition, only portion of wage bill met by Government)
Lira University	• Incomplete facilities • Funding Gaps (infrastructure and staff)
Gulu University	• Funding Gaps (development budget)
Busitema University	• Medical School no premises of its own • Lacks staff and equipment • Funding Gap (presidential pledge not met)
Soroti University	• Funding Gap (delayed construction)

Source: Parliament of the Republic of Uganda (2016)

Table 1-11: *Gaps at public universities in Uganda*

Discussion

The formation process of public universities in Uganda consisted of three major steps: start-up, takeover, and upgrade. Startups made use of resources provided by the government to develop universities from scratch. Upgrade on the other had involves the government taking up existing educational institutions and developing them into fully fledged universities. Takeovers were defined by privately owned universities taken over by government. Six of the universities emerged from out of an upgrading process. These include: Busitema, Gulu, Kyambogo, Lira, Makerere and Mbarara. Two universities (Soroti and Muni) were set up from scratch, while Kabale was taken over from private entrepreneurs.

Upgrades display an advantage over others in that they provide a starting foundation for the universities to build on pre-existent premises, infrastructure, facilities, and staff. On the other hand, upgrades dissolve other tertiary institutions that offer educational services. Startups are more difficult to set up because land, premises, infrastructure, and staff are to be sourced. This may affect the timely implementation of the project. Like upgrades, takeovers are easier to implement because the basic capacity to operate the university is in place.

The creation of a clear legal framework for the establishment of the public universities served to empower these institutions and guide the implementation of the projects. For example, the overarching Universities and other Tertiary Institutions Act prescribed the full components and processes of public universities in Uganda. The

statutory instruments derived from the act established for each university a specific mandate, objective, and function. The dates of each statutory instrument of the public universities in Uganda also demonstrate that the setting up of some of the institutions was rushed. For example, three institutions were set up between 2002 and 2007 and three others were set up or taken over in 2015.

This overburdened the government in providing proper resources and explains why most of the public universities continue to face teething problems. According to the Ministry of Finance Planning and Economic Development, the increase in the number of public universities amplified the burden of funding six-fold from Ug shs 167.94 billion in Financial Year 2012/2013 to Ug shs 606.09 billion in Financial Year 2017/2018. The formation of Soroti, Lira and Kabale universities forced government to divert some of the money meant for payment of non-teaching staff in the other public universities.

The statutory instruments to a certain extent tried to define the character of each public university in Uganda. Each had a distinct vision and mission except for Lira University, Soroti University, and Kabale

University, which were all formed in 2015. However, their web portals stated their vision and mission statements. The vision and mission statements for Makerere University were not found, while those for MUST were found to be available on their web portals.

Theoretically, differentiating the vision and mission statements of each university is aiming at creating unique and specialized public universities. The focus of their colleges however paints a very different picture since there are striking duplications of courses. Apart from Makerere and MUST, each of the other public universities display objectives of formation. However, four universities (Busitema, Kabale, Lira and Soroti public universities) were revealed to use the same objectives written word for word. This potentially makes it difficult to differentiate these institutions.

Gulu and Muni universities shared the same first objective. Similarity in the objectives of some of the universities implies that there was little effort made to create unique institutions. This circumstance seemed to have an impact on the creation of duplicated courses, which could have hampered enrollment in public universities in Uganda. Kyambogo university's objective (c) recognizes this problem by stating that the university intends to reduce duplication of areas of study in institutions within proximity. None of the other public universities provided a stated objective to do so.

The same situation applies to the stated functions of the universities. Six of them (Busitema, Gulu, Kabale, Lira, Muni and Soroti) listed the same functions except for a slight variation regarding the last function in the case of Muni university. This is likely to cause similarity in the services offered by the respective universities.

The data indicates that regionalism underpinned the formation of many if not all the new public universities that were established after 2001. The desire to have regional balance in the establishment of the institutions was commendable. So far, all the regions of Uganda host at least two public universities. At the level of subregion, a lot more work needs to be done. There is a disproportionate representation of public universities and yet in Uganda, the subregions are critical markers of identities for the people. For example, Bugisu, Bunyoro, Busoga, Karamoja, Rwenzori, Sebei, and Toro lack public universities. This pattern could spark off a sense of alienation and deprivation amongst the affected subregions.

At least half of the public universities employ vice chancellors who hail from the subregions in which they are situated. It is not clear if this is intended, because the statutory instruments and the Universities and other Tertiary Institutions Act 2001 do not specify this as a requirement for their operations. In fact, the only local involvement in the governance of the university is in the membership of the University Council, where one representative from the District Council in the district in which the university is located, is referenced. Nonetheless, this trend is equally commendable since it creates a feeling of ownership of these university projects within the communities in which they are located.

The biggest challenge, however, is the stunning similarity in the colleges and faculties constituting the institutions. Most of the universities offer similar colleges and faculties and therefore offer similar courses as well. The aim of this structure was to deconcentrate courses offered by the pioneering public university, Makerere. This would have had a positive effect if the universities were only mandated to enroll students from their regional locations. Without this precondition, the institutions find themselves competing for students from across the country, for which a clear specialization and positioning of each university would have been necessary. This has grossly affected enrollment in the public universities.

Thirty-two of the forty-seven colleges and faculties in the public universities were science based, leaving only fifteen oriented towards the humanities. This suggests that the government is aggressively pursuing its science first policy. There is, however, a danger of eventually pushing the humanities aside, which would have adverse consequences for Uganda. All the public universities examined demonstrate the same three-part funding model of government funds, private student tuition, and grants. The failure to think beyond this model has negatively affected the public universities operations that are perennially beset by funding gaps.

Several gaps at the public universities have been identified since the enactment of the Universities and other Tertiary Institutions Act 2001. A report from the committee of education in parliament, listed funding, infrastructure, and inadequate staff as some of the persistent problems that asked for immediate attention. The data indicates that some of the gaps emanate from the structural process of setting up these universities, during which there has been limited attention being paid to the criteria for how the universities are supposed to be set up.

Conclusions

This chapter revealed that Uganda has made strides in the establishment of at least seven new public universities since 2001. The universities have boosted enrollment and graduation of students and in many of them, research output has moderately improved. The universities are proportionately distributed across regions, but there is need to situate more public universities in the subregions, to avoid a feeling of bias amongst communities that do not have any. This should however only be done when there are sufficient resources to fund the development of new universities.

Public universities in Uganda were founded with strong legislation in the Universities and other Tertiary Institutions Act, which created the foundation for the establishment of the universities. The statutory instruments are good tools for guiding the operations of the institutions. Where duplications exist, there should be revisions to afford these universities a chance to be unique spaces for offering public university education in the country.

Due to the global trend in decline in funding of public universities, these institutions are advised to look for more recent models of funding that will support their search for resources to operate. These funding models may have to do with engaging the private sector of coming up with plans and packages for students and external stakeholders. Additionally, there should be more local participation in the governance structure of the universities. Representation of districts, local governments and regional and cultural institutions should be increased as well.

Bibliography

American Academy of Arts & Sciences. 2015. *Public Research Universities: Why They Matter*. Cambridge:

American Academy of Arts & Sciences.

Anomaly, Jonathan. "Public goods and education." In *Philosophy and Public Policy* , ed. Andrew I. Cohen, 105–

120 (Lanham: Rowman & Littlefield, 2018).

Bisaso, Ronald. "Makerere University as a flagship institution: Sustaining the quest for relevance." In *Flagship universities in Africa,* ed. Damtew Teferra, 425–466 (London: Palgrave Macmillan Cham, 2017).

Coetzee, Susanna Abigael, and Mbanze, C. V. "Merging into a private university: Law regulating the transfer of academic employees in Swaziland." *Journal of Asian and African Studies* 49, No.5 (2014): 584–596, doi: 10.1177/0021909613507043.

Cortés-Sánchez, Julián. "Mission and vision statements of universities worldwide: A content analysis." *Documentos De Investigación, Facultad de Administración* 152 (2017): 2463–1892.

Courant, Paul N., McPherson, Michael, and Resch, Alexandra M. "The public role in higher education." *National Tax Journal* 59, No. .2 (2006): 291–318.

Court, David. "Financing higher education in Africa: Makerere, the quiet revolution." *Perspectives in Education* 19, No. 2 (2001): 3–22.

De La Warr, Earl. *African Affairs* 49, No. 196 (July 1950): 250–252, doi.org/10.1093/oxfordjournals.afraf.a093826.

Ezati Azikuru, Luija Marie, Onen, David, and Ezati, Betty A. "The Influence of Planning on the Quality of Teaching in Public Universities." *International Journal of Education and Research* 4, No.12 (December 2016): 121–132.

Hyuha, Mukwanason A. "Uganda: Higher Education Modernization Needed." *International Higher Education* 90 (2017): 21-22, doi/org/10.6017/ihe.2017.90.9791

Itaya, Jun-ichi, de Meza, de Meza, and Myles, Gareth D. "Who should provide public goods?." In *Incentives, Organization, and Public Economics: Papers in Honour of Sir James Mirrlees* , eds. Peter Hammond, and Gareth D. Myles, 123–150 (New York: Oxford University Press, 2000).

Kaggwa, Victoria Tamale, Sekiwu, Denis, and Naluwemba, Frances Esther. "Student expectations and quality of postgraduate education: the case for public universities in Uganda." *Advances in Social Sciences Research Journal* 4, No. 21 (November 2018): 25–50, doi: 10.14738/assrj.421.3756.

Lo, William Yat Wai Lo. "Decentralization of higher education and its implications for educational autonomy in Taiwan." *Asia Pacific Journal of Education* 30, No.2 (2010): 127–139, doi: 10.1080/02188791003721572.

Lubaale, Grace. "Inclusive Education Implementation in Public Universities of Uganda and Development Implications." *Research Journal of Educational Studies and Review* 6, No. 2 (2020): 29–39.

Lunenburg, Fred C. "The Legal Framework for Public Education." *Focus on Colleges, Universities, and Schools* 6, No. 1 (2012): 1–9.

Menashy, Francine. "Education as a global public good: The applicability and implications of a framework," *Globalisation, Societies and Education* 7, No. 3 (2009): 307–320, doi.org/10.1080/14767720903166111.

Moşteanu, Tatiana, and Creţan, Georgiana. "Education and the Characteristics of Public Goods. Overlaps and Differences." *Theoretical & Applied Economics* 18, No. 9 (2011): 33–40.

Mugaga, Robert. "Makerere Graduated 13 at first graduation." *observer.ug*. January 17, 2010, https://www.observer.ug/component/content/article?id=6824:makerere-graduated-13-at-first-graduation.

Nakimuli, Amina, and Turyahebwa, Abanis. "Institutional efficiency in selected universities in Uganda." *Journal of Education and Practice* 6, No. 10 (2015): 90-96. "How Museveni has revolutionalized the Education sector." *nrm.ug*. (n.d.). https://nrm.ug/blog/how-museveni-has-revolutionalized-education-sector.

Ogulei, John. "New Soroti University in Illegal Eviction Scandal." *chimpreports.com*. May 23, 2017, https://chimpreports.com/new-soroti-university-in-illegal-eviction-scandal/.

Oloka-Onyango, Joseph. "The Legal Control of Tertiary Institutions in East Africa: The Case of Makerere University." *Africa Development/Afrique et Développement* 17, No. 4 (1992): 47–66, https://www.jstor.org/stable/43658275.

Omona, Julius. "Funding higher education in Uganda: modalities, challenges and opportunities in the twenty-first century." *Makerere Journal of Higher Education* 4, No.1 (2012): 11–44.

Parliament of the Republic of Uganda. 2016. *Report of the Sectoral Committee on Education and Sports on the State of Universities in Uganda, November 2016*. Kampala: Parliament of the Republic of Uganda.

Piereson, James, and Schaefer Riley, Naomi. "Reimagining the Public University." *nationalaffairs.com*. Winter 2020, https://www.national affairs.com/PUBLICATIONS/DETAIL/REIMAGINING-THE-PUBLIC-UNIVERSITY.

Chapter Two
Instructional approaches and academic performance of university students in Uganda

Ayodeji O. Awobamise, Yorsa Jarrar
Adebola Adewunmi Aderibigbe

Introduction

According to Nwachukwu[1], instructional strategies are those decisions made about organizing materials, ideas, and people in order to provide learning. Weston and Cranton[2] posit that instructional strategies are teaching methods and materials used in the process of passing across knowledge in a formal academic setting. Changes and improvements in educational technology are drastically impacting teaching and learning at all levels[3].

Technologies now allow for a more inclusive and holistic approach to learning. Students that would have had little or no access to important learning materials, thanks to the internet and the resources it allows, now have access[4]. More importantly, there is a growing belief that the old approaches might no longer be effective in today's world. Therefore, institutions at all levels are experimenting with different

---

1 C. E. Nwachukwu, *Designing appropriate methodology in Vocational and Technical Education in Nigeria* (Enugu: University Trust Publishers, 2005).

2 Cynthia Weston, and Patricia A., Cranton, "Selecting instructional strategies," *The Journal of Higher Education* 5, No. 3 (1986): 260–254.

3 Susan Imel. *E-learning—Trends and Issues Alert. Report No-40* (Washington, DC: Office of Educational Research and Improvement, 2002).

4 Afam Ituma, "An evaluation of students' perceptions and engagement with e-learning components in a campus-based university," *Active Learning in Higher Education* 12, No. 1 (2011): 57–68.

methods to ensure that students optimally benefit from the education experience.

For instance, schools in Nigeria and some other parts of Africa did away with ranking positions at primary and secondary education levels because of the negative psychological impact those grades and ranks might have on students that are not performing at a very high level. Inclusivity is another hot-button topic in the academic world and institutions are working hard at ensuring that students feel like a part of the community by recruiting faculty staff from minority backgrounds and pushing and ensuring affirmative action in the admission of students. All these are efforts to ensure that the learning experience of the students is very productive.

Technological changes have resulted in creative ways in teaching students especially in the African continent, where there are very limited reading and instructional materials. It was not too long ago, that a Ghanaian lecturer was featured teaching Microsoft Word application by drawing the user interface of the application on a blackboard and instructing the students by word of mouth. He could not practically show what a computer is and how Microsoft Word operates because he did not have access to a computer—so he improvised. These innovations are not always a result of lack of equipment or access to reading materials, but sometimes due to the fact that some modules require a unique approach to be taught.

The dynamics and the reality of the African academia is such that courses like chemistry, biology, and other pure science courses are taught without students entering a fully equipped laboratory, if they enter any at all. This made institutions in many parts of the continent, tout their ability to provide good materials, internet access and qualified teachers in their marketing materials. Institutions are sometimes distinguished by their ability to provide some of the basic materials and equipment for learning.

Some African countries and organizations have been skeptical about distance learning. For example, it is a well-known fact in Nigeria, that online degrees, as they are popularly called, are not recognized. This is also the case in a lot of other African ad developing nations. This is probably due to the belief that students cannot learn properly via e-Learning platforms.

However, the Covid-19 pandemic that started in China and rapidly spread to the rest of the world ensured that the issue of online teaching and instruction is revisited. Most countries around the world, including Uganda, were forced to 'lockdown', effectively making face-to-face teaching all but impossible. Schools were already in session and had to devise new ways to teach their students. Several approaches were adopted; some schools made use of the WhatsApp platform and other Instant messaging applications, while most schools adopted the use of Zoom meeting application to host and hold classes.

Schools like Kampala International University already had a Learning Management Software that was already used before the lockdown, so the university simply migrated classes online. It became immediately clear that teaching online might be the only option because no one knew how long the lockdown will last and when schools will be allowed to resume regular activities.

This lockdown presented to the researchers a unique opportunity to test and compare the effect and efficacy of online teaching methods (computer assisted learning), blended learning method and the traditional face-to-face teaching approach. It is against this backdrop that the study was conceived. The study seeks to find out the effect of various teaching approaches (computer assisted, face-to-face or blended) on academic performance of university students in Uganda. The study also sought to identify the most effective approach to teaching in Uganda.

Literature review

In his study on teaching methods and educational performance, Okoye[5] stated that one of the factors that influences student's performance apart from the physical environment is the teaching method. In a similar study carried out by Anil and Ozer,[6] it was found out that one of the reasons behind poor academic performance of students is the implementation of ineffective teaching methods. In view of this, the authors shall briefly explain the three teaching methods studied in this chapter, namely, Computer-based learning, face-to-face learning, and blended learning approach.

Computer-based learning

Computer based Learning, also referred to as e-Learning, online learning and computer assisted learning, can be described as an approach were part or all the teaching is delivered digitally.[7] Machumu[8] explained that e-Learning is becoming more popular in Africa and in Tanzania due to the fact that the cost of technology has significantly reduced over the years and broadband internet is now available in most cities in Africa. This has made the growth and popularity of e-Learning and all other ePlatforms possible in Africa.

Machumu[9] goes on to explain that e-learning can make use of platforms such as emails, skype and other eLearning platforms. Teleconferencing, and web conferencing are now popular for small group tutorials or

---

[5] R. O. Okoye, *Educational and Psychological Measurement and Evaluation* (Lagos: ED-solid foundation publishers, 1996).

[6] Duygu Anil, and Yesim Ozer, "The effect of the aim and frequency of computer usage on student achievement according to PISA 2006," *Procedia-Social and Behavioral Sciences* 46 (2012): 5484–5488.

[7] Velazquez, Franzoni and Assar, Said. "Using learning styles to enhance an e-learning system." Proceedings of the 6th European Conference on e-Learning, Copenhagen, Denmark, 2017.

[8] Machumu, Paul. "The e-learning and computer-based instruction in engineering education: The case study in Tanzania." AIP Conference Proceedings Vol. 1778, AIP Publishing, 2016.

[9] Ibid

teaching. Computer based learning has grown quite popular over the years, because almost every aspect of face-to-face teaching can be replicated on the appropriate e-learning platform.

For instance, students can ask questions by virtual hand which gives them access to the virtual microphone and allows other participants to hear them. Documents (PowerPoints, and other documents) can be shared, so everyone can follow along. Also, for courses that require the teacher to show how a computer application is used, screen sharing is now a feature that most virtual classrooms allow. So, there is no gainsaying the fact that while computer-based learning can be an effective method of teaching if done properly. According to Olojo, Adewumi and Ajisola[10] e-learning is just as effective, as traditional face-to-face teaching.

Gibbons and Fairweather[11] concluded that students that made use of computer-based learning had better levels of retention and learned more efficiently than students that participated in only face-to-face studies. However, a study by Davis, James, Chryssafidou, Evi, Zamora, Javier, Davies, David, Khan, Khalid and Coomarasamy, Arri[12] comparing the efficacy of computer-based teaching and lecture-based teaching found out that both groups performed very similarly and there was no significant difference between the academic performance of students in both groups.

A study by Bayrak and Bayram[13] on the effect of computer aided teaching on students' academic performance, found out that computer-

---

[10] Jethro Olojo, Grace Adewumi, and Thomas Ajisola, "E-Learning and its effects on teaching and learning in a global age," *International Journal of Academic Research in Business and Social Sciences* 2, No 1, 203–210.

[11] Ibid

[12] James Davis, Evi Chryssafidou, Javier Zamora, David Davies, Khalid Khan, and Arri Coomarasamy, "Computer-based teaching is as good as face-to-face lecture-based teaching of evidence-based medicine: a randomized controlled trial," *BMC Medical Education* 7 No. 1 (2007): 1–6.

[13] Beyza Bayrak, and Hale Bayram, "The effect of computer aided teaching method on the students' academic achievement in the science and technology course," *Procedia Social and Behavioural Sciences* 9 (2010): 235–238.

aided teaching boosted the academic performance of students. In their study, computer aided teaching made use of interactive animations and simulations without face-to-face interactions. This goes to show that computer aided teaching is not limited to online teaching. Taking a different approach to studying

the effectiveness of computer-based learning Schindler, Burkholder, Morad, and Marsh[14] sought to measure student engagement instead of measuring students' performance as a lot of studies have done in the past.

They conceptualized that computer-aided technology does not only include educational platforms as Moodle, blackboard and different LMS platforms, but also includes social media platforms as well as blogs, web conferencing, wikis, and even digital games. The rationale was to look at how these technologies might be aiding learning by improving cognitive engagement of the students. Their findings showed that there is indeed a positive relation between computer-based technology and student engagement.

A study conducted by Senteni[15] sought to examine the relationship between computer-based instruction and student academic achievement. His findings showed that students that are taught using this method tend to have a higher level of motivation and achievement. His confirmed that students that are taught using this method generally tend to develop a more positive outlook towards academics.

---

[14] Laura A. Schindler, Gary J. Burkholder, Osama A. Morad, and Craig, Marsh, "Computer-based technology and student engagement: a critical review of the literature," *International Journal of Educational Technology in Higher Education* 14, No. 25 (2017): 1–28.

[15] Alain Senteni, "Mathematics and computer-aided learning," *Academic Exchange Quarterly* 22 (2004).

These findings are also supported by Serin[16] who found out that computer-based instruction significantly improved students' achievements and problem-solving skills. He arrived at this conclusion by carrying out an experimental study, that compared students' problem-solving skills before and after they were introduced to computer-based instruction.

A shortcoming of most of the studies that sought to understand the effectiveness of computer-based instruction is that most of them tend to simply study pre and post computer-based instruction and do not necessarily compare it to other methods of instruction. This is counterintuitive as it is possible for it to be effective at improving students' performance while not necessarily being better than other instructional methods at improving students' performance. It is on this basis that the researchers decided to compare the academic performance of students taught using three different instructional methods, namely, face-to-face, computer based and blended methods

Blended learning

Blended learning is a relatively new topic the academic debate. According to Taylor,[17]blended learning, also referred to as hybrid and mixed learning, started to emerge as a method of teaching for distance learning studies by including technology and the internet in order to improve the learning experience of students.

The blended teaching approach combines elements of both online and face-to-face learning. It is generally agreed that blended learning combines the best features of both the online and face-to-face learning approaches (see Figure 1) Scholars generally agree that blended

---

16 Oguz Serin, "The effect of the computer-based instruction on the achievement and problem-solving skills of the science and technology students," *The Turkish Online Journal of Educational Technology* 10, No 1 (2011): 183–201.

17 James C. Taylor, "Distance education technologies: the fourth generation," *Australasian Journal of Educational Technology* 11, No. 2 (1995): 1–7.

learning is a method that combines the models of traditional (face-to-face) and distance learning (online).[18]

Dziuban, Hartman and Moskal[19] explained that blended learning should be approached not merely as a temporal construct, but rather as a fundamental redesign of the instructional model with the following characteristics:

- a shift from lecture- to student-centered instruction in which students become active and interactive learners (this shift should apply to the entire course, including face-to-face contact sessions);
- increases interaction between student-instructor, student-student, student-content, and student-outside resources;
- integrated formative and summative assessment mechanisms for students and instructor.

Numerous scholars have attempted to study the efficacy of blended learning compared to other forms of learning such as face-to-face or online learning. Majority of these studies has been conducted at university level, but studies have also shown that blended learning is an approach that can be effective even at secondary school level.[20]

According to Chen and Jones[21], numerous studies have shown that blended learning is positively associated with academic performance of students. Kagohara, Van der Meer, Achmadi, Green, et al[22] found that

---

[18] Azamat Akbarov, Kemal Gönen, and Hekan Aydogan, "Students' attitudes toward blended learning in EFL context," *Acta Didactica. Napocenesia* 11, No. 1 (2018): 61–68.
[19] Chuck Dziuban, Joel Hartman, Joel, and Patsy Moskal, "Blended Learning," *EDUCAUSE Review* 7 (2004).
[20] Najeh Alsalhi, Mohd Eltahir and Sami Al-Qatawneh. "The effect of blended learning on the achievement of ninth grade students in science and their attitudes towards its use," *Heliyon* 5 (2019): e02424.
[21] Clement Chen, and Keith Jones, "Blended learning vs. traditional classroom settings: assessing effectiveness and students' perceptions in an MBA accounting course," *Journal of Educators Online* 4, No. 1 (2007): 1–15.
[22] Deborah Kagohara, Larah Van der Meer, Donna Achmadi, Vanessa Green, Mark O'Reilly, Austin Mulloy, Giulio Lancioni, Russell Lang, and Jeff Sigafoos, "Behavioral

multimedia tools such as simulation software and videos are more effective at explaining complex topics than textbooks and as such aids learning. In their study on the effectiveness of blended learning on teaching and learning,

Dowling, Godfrey and Gyles[23] found out that students generally prefer blended learning to traditional learning because it improves teaching and makes learning a lot easier.

A study by Tosun, Sucuz and Yigit[24] compared the effect of computer assisted teaching and computer-based teaching on computer course success of students. The study conceptualized computer assisted teaching as the transfer of instructional content and other teaching activities via computers complementing traditional teaching methods while computer-based teaching referred to teaching that is concluded exclusively online.

The study was conducted in Turkey and the findings showed that students that received instructions and materials via computer assisted methods showed a higher level of success in their practical test than students that were taught using the computer-based method. A meta-analysis of fifty-one different studies on the effectiveness of the blended learning method in improving students' performance was carried out by Vo, Zhu, and Diep[25] and the findings showed a significant positive

intervention promotes successful use of an iPod-based communication device by an adolescent with autism," *Clinical Case Studies* 9, No. 5 (2010): 328–338.

[23] Carlin Dowling, Carlin, Jayne Godfrey, Jayne, and Nicole Gyles, "Do hybrid flexible delivery teaching methods improve accounting students' learning outcomes?," *Accounting Education* 12, No. 4 (2003): 373–391.

[24] Nilgun Tosun, Nursen Sucsuz, and Birol Yigit, "The effect of computer assisted and computer-based teaching methods on computer course success and computer using attitudes of students," *The Turkish Online Journal of Educational Technology* 5 No. 3 (2006): 46–53.

[25] Minh Vo, Chang Zhu and Anh Diep, "The effect of blended learning on student performance at course-level in higher education: A meta-analysis," *Studies in Educational Evaluation* 53 (2017): 17–28.

relation between blended learning and academic performance of students in STEM disciplines.

On the other hand, Wei, Shi, Yang and Liu[26] found that there is no significant effect when using blended learning over any other method. Their studies concluded that there was no positive impact on student performance or achievement when using blended learning. A similar study by Tosun[27] also found no significant improvement in students' academic performance when using blended learning. The conflicting results show that the jury is still out on whether blended learning is more or even as effective as traditional learning. This makes it imperative for a study that specifically measures and compares different teaching methods using students' scores as the basis of measurement.

Face-to-face learning

This is the traditional mode of teaching that requires both the teacher and the students to be at the same place at the same time imparting and receiving knowledge respectively. Over the years, this method has shown to be effective at teaching students in a formal setting. The effectiveness of this approach to learning has been well documented in literature over the years.

A study by Kemp and Grieve[28] compared face-to-face and face-to-screen learning modes. The study was carried out among psychology students and the results showed that students preferred face-to-face learning and indicated that they strongly preferred class discussion to be had face-to-face than through online platforms. A follow-up study

---

[26] Yitong Wei, Yinghui Shi, Harrison Yang and Jianging Liu. "Blended learning versus traditional learning: a study on students' learning achievements and academic press." International Symposium on Educational Technology 2017, 219–223.

[27] Tosun, Sezen. 2015. "The effects of blended learning on EFL students' vocabulary enhancement." *Procedia Social and Behavioral Science, 199*, 641–647.

[28] Nenagh Kemp. and Rachel Grieve, "Face-to-face or face-to-screen? Undergraduates' opinions and test performance in classroom vs. online learning," *Frontiers in Psychology* 5 (2014): 1–11.

by the same researcher had similar findings, which showed that while students like and appreciate the convenience of online; they would rather have face-to-face class activities.

Numerous studies have been carried out comparing the effect of face-to-face or traditional teaching methods and other forms of teaching (computer-based and blended method) on academic performance. The findings generally suggest that the face-to-face teaching method is not very effective when compared to the blended method.[29] However, some studies have also found no significant difference in academic performance between groups of students that were taught using face-to-face methods and those that were taught using computer assisted methods.[30]

A lot of studies have been conducted on the effect of instructional methods on academic performance, but very few have actually studied the three approaches together in order to find the most effective approach to teaching especially in more recent times. It is the opinion of the researchers that, as the world gravitates towards online teaching and business, and as Africa is forced, due to the covid-19 pandemic to embrace e-learning, it is important that a study on the most appropriate methods is carried out in an African context in order to confirm which of the approaches best works.

This study therefore differs from previous studies in the sense that it does not simply look at the effect of one method of teaching on academic performance, as seen in most studies, but takes it a step further to compare the impact of three methods of teaching on academic performance of students while also identifying which of them is more

---

29 Luisito Lacatan, "Hybrid method and face to face method in teaching mathematics: Effects on students' performance," *International Journal of Information and Education Technology* 3, No. 2, (2013): 143–146; Nahid Elfaki, Itedal Abdulraheem, and Rashida Abdulrahim, "Impact of E-Learning vs Traditional learning on student's performance and attitude," *International Journal of Medical Research & Health Sciences* 8, No. 10 (2019): 76–82; Kagohara et al., "Behavioral intervention."

30 Kemp and Grieve, "Face-to-face;" Smith, ""Face-to-face." Wei, "Blended learning."

effective. It is based on this background that the researchers hypothesize the following:

Hypothesis 1: there is a significant difference in the academic performance of students making use of either computer-based learning, face-to-face or the hybrid approach.

Hypothesis 2: students that studied using the blended approach will perform significantly better than students that made use of either face-to-face or computer-based learning approaches.

Methodology

This study made use of the non-equivalent control group quasi-experimental design. Since the researchers made use of already established groups- students in the department of communication at Victoria University and

Kampala International University- they had no control over how the participants in this study were assigned. Three groups of students were used in this study, namely:

1. Students of Journalism and Media Studies of Kampala International University. This group was selected because the students were exposed to the face-to-face learning approach. They are considered as the control group for this study.
2. Students of Journalism and Media Studies at Victoria University. They were selected because Victoria University has a policy of making use of the blended approach. This involves making use of face-to-face communication, as well as online materials from educational websites and social media to complement face-to-face learning.
3. Students of communication at Virtual University of Uganda, an online university that conducts only virtual or online classes.

These three institutions were chosen because they make use of a unique approach to teaching and therefore will fit into the 3 categories of instructional methods examined in this study. In order to ensure that there is no bias, the researchers chose to select only students of communication from the three institutions, because the admission requirements are the same and the curricula are regulated and monitored by a central body- the National Council for Higher Education in Uganda. To test students' performance, results of the participating students from the three universities were collected and analyzed.

Participants

The population of this study consisted of students from three unique universities in Uganda- Virtual University, Kampala International University and Victoria University. Virtual University was selected because it teaches exclusively online. Kampala International University makes use of face-to-face learning approach while Victoria University makes use of the blended learning approach. Table 1 below shows the breakdown of the study participants.

<table>
<tr><th>Groups</th><th>Institution</th><th>Mode of instruction</th><th>Modules covered</th><th>No. of students</th></tr>
<tr><td>1</td><td>Victoria University</td><td>Blended learning</td><td rowspan="3"><ul><li>Introduction to Mass Communication</li><li>Economics</li><li>Political Science</li></ul></td><td>90</td></tr>
<tr><td>2</td><td>Virtual University</td><td>Computer-based learning</td><td>124</td></tr>
<tr><td>3</td><td>Kampala International University</td><td>Face-to-Face</td><td>211</td></tr>
<tr><td></td><td colspan="3">TOTAL STUDY PARTICIPANTS (N)</td><td>425</td></tr>
</table>

Table 2-1: *Study participants*

Study variables

The independent variables for this study are blended learning, computer-based learning, and face-to-face learning.

The dependent variables are the scores in introduction to mass communication, economics, and political science courses of the students in the selected universities and the responses of the experimental groups on their perception of the different teaching methods.

Instrument/experimental conditions

Three modules taught in each of the selected institutions were chosen. The primary reason for choosing these modules is because all three schools teach them at 100 level and therefore would ensure that all participants are tested for the same thing. Also, the students were not aware that the experiment was going on, they attended their classes as they normally would and were tested as they normally would. The agreed standard is that all questions asked in the final examination must be based on subjects covered in the course of the semester. So, the results of these three modules from the three universities were imputed and analyzed for this study.

Time frame

The timeframe for this study was between August 2019 to January 2020. The three universities started the semester either in August or September and wrote their final examinations in December 2019. All results were marked and collated by end of January 2020. The results of the selected modules were used in the analysis.

Findings and discussion

This study sought to find out if there is a difference in students' academic performance based on the teaching approach adopted by their respective institutions. To find out if there is difference in the academic performance of the 3 groups, namely, students from Kampala International University, Victoria University and Virtual University. A one-way ANOVA test was carried out and the results are presented in the table below.

						95% Confidence Interval for Mean			
		N	Mean	Std. Deviation	Std. Error	Lower Bound	Upper Bound	Minimum	Maximum
Perception of News credibility	Group 1	90	69.86	11.97	1.26	67.35	72.36	34	91
	Group 2	124	63.46	13.22	1.19	61.11	65.81	32	87
	Group 3	211	61.93	15.33	1.06	59.85	64.01	28	87
	Total	425	64.05	14.38	.70	62.68	65.42	28	91

Table 2-2: *Descriptive statistics of data*

The table above shows that the mean score of those that were taught using the blended learning method was higher (M= 69.86, SD = 11.97) than those taught using the computer-based method (M= 63.46, SD= 13.22) and the face-to-face learning method (M= 61.93, SD= 15.33).

		Sum of Squares	df	Mean Square	F	Sig.
Academic Performance	Between Groups	4025.90	2	2012.95	10.16	.000
	Within Groups	83607.85	422	198.12		
	Total	87633.76	424			

Table 2-3: *ONE-WAY ANOVA*

The one-way ANOVA test results show a significant difference in the academic performance at $p<.05$ level for students from the 3 different categories [$F(2,422)=10.16$, $p<.05$]. Therefore Hypothesis 1, which states that, "there is a significant difference in academic performance of students making use of either computer-based learning, face-to-face or the hybrid approach" is accepted.

Since the one-way ANOVA test showed a significant result, the researchers then ran post hoc comparisons using Fisher's Least Significant Difference (LSD) test. LSD test was used because the sample size for each group was not equal, and homogeneity of variances was not achieved. The result of the post hoc is presented in the table below.

Table: Multiple Comparisons (Final Marks)							
			Mean Difference			95% Confidence Interval	
	(I) Groups	(J) Groups	(I - J)	Std. Error	Sig.	Lower Bound	Upper Bound
LSD	Blended Learning	Computer based learning	6.4	1.95	0.001	2.56	10.23
		Face-to-face learning	7.93	1.77	.000	4.44	11.41
	Computer based learning	Blended Learning	-6.4	1.95	0.001	-10.23	-2.56
		Face-to-face learning	1.53	1.59	0.337	-1.6	4.66
	Face-to-face learning	Blended Learning	-7.93	1.77	.000	-11.41	-4.44
		Computer based learning	-1.53	1.59	0.337	-4.66	1.6

Table 2-4: *Fisher's Least Significant Difference (LSD) test result*

From the table above, the results show that there is a significant difference between blended learning and computer-based learning ($p=0.001$) and a significant difference between blended learning and face-to-face learning ($p<.001$). The table also shows that there is no significant difference in the academic performance of students taught using computer-based learning ($P=.337$).

Based on the findings, Hypothesis 2 which states that students that studied using the blended approach will perform significantly better than students that made use of either face-to-face or computer-based learning approaches, is accepted. The findings of this study show that the blended method is the most effective method if the final grade is the mode of measuring academic performance. This goes to show that while online methods might be gaining a lot of traction in recent times, the role of face-to-face interactions cannot be overlooked, because blended learning combines the benefits of computer-based teaching with that of face-to-face learning.

All in all, technological advances have greatly influenced our lives in a lot of different ways- communication, travel, business and even art. The education sector is not left out in this technological revolution. Africa has been reluctant to adopt eLearning, arguing that the traditional classroom cannot be replaced, but the Covid-19 pandemic of 2019/2020 has proven that if education is to be continued in Africa, then there needs to be an adoption and appreciation of eLearning.

This chapter however argues that, while we are negotiating this new path, there is a need to not just adopt a new approach blindly, but rather to understand and study which teaching approach is more appropriate. It was on this basis that this study compared the academic performance of students that were taught using three different teaching approaches, namely, face-to-face, blended and computer-based learning.

The findings show that the blended learning approach has a significant positive effect on academic performance. This finding supports the submission of other similar studies.[31] Their findings showed that students taught using the blended approach perform better than students taught using the computer-based or the face-to-face learning methods. The findings of this study do not support the submission of Wei et al.,[32] who found no significant difference in the academic performance of students.

While this study is extensive and covers a wider scope than most of the studies reviewed in literature, there are still areas for improvement. From the review of literature, it is clear that a consensus on the effectiveness of blended learning method over other methods has still

31 Vo, Zhu, and Diep, "The effect of blended learning."

32 Wei, Shi, Yang, and Liu, "Blended learning."

not been arrived at. The reason for this is not far-fetched, literature has shown that most of the studies conducted focused on one institution or a single field of study, thereby making generalization difficult. Based on these gaps in literature and the limitations of our current study, the following areas of research in future studies are recommended:

1. A study that examines the effect of collaborative technologies such as blogs and social networking sites on academic performance. The study should look at social media sites and blogs as educational aids and examine how they might influence the academic performance of students.
2. Due to the fact that the researchers could not randomize the participants, as we had to rely on students already enrolled in a particular program making use of a particular method, it is possible that fundamental differences between groups could have affected the results. For instance, it is quite possible that students that enrolled in the online class, find it easier to learn using online platforms than traditional methods, which might impact the results of this study. It is therefore our recommendation that future studies seek to randomize the participants, so a more reliable results can be derived from the study.
3. In this study, we have limited blended learning to only learning where digital instructional materials are used as a complement to face-to-face learning. There are different forms of blended learning, and this study did not consider all of them. It is therefore necessary that future studies consider the different forms of blended learning and ascertain which of them is most effective at improving academic performance of students at university level.

Conclusion

This study contributes to debate on the efficacy of online and eLearning approaches in higher education. It furthers the global debate surrounding the effect of eLearning on academic performance and sheds light on the effectiveness of blended learning in the Ugandan context. The findings of this study showed that there is a significance difference in the academic performance of students from three different groups (blended, computer-based and face-to-face learning methods). This study also confirmed that students that are taught using the blended approach, perform significantly better than students that are taught using the computer based or face-to-face learning approaches. Further studies are recommended to be conducted in the context of sub-Saharan Africa, in order to examine the most effective method of teaching taking into consideration the peculiarities of the African reality.

Bibliography

Akbarov, Azamat, Gönen, Kemal, and Aydogan, Hekan. "Students' attitudes toward blended learning in EFL context." *Acta Didactica. Napocenesia* 11, No. 1 (2018): 61–68.

Alsalhi, Najeh, Eltahir, Mohd, and Al-Qatawneh, Samir. "The effect of blended learning on the achievement of ninth grade students in science and their attitudes towards its use." *Heliyon* 5 (2019): e02424.

Anil, Duygu Anil, and Ozer,Yesim. "The effect of the aim and frequency of computer usage on student achievement according to PISA 2006." *Procedia-Social and Behavioral Sciences* 46 (2012): 5484–5488.

Bayrak, Beyza and Bayram, Hale. "The effect of computer aided teaching method on the students' academic achievement in the science and technology course." *Procedia Social and Behavioural Sciences* 9 (2010): 235–238.

Chen, Clement. and Jones, Keith. "Blended learning vs. traditional classroom settings: assessing effectiveness and students' perceptions in an MBA accounting course." *Journal of Educators Online* 4, No. 1 (2007): 1–15, doi: 10.9743/JEO.2007.1.3.

Clark, Ruth C., and Mayer, Richard.E. 2003. *E-learning and the Science Instruction*. San Francisco: Preiffer.

Davis, James, Chryssafidou, Evi, Zamora, Javier, Davies, David, Khan, Khalid, and Coomarasamy, Arri. "Computer-based teaching is as good as face-to-face lecture-based teaching of evidence-based medicine: a randomized controlled trial," *BMC Medical Education* 7 No. 1 (2007): 1–6.

Dowling, Carlin, Godfrey, Jayne, and Gyles, Nicole. "Do hybrid flexible delivery teaching methods improve accounting students' learning outcomes?." *Accounting Education* 12, No. 4 (2003): 373–391.

Dziuban, Chuck, Graham, Charles, Moskal, Patsy, Norberg, Anders, and Sicilia, Nicole. "Blended learning: the new normal and emerging technologies." *International Journal of Education Technology in Higher Education* 15, No.3 (2018): 1–16.

Dziuban, Chuck, Hartman, Joel, and Moskal, Patsy. "Blended Learning." *EDUCAUSE Review* 7 (2004).

Elfaki, Nahid, Abdulraheem, Itedal, and Abdulrahim, Rashida. 2019. "Impact of E-Learning vs Traditional learning on student's performance and attitude." *International Journal of Medical Research & Health Sciences* 8, No. 10 (2019): 76–82.

Imel, Susan. 2002. *E-learning—Trends and Issues Alert. Report No-40.* Washington, DC: Office of Educational Research and Improvement.

Ituma, Afam. 2011. "An evaluation of students' perceptions and engagement with e-learning components in a campus-based university." *Active Learning in Higher Education.* 12, No. 1 (2011): 57–68.

Kagohara, Deborah, Van der Meer, Larah, Achmadi, Donna, Green, Vanessa, O'Reilly, Mark, Mulloy, Austin, Lancioni, Giulio, Lang, Russell, and Sigafoos, Jeff. "Behavioral intervention promotes successful use of an iPod-based communication device by an adolescent with autism." *Clinical Case Studies* 9, No. 5 (2010): 328–338.

Kemp, Nenagh. and Grieve, Rachel. "Face-to-face or face-to-screen? Undergraduates' opinions and test performance in classroom vs. online learning." *Frontiers in Psychology* 5 (2014): 1–11.

Lacatan, Luisito. "Hybrid method and face to face method in teaching mathematics: Effects on students' performance." *International Journal of Information and Education Technology* 3, No. 2, (2013): 143–146.

Machumu, Paul. "The e-learning and computer-based instruction in engineering education: The case study in Tanzania." AIP Conference Proceedings Vol. 1778, AIP Publishing, 2016.

Nwachukwu C.E. 2005. *Designing appropriate methodology in Vocational and Technical Education in Nigeria.* Enugu: University Trust Publishers.

Okoye, R. O. 1996. *Educational and Psychological Measurement and Evaluation.* Lagos: ED-solid foundation publishers.

Olojo, Jethro, Adewumi, Grace, and Ajisola, Thomas. "E-Learning and its effects on teaching and learning in a global age," *International Journal of Academic Research in Business and Social Sciences* 2, No 1, 203–210.

Schindler, Laura A., Burkholder, Gary J., Morad, Osama A., and Marsh, Craig. "Computer-based technology and student engagement: a critical review of the literature." *International Journal of Educational Technology in Higher Education* 14, No. 25 (2017): 1–28.

Senteni, Alain. "Mathematics and computer-aided learning." *Academic Exchange Quarterly* 22 (2004).

Serin, Oguz. "The effect of the computer-based instruction on the achievement and problem-solving skills of the science and technology students." *The Turkish Online Journal of Educational Technology* 10, No 1 (2011): 183–201.

Smith, Nigel. "Face-to-face vs. blended learning: Effects on secondary students 'perceptions and performance." *Procedia – Social and Behavioral Sciences* 89 (2013): 79–83.

Taylor, James C. "Distance education technologies: the fourth generation." *Australasian Journal of Educational Technology* 11, No. 2 (1995): 1–7.

Tosun, Nilgun Sucsuz, Nursen, and Yigit, Birol. "The effect of computer assisted and computer-based teaching methods on computer course success and computer using attitudes of students." *The Turkish Online Journal of Educational Technology* 5 No. 3 (2006): 46–53.

Tosun, Sezen. 2015. "The effects of blended learning on EFL students' vocabulary enhancement." *Procedia Social and Behavioral Science, 199*, 641–647.

Velazquez, Franzoni and Assar, Said. "Using learning styles to enhance an e-learning system." Proceedings of the 6th European Conference on e-Learning, Copenhagen, Denmark, 2017.

Vo, Minh, Zhu, Chang and Diep, Anh. 2017. "The effect of blended learning on student performance at course-level in higher education: A meta-analysis." *Studies in Educational Evaluation.*53 (2017): 17–28.

Wei, Yitong, Shi, Yinghui, Yang, Harrison, and Liu, Jianging. "Blended learning versus traditional learning: a study on students' learning achievements and academic press." International Symposium on Educational Technology 2017, 219–223.

Weston, Cynthia, and Cranton Patricia A. "Selecting instructional strategies." *The Journal of Higher Education* 5, No. 3 (1986): 254–260.

Chapter Three

The moderating role of academic resilience on the relationship between student satisfaction and academic burnout among graduate students

Yosra Jarrar, Ayodeji O. Awobamise
Gabriel E. Nweke

Introduction

Education and academic progress are usually measured by certain outcomes and as such learners are expected to meet certain standards and benchmarks set for them by their various academic institutions where they currently study or hope to study. For instance, a student that hopes to study medicine is expected to do very well in certain courses including biology, chemistry, and mathematics. Hence, a lot of learners spend most of their time in school ensuring they meet the standards to achieve their academic goals and aspirations. In the process of going about their regular school activities, students can become emotionally and physically exhausted; this exhaustion is often referred to as academic burnout.

Academic burnout can be described or defined in many ways, but the most widely used definition is that proposed by Schaufeli, Pinto, Salanova, and Bakker,[1] who describe it as the feeling of exhaustion that is caused by academic requirements and demands of school which is

---

1 Wilmar Schaufeli, Isabel Martinez, Alexander Pinto, Marisa Salanova, and Arnold Bakker, "Burnout and engagement in university students, a cross-national study," *Journal of Cross-Cultural Psychology* 33, No. 5 (2002): 464–481.

accompanied by pessimism, and disinterest about school assignments on the part of students. Oyoo et al.[2] explain that academic burnout is constituted of three main sub-categories, namely, emotional exhaustion, academic inefficiency, and cynicism[3].

Emotional exhaustion is often caused by academic pressure which again is directly linked to undue or unnecessary pressure imposed on the learners due to the hyper-competitive academic environment and the need to stand out. Cynicism emerges when students become disappointed or frustrated by their inability to succeed as much as is expected of them. This inability to meet expectations leads students to believe that education is not worth the stress which can cause academic burnout.[4]

Academic inefficiency, which is the third sub-category under academic burnout stems from the belief in the minds of students that they are not capable of achieving academic excellence in a particular field or area. For instance, some students believe they cannot study engineering and defeat themselves even before resuming school.

Academic burnout is often caused by stress which in turn can be a result of students' inability to meet excessively stressful school demands and deadlines.[5]

---

[2] Syprine Aoko Oyoo, Peter Mucheru Mwaura, and Theresia Kinai, "Academic resilience as a predictor of academic burnout among form four students in Homa-Bay County, Kenya," *International Journal of Educational Research* 6, No. 3 (2018): 187–200.

[3] Ibid

[4] Zeinab Rahmati, "The study of academic burnout in students with high and low level of self-efficacy," *Procedia - Social and Behavioral Sciences* 171 (2015): 49–55; Katariina Salmela-Aro, and Katja Upadyaya, "School burnout and engagement in the context of demands-resources model," *The British Journal of Educational Psychology* 84, No. 1 (2014):137–151.

[5] Caterina Fiorilli Virna Galimberti, Simona De Stasio, Carlo Di Chiacchio, and Ottavia Albanese, "L'utilizzazione dello School Burnout Inventory (SBI) constudenti Italiani di scuola superiore di primo e secondo grado," *Psicologia clinica dello sviluppo* 18, No. 3 (2014): 403–423.

Similarly, Ajam and Bayani explain that academic burnout or school burnout is often caused when the academic demands far exceed the students' resources to meet those demands[6]. Academically resilient students usually demonstrate a strong ability to recover quickly from traumatic events related to their school activities and also manage to complete their studies while getting good grades even in the face of failure.

Furthermore, resilient students are known to explore their school environment and develop relationships that help in furthering their desire for academic excellence. In a nutshell, academic resilience stems from students' ability to adapt to a changing and often challenging environment which in turn leads to personal growth.

Also, unsatisfactory social relationships developed within the school context can negatively impact students' resilience and lead to maladjustments. For instance, if a child finds themselves in an environment where they do not feel welcome or are continuously bullied and treated as outsiders, then such a child or student might have a lower threshold of resilience. Conversely, if one finds themselves in a highly satisfying social relationship, then it can be hypothesized that they will have a higher level of resilience and will be able to avoid academic burnouts more.

Academic resilience as a concept focuses on the strengths and the optimal performance of students. Jensen et al.[7] describe resilience as the effective strategy and positive attitude that individuals adopt when responding to stressors or stressful situations. Learners from all over the world experience challenging and stressful situations academically and only academically resilient students can cope with such situations

---

[6] Ekrami Asieh Ajam, Tahereh Rezaei, and Ali Asghar Bayani, "Relationship between hope to work and academic motivation with academic burnout," *Knowledge and Health* 10 (2015): 44–50.

[7] Jensen Phyllis Marie Jense, Karen Trollope-Kumar, Heather Waters, and Jennifer Everson, "Building physician resilience," *Canadian Family Physician* 54, No. 5 (2008): 722–729.

by turning stress-inducing events into opportunities for personal development, benefit, and growth[8].

Therefore, it can be said that such students can adapt successfully and respond efficiently to the demand of their situation. The implication is that academically resilient students are going to be more likely to maintain a high level of academic motivation and performance irrespective of the challenges they face that could negatively affect their grades. Studies by different scholars all point to the fact that academic resilience is a major predictor of academic performance and plays a major role in reducing academic burnout among students.[9]

It is therefore the aim of the current study to examine the relationship between academic resilience and academic burnout and to further explore the moderating role of student satisfaction on the relationship between academic resilience and academic burnout.

Theoretical framework

This study made use of the conservation of resource theory developed by Hobfoll.[10] The theory explains how students make use of internal and external resources to cope with challenging or stressful situations within their learning environment. Conservation of resource theory (COR) assumes that individuals seek to obtain, retain, foster, and protect their resources to maintain their well-being and positive outlook towards life and their sense of self. Resources in the context of this theory refer to entities that have instrumental and intrinsic value.

---

[8] Kareepadath Rajan Santhosh, and Jimmy James, "The effect of resilience on burnout among the blue collared employees in metal factories," *International Journal of Multidisciplinary Management Studies* 3, No. 6 (2013): 48–55.

[9] Khadijeh Abolmaali, and Roghayeh Mahmudi, "The prediction of academic achievement based on resilience and perception of the classroom environment," *Open Science Journal of Education* 1, No. 1 (2013): 7–12.

[10] Stevan E. Hobfoll, "Conservation of resources. A new attempt at conceptualizing stress," *American Psychologist* 44, No. 3 (1989): 513–524. doi:10.1037//0003-066x.44.3.513

Hobfoll explains that personal resources include self-esteem, motivation, self-efficacy, optimism, and resilience. Other resources include a supportive network of friends, teachers, parents, and romantic partners. He goes on to explain that personal resources combined with a strong and supportive social network are generally related to the well-being of students and therefore can reduce academic burnout. According to Hobfoll, the more resources people have, the more they are likely to be able to cope with the demands and will be able to deal with organizational and institutional stressors.

He explains that "the degree to which individuals appraise something as threatening, and the coping choices they make, are largely determined by the resources they have."11 Furthermore, anything that poses a threat to valued and important resources will most likely lead to burnout.12

This theory is particularly relevant to this study because it considers the factors that can lead to academic burnout and posits that if certain resources are present, then individuals can avoid or mitigate burnouts. Since the current study seeks to understand the relationship between academic resilience and academic burnout, and how student satisfaction moderates this relationship, then this theory is appropriate. The theory explains that individuals that have a strong support system are also less likely to experience burnout.

This theory has been used by other scholars who sought to understand how job demands lead to burnout[13] and it was found that higher demands at the workplace are associated with burnouts. Similarly, Zhang, Klassen, and Wang in their study on middle school students, found out that individuals experience high levels of burnout when

---

11 Hobfoll, "Conservation," 312.

12 Ibid

13 Gene M. Alarcon, Jean M. Edwards, and Lauren E. Menke, "Student burnout and engagement: A test of the conservation of resources theory," *The Journal of Psychology* 145 No. 3 (2011): 211–227.

there is an imbalance between requirements and available resources.[14] Based on the foregoing it will therefore be beneficial to examine if this theory holds in the context of the current study.

Student satisfaction in this study is linked to their support system and the researchers assume that the stronger the students' support system is (in terms of relationships in and outside of school), the more satisfied they will be. Consequently, the study seeks to test the following hypothesis:

H1: *Student satisfaction will be negatively associated with academic burnout.*

Review of literature

The teaching and learning process at the university level and especially at the postgraduate level is rigorous enough that stress can be and is usually expected. In addition to the academic stress associated with obtaining a postgraduate degree, students are also often reminded about the progress they could have been making in other aspects of life if they have not opted for graduate studies. These reminders come in the form of observing their friends and colleagues who are doing well professionally and personally, getting married, getting promoted, and much more, while they might be stuck in the rigmarole of academia.

High levels of stress in the academic environment can lead to academic burnout which often manifests in the form of emotional exhaustion, feelings of inadequacy, and a cynical attitude towards learning and other school activities, among others. Academic burnout can lead to unprofessional performance, failure in academics, and a general reduction in life satisfaction. Considering these consequences, students must develop coping mechanisms to mitigate the negative effects of academic burnout or avoid it completely.

---

[14] Xiaozhou Zhang, Robert M. Klassen, and Yun Wang, "Academic burnout and motivation of Chinese secondary students," *International Journal of Social Science and Humanity* 3, No.2 (2013): 134–138.

Numerous studies have investigated the relationship between academic resilience and academic burnout. Kamalpour, Azizzadeh-Forounzi, and Tirgary carried out a study to find out the relationship between academic resilience and academic burnout among students of nursing at Kerman University in Iran. The findings of the study showed that students with a higher level of academic resilience reported lower levels of burnout than students with low levels of academic resilience[15]. Similarly, a study by Garcia-Izquierdo et al. sought to analyze the impact of academic resilience on students' academic burnout and mental health. Their findings suggest that there was a significant negative relationship between academic resilience and the exhaustion dimension of burnout. The findings further revealed that academic resilience was positively associated with academic efficacy[16]. This can be interpreted to mean that students with a higher level of academic resilience score higher on academic efficacy and lower on emotional exhaustion.

A study by Kotze and Kleynhans which sought to find out whether academic burnout, engagement, and resilience were predictors of academic performance among undergraduate students at a university in South Africa, found out that academic resilience, cynicism, and emotional exhaustion were all significant predictors of academic achievement[17]. Furthermore, studies by Fiorilli, et al[18], May, Bauer and

---

[15] Somayeh Kamalpour, Mansoureh Azizzadeh-Forouzi, and Batool Tirgary, "A study of the relationship between resilience and academic burnout in nursing students," *Journal of Medical Education Development Center* 13, No.5 (2017): 476–487.

[16] Mariano García-Izquierdo, Isabel M. Ríos-Risquez, Cesar Carrillo-García, and Emiliana Sabuco-Tebar, "The moderating role of resilience in the relationship between academic burnout and the perception of psychological health in nursing students," *Educational Psychology* 38, No. 8 (2015): 1068–1079.

[17] Martina Kotzé, and Ronel Kleynhans, "Psychological well-being and resilience as predictors of first-year students' academic performance," *Journal of psychology in Africa* 23, No. 1 (2014): 37– 41.

[18] Fiorilli et al., "L'utilizzazione."

Fincham[19], and Salmela-Aro et al.[20] all sought to understand the relationship between stress in academic settings and academic burnout, and they all arrived at the conclusion that high levels of stress in the academic environment or the context of academia can result in burnout among students and is often manifested in cynical attitude towards learning and school in general, emotional exhaustion and an increased feeling of inadequacy among the affected students.

According to Kim et al, emotional exhaustion is often the first and most prominent sign of academic burnout[21]. Cynicism on the other hand is how students try to cope with this burnout which serves to counteract the toll their emotional exhaustion is taking on their psyche[22]. Finally, a sense of inadequacy increases as the student performance drops as a result of academic burnout.

A study by Kiuru et al. on the relationship between peer group influence and adolescents' school burnout found out that students that benefit from a reasonable amount of external and internal resources and are in high-achieving groups are significantly more likely to develop proper coping mechanisms and to be shielded from the negative effects of burnout[23]. Other studies have considered the relationship between resilient behavior and school burnout, documenting that most students that are resilient or have a high level of resilience are generally

---

[19] Ross May, Kristina Bauer, and Frank Fincham, "School burnout: Diminished academic and cognitive performance," *Learning and Individual Differences* 42 (2015): 126–131.

[20] Katariina Salmela-Aro, Noona Kiuru, Esko Leskinen, and Jari-Erik Nurmi, "School burnout inventory (SBI) reliability and validity," *European Journal of Psychological Assessment* 25, No. 1 (2009): 48–57.

[21] Boyoung Kim, Minyoung Lee, Keunhwa Kim, Hyunju Choi, and Sang Lee, "Longitudinal analysis of academic burnout in Korean middle school students," *Stress Health* 31, No. 4 (2015): 281–289.

[22] Milja Parviainen, Kaisa Aunola, Minna Torppa, Marja-Kristiina Lerkkanen, Anna-Maja Poikkeus, and Kati Vasalampi, "Early antecedents of school burnout in upper secondary education: A five-year longitudinal study," *Journal of Youth and Adolescence* 50 (2021): 231–245.

[23] Noona Kiuru, Kaisa Aunola, Jari-Erik Nurmi, Esko Leskinen, and Katariina Salmela-Aro, "Peer group influence and selection in adolescents' school burnout: A longitudinal study," *Merrill-Palmer Quarterly* 54, No. 1 (January 2008): 23–55.

protected from experiencing severe forms of maladjustment, most notably, school burnout.[24] Resilience has often been described as the individual capacity to handle pressure, challenges, and setbacks effectively and efficiently.[25] It is also about the ability to adapt to varying levels of adverse circumstances.

In the context of this study, resilience is described as the ability to maintain high levels of motivation, performance, and achievement even when faced with a negative academic environment. Highly resilient students believe in themselves and their ability to excel and therefore know how to regulate their behaviors and carry out actions in a way that helps them achieve their objectives and academic goals.

Studies by various authors show that academic resilience serves as an effective shield against the negative emotions directly linked to academic stress and the stressful environment of academia.[26] Furthermore, it has been found that highly resilient students tend to recover faster from academic burnout than non-resilient students.

Based on the foregoing, the researchers, therefore, seek to confirm the following hypothesis:

H2: *Academic Resilience will be negatively associated with academic burnout.*

---

[24] Fiorilli et al., "L'utilizzazione;" Luciano Romano, Xin Tang, Lauri Hietajärvi, Katariina Salmela-Aro, and Caterina Fiorilli, "Students' Trait Emotional Intelligence and Perceived Teacher Emotional Support in Preventing Burnout: The Moderating Role of Academic Anxiety," *International Journal of Environmental Research and Public Health* 17, No. 13 (2020): 4771.

[25] Fred Luthans, Gretchen R. Vogelgesang, and Paul B. Lester, "Developing the psychological capital of resiliency," *Human Resource Development Review* 5, No.1 (2006): 25–44.

[26] Antonio Arrebola-Moreno, Rocio Garcia-Retamero, Andres Catena, Rafael Marfil-Álvarez, Rafael Melgares-Moreno, and Jose Ramírez-Hernández, "On the protective effect of resilience in patients with acute coronary syndrome," *International Journal of Clinical and Health Psychology* 14, No. 2 (2014): 111–119; Mir M. Ali, Debra S. Dwyer, Elizabeth A. Vanner, and Alexander Lopez, "Adolescent propensity to engage in health risky behaviors: The role of individual resilience," *International Journal of Environmental Research and Public Health* 7, No. 5 (2010): 2161–2176.

Student satisfaction in the context of this study is directly linked to how available internal and external resources are to them. Internal and external resources in the context of this study refer to self-esteem, motivation, self-efficacy, optimism, and resilience. Other resources include a supportive network of friends, teachers, parents, and romantic partners. So, student satisfaction in the context of this study has to do with the presence of these resources in the academic context of students' life. It should be noted that university students deal with a lot of challenges since they interact with the same group of students and lecturers for an extended period of time.

It should also be noted that during school years, students develop relationships that are maintained for at least the period of their school years and even beyond, sharing their successes and failures. According to Romano et al., students usually need relationships outside of their immediate family in order to build their identity and shape their beliefs.[27] It can therefore be concluded that the academic well-being of students at any level of their academic journey is often related to the quality of the relationships with their teachers and peers which are categorized as external resources.[28]

Furthermore, studies have shown that school environment in terms of classroom climate, which has to do with friendliness, and cordial relationships with students and teachers in the classroom, plays a major role in school maladjustment. For instance, scholars have suggested that students who have a positive disposition to their teachers and fellow students experience a higher sense of involvement which in turn improves academic achievement and engagement levels which also improves their chances of completing their studies and not dropping

---

[27] Luciano Romano, Ilaria Buonomo, Antonio Callea, Caterina Fiorilli, and Katerina Schenke, "Teacher Emotional Support Scale on Italian High School Students: A contribution to validation," *The Open Psychology Journal* 13, No. 1 (2020): 123–132.

[28] Young, Lauryn, Mulloy,. Maura, Huckabee, Sloan, Landoll, Ryan, Miller, Elaine, Miller, Marissa, and Weist, Mark D. "Child and Adolescent Mental Health and the Schools." In *Transition of Youth and Young Adults; Advances in Learning and Behavioral Disabilities*, eds. Bryan G. Cook, Melody Tankersley, and Timothy J. Landrum (Bingley: Emerald Group Publishing, 2015), 197–224.

out.[29] As earlier discussed in the conceptualization of resilience, previous studies have mostly considered resilience as a unique trait that a few individuals possess or self-develop. However, more recent studies point to the fact that resilience is something that students can develop based on the interaction with their environment and their evaluation of stressful events.[30]

Previous studies suggest that resilient students are significantly more likely to view their academic environment as a supportive and satisfying place and that low-resilient students view their academic environment as unsatisfying and unsupportive[31]. Furthermore, Drybye et al.[32] found that resilient students are less likely to experience academic burnout when they have a positive perception towards their academic environment and the relationships developed within. Other studies also highlighted the fact that resilient students who have a higher level of satisfaction tend to experience lower burnouts.

---

[29] Clea A. McNeely, James M. Nonnemaker, and Robert W. Blum, "Promoting school connectedness: Evidence from the national longitudinal study of adolescent health," *Journal of School Health*,72, No. 4 (2002): 138-146; Michael D. Resnick, L. James Harris, Robert W. Blum, "The impact of caring and connectedness on adolescent health and well-being," *Journal of Paediatrics and Child Health* 29, No. 1 (1993): S3–S9.

[30] Luciano Romano, Giacomo Angelini, Piermarco Consiglio, and Caterina Fiorilli, "Academic Resilience and Engagement in High School Students: The Mediating Role of Perceived Teacher Emotional Support," *European Journal of Investigation in Health, Psychology and Education* 11, No. 2 (2021): 334-344; Claudia Russo, Daniela Barni, Ioana Zagrean, Maria Lulli, Giorgia Vecchi, and Francesca Danioni, "The Resilient Recovery from Substance Addiction: The Role of Self-transcendence Values and Hope," *Mediterranean Journal of Clinical Psychology* 9, No. 1 (2021).

[31] Robert Pietrzak, Douglas Johnson, Marc Goldstein, James Malley, Alison Rivers, Charles Morgan, and Stven Southwick, "Psychosocial buffers of traumatic stress, depressive symptoms, and psychosocial difficulties in veterans of Operations Enduring Freedom and Iraqi Freedom: The role of resilience, unit support, and postdeployment social support," *Journal of affective disorders* 120, No. 1-3 (2010): 188–192.

[32] Liselotte Dyrbye, David Power, Stanford Massie, Anne Eacker, William Harper, Matthew Thomas, Daniel Szydlo, Jeff Sloan Jeff, and Tait Shanafelt, "Factors associated with resilience to and recovery from burnout: a prospective, multi-institutional study of US medical students," *Medial Education* 44, No.10 (2010):1016–1026.

For instance, Masten et al.[33] explained that students who have a more positive outlook on the attributes of their teachers are more likely to be able to overcome academic burnout than students who rate their teachers lowly. Conversely, when students have a negative impression of their teachers and rate them low in terms of their quality of teaching and interaction, they tend to find it more difficult to cope with academic rigor and are significantly more likely to experience academic burnout.

From the foregoing, it appears that a consensus on the mediating role of student satisfaction on the relationship between academic resilience and academic burnout has been arrived at. However, it is worth noting that most of the studies reviewed focused on high school students who generally are exposed to a different academic environment and stressors than postgraduate students that this study focuses on. It is therefore based on this premise that this study seeks to test the following hypotheses:

H3: *Academic Resilience and student satisfaction will significantly predict academic burnout*

H4: *Academic Resilience will moderate the associations between student satisfaction and academic burnout*

Materials and methods

Research approach

Since this study seeks to investigate the moderating role of student satisfaction on the relationship between academic resilience and academic burnout among graduate students, the study made use of the quantitative research approach and involved the administration of questionnaires to a sample of the study population.

---

[33] Ann Masten, Janette Herbers, J. J. Cutuli, Theresa Lafavor, "Promoting competence and resilience in the school context," *Professional School Counseling* 12, No. 2 (2008).

Participants

The study participants included postgraduate students at Kampala International University (KIU) and Makerere University. According to the latest (2022) webometrics ranking, Makerere University and Kampala International University ranked number one and two among Ugandan universities. The fact they rank this high in the country also ensures that they attract a wide range of students from various backgrounds which makes them suitable for this study. Also, the two universities have the most robust postgraduate programs in Uganda and attract a lot of professors and senior lecturers in the country, who in turn ensure rigor and thoroughness in research. Based on these conditions, the researchers opted to select these institutions to sample.

In total, 402 students participated in this study. 256 of the participants were from Makerere University and 146 were from Kampala International University. Fifty-two percent of the total respondents were male and forty-eight were female. Their ages range from twenty-four to forty-five years. The average age was 31,3 for male students and 27,8 for female students.

Measures

This study measured three different variables, namely, academic resilience, student satisfaction, and academic burnout. To test the hypotheses, the researchers made use of a questionnaire that combined the following scales: the Maslach Burnout Inventory-Student Survey developed by Schaufeli, Martinez, Pinto, and Bakker,[34] the Brief Resilience Scale developed by Smith et al.[35] and the Student Satisfaction Inventory developed by Juillerat.[36] The Maslach Burnout Inventory-

---

[34] Schaufeli et al., "Burnout and engagement."

[35] Bruce Smith Bruce, Jeanne Dalen, Kathryn Wiggins, Erin Tooley, Paulette Christopher, and Jennifer Bernard, "The brief resilience scale: assessing the ability to bounce back," *International Journal of Behavioral Medicine*, 15 (2008): 194–200.

[36] Stephanie Lee Juillerat, "Investigating a two-dimensional approach to the assessment of student satisfaction: Validation of the student satisfaction inventory," Dissertation, Temple University, 1995.

Student Survey (MBI-SS) was used to measure academic burnout. The instrument measures cynicism (CY), academic efficacy (AE), and emotional exhaustion (EE). This instrument uses a seven-point frequency rating scale that ranges from 0 (never) to 6 (every day). A student that ranks high on EE and CY subscales and low on AE is said to suffer from academic burnout.

The Brief Resilience Scale was used to measure the ability of students to recover or bounce back from stress. The scale scored responses on a range from 1 (low resilience) to 5 (high resilience). Finally, ten questions from the Student Satisfaction Inventory were included in the questionnaire. The original scale has over seventy questions but not all the questions apply to the current study and therefore after validating the questionnaire in line with the current study, ten questions were selected. In total, the questionnaire had twenty-five questions and could be answered in about thirty minutes.

Procedure

To ensure that the questionnaire was distributed equitably, the researchers made use of stratified random sampling. This sampling approach involves sub-dividing the study population into different strata. These strata were created based on the faculties in each of the institutions, and then students within each faculty were randomly selected based on their proportion to the general population. By doing this, every faculty is properly represented in the study which improves the reliability and generalizability of the findings and conclusions. The breakdown of the distribution is as follows:

S/N	Institution	Faculty	Sample size
1	Makerere University	College of Agricultural and Environmental Sciences	21
		College of Business and Management Sciences	35
		College of Computing and Information Sciences	20

S/N	Institution	Faculty	Sample size
		College of Education and External Studies	30
		College of Engineering, Design, Art, and Technology	20
		College of Health Sciences	20
		College of Humanities and Social Sciences	40
		College of Natural Sciences	20
		College of Veterinary Medicine, Animal Resources and Bio-Security	20
		School of Law	30
		Subtotal	**256**
2	Kampala International University (main campus)	College of Humanities and Social Sciences	35
		College of Economics and Management	25
		College of Education, Open and Distant Learning	30
		School of Mathematics and computing	16
		School of Engineering and Applied Sciences	20
		School of Law	20
		Subtotal	**146**
Grand Total			**402**

Table 3-1: *Sample size distribution*

Results and discussion

H1: *Student satisfaction will be negatively associated with academic burnout.*

To test this hypothesis, a Pearson's correlation analysis was carried out and the results are presented in Table 2 below.

Variable	academic burnout	p-value
Student satisfaction	-.470**	< .001

Table 3-2: *Correlation between student satisfaction and academic burnout*

The result shows a significant negative relationship between student satisfaction *and* academic burnout ($r = -.470, p < .001$), which means that students with a higher level of satisfaction are less likely to experience academic burnout. Student satisfaction is conceptualized in this study as the availability of internal and external resources in the form of friends, and a good support system both in school and at home. This shows that if students have a good support system and they are not in a hostile academic environment, then they are significantly less likely to experience academic burnout.

This finding supports those by Zhang, Klassen, and Wang[37] in their study on middle school students which revealed that participants experienced high levels of burnout when there was an imbalance between requirements and available resources. Similarly, Kiuru et al.[38] concluded that students with a high level of external and internal resources, which leads to higher levels of satisfaction, tend to be shielded from the negative effects of academic burnout. Based on the foregoing, it can be concluded that Hypothesis 1 is accepted.

H2: *Academic Resilience will be negatively associated with academic burnout.*

To test this hypothesis, a Pearson's correlation test was carried out. The result of the analysis is presented in the table below.

[37] Zhang, Klassen, and Wang, "Academic burnout."

[38] Kiuru et al., "Peer group influence."

Variable	Academic burnout	p-value
Academic Resilience	-.499**	< .001

Table 3-3. *Correlation between academic resilience and academic burnout*

The result shows a significant negative relationship between academic resilience *and* academic burnout (r = -.499, $p < .001$), suggesting that students that possess a high level of academic resilience tend to experience less academic burnout. Therefore, it can be concluded that Hypothesis 2 is accepted.

Furthermore, the results of this study support those by Fiorilli et al.[39] and Romano et al.[40] who found out that academically resilient students are significantly less likely to experience academic burnout. Resilience in the context of this study means that students can effectively and efficiently handle pressure, setbacks, and challenges. What this means in the context of this study is that while it is almost inevitable that challenges will arise in students' academic journey, how students respond to these challenges and how they manage stress significantly impacts their likelihood of experiencing burnout.

H3: *Academic Resilience and student satisfaction will significantly predict academic burnout*

To test this hypothesis, a multiple regression analysis was carried out. The result of the analysis is presented below.

[39] Fiorilli et al., "L'utilizzazione dello."

[40] Romano et al., Students' Trait. "

Model Fit Measures

			Overall Model Test			
Model	**R**	**R^2**	**F**	**df1**	**df2**	**p**
1	0.583	0.340	103	2	399	< .001

Model Coefficients - Academic burnout

Predictor	Estimate	SE	t	p
Intercept	96.183	4.5602	21.09	< .001
Student Satisfaction	-0.458	0.0618	-7.41	< .001
Academic Resilience	-0.992	0.1167	-8.50	< .001

Results of the multiple regression show that there is a collective significant relationship between, student satisfaction, academic resilience and academic burnout, ($F(2, 399) = 103$, $p < .001$, $R^2 = .340$). The individual predictors were examined further and revealed that student satisfaction ($t = -7.41$, $< .001$) and academic resilience ($t = -8.50$, $< .001$) are significant predictors in the model.

The result suggests that high student satisfaction and academic resilience negatively impact academic burnout, which means that high levels of student satisfaction and academic resilience are associated with low academic burnout.

This finding lends support to the conservation of resource theory[41] by showing that students who try to be resilient and surround themselves with like-minded and people that support them are significantly less likely to experience burnout. The theory also suggests that if certain factors are present, in this case, internal and external resources, then

[41] Hobfoll E. Steven, "Conservation of resources. A new attempt at conceptualizing stress," *Am Psychol.*;44, No. 3(1989):513–524. doi:10.1037//0003-066x.44.3.513

such individuals can avoid or mitigate burnout. Based on the foregoing, Hypothesis 3 is also supported.

H4: *Academic Resilience will moderate the associations between student satisfaction and academic burnout*

	Estimate	**SE**	**Z**	**p**
Student Satisfaction	-0.4805	0.06211	-7.74	< .001
Academic Resilience	-1.1614	0.10700	-10.86	< .001
Student Satisfaction ✻ Academic Resilience	0.0172	0.00768	2.24	0.025
	Estimate	**SE**	**Z**	**p**
Average	-0.481	0.0624	-7.70	
Low (-1SD)	-0.601	0.0978	-6.15	
High (+1SD)	-0.360	0.0638	-5.64	

Note. shows the effect of the predictor (Student Satisfaction) on the dependent variable (Academic burnout) at different levels of the moderator (Academic Resilience)

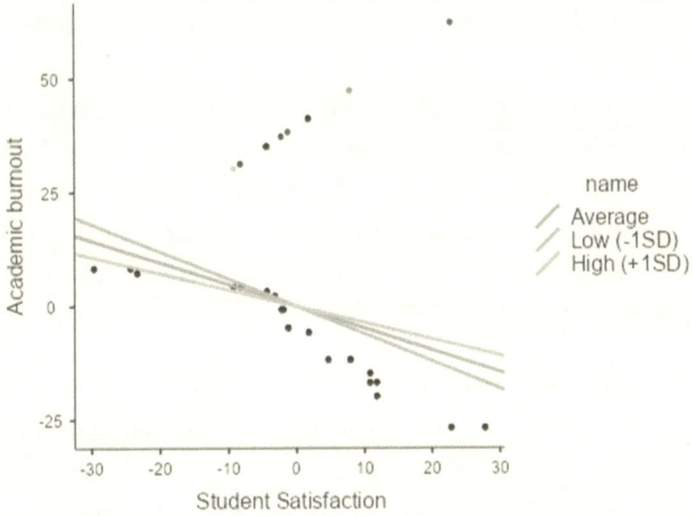

According to the results from JAMOVI, the overall moderation model has significant effects F (2, 399) = 103, p < .001. Also, the overall interaction effect is significant (p = .025) which means that academic resilience significantly moderates the relationship between student satisfaction and academic burnout.

Examining the interaction plot shows an enhancing effect: as student satisfaction increased, academic burnout decreased. At low, average, and high levels of academic resilience, student satisfaction significantly impacted academic burnout.

The results of this study support those by Drybye et al,[42] who found that resilient students are less likely to experience academic burnout when they have a positive perception towards their academic environment and the relationships developed within. In the same vein, the result supports those by Masten et al.,[43] who concluded that students who have a more positive outlook on their teachers' attributes are more likely to be able to overcome academic burnout than students who rate their teachers lowly. Based on the foregoing, it can be concluded that Hypothesis 4 is accepted.

Conclusions and recommendations

This study examined the relationship between student satisfaction, academic resilience, and academic burnout among postgraduate students at two universities in Uganda. The findings showed the importance of a good and healthy academic environment and culture, a good support system for students, and academic resilience on their likelihood to experience academic burnout. The study explains why some students, despite having great academic resilience, still end up experiencing academic burnout.

The study explained that even when a student has a high level of resilience but a very low level of satisfaction, then academic burnout remains a possibility. Based on this, it is the recommendation of the researchers that care is taken by institutions of higher education to not

[42] Drybye et al., "Factors."

[43] Masten et al., "Promoting competence."

only monitor the academic performance of students but to also support their mental health and ensure that the academic environment is such that encourages positive interactions and cordial relationships between all academic stakeholders (students, professors, and school management).

An environment that encourages open discourse and interaction in a fair and friendly environment can make the difference between a dropout and a student who completes their program. Furthermore, relationship satisfaction with family members and the environment of friends also plays a role in academic burnout and therefore needs to be managed. The researchers suggest that parents, spouses, and siblings of postgraduate students should encourage and support them to increase their chances of completing their studies.

School burnout is often the most quoted reason for dropping out of post-graduate students and this is usually in response to negative support from family and friends. This is particularly worrisome in the global south as parents and society expect that at a certain age, one is making money and taking care of their parents. So, going to school and relying on support from family, and aged in late twenties, is largely frowned upon. This attitude, widespread in African society, towards individuals who study into their twenties or thirties can be a source of stress for postgraduate students and therefore can lead to academic burnout if care is not taken.

The researchers, therefore, recommend the government in Uganda and other African countries to support postgraduate students by encouraging academic institutions to employ some of them as teaching/research assistants, so they are contributing professionally while still progressing academically. Also, a stipend from the government for postgraduate students will encourage studies while also helping students cope with the burden of pursuing further degrees without a job to support their family and themselves.

Bibliography

Abolmaali, Khadijeh, and Mahmudi, Roghayeh. "The prediction of academic achievement based on resilience and perception of the classroom environment." *Open Science Journal of Education* 1, No. 1 (2013): 7–12.

Ajam, Ekrami Asieh, Rezaei, Tahereh, and Bayani, Ali Asghar. "Relationship between hope to work and academic motivation with academic burnout." *Knowledge and Health* 10 (2015): 44–50.

Alarcon, Gene M., Edwards, Jean M., and Menke, Lauren E. "Student burnout and engagement: A test of the conservation of resources theory." *The Journal of Psychology* 145, No. 3 (2011): 211–27.

Ali, Mir M., Dwyer, Debra S., Vanner, Elizabeth A., and Lopez, Alexander. "Adolescent propensity to engage in health risky behaviors: The role of individual resilience." *International Journal of Environmental Research and Public Health* 7, No. 5 (2010): 2161–2176, doi:10.3390/ijerph7052161.

Arrebola-Moreno, Antonio, Garcia-Retamero, Rocio, Catena, Andres, Marfil-Álvarez, Rafeal, Melgares-Moreno, Rafeal, and Ramírez-Hernández, Jose. "On the protective effect of resilience in patients with acute coronary syndrome." *International Journal of Clinical and Health Psychology* 14, No. 2 (2014): 111–119. doi: 10.1016/S1697-2600(14)70044-4.

Dyrbye, Liselotte, Power, David, Massie, Stanford, Eacker, Anne, Harper, William, Thomas, Matthew, Szydlo, Daniel, Sloan, Jeff, and Shanafelt, Tait. "Factors associated with resilience to and recovery from burnout: a prospective, multi-institutional study of US medical students." *Medical Education* 44, No.10 (2010):1016–1026, doi:10.1111/j.1365-2923.2010.03754.x.

Fiorilli, Caterina, Galimberti Virna, De Stasio, Simona, Di Chiacchio, Carlo, and Albanese, Ottavia. "L'utilizzazione dello School Burnout Inventory (SBI) constudenti Italiani di scuola superiore di primo e secondo grado." *Psicologia clinica dello sviluppo* 18, No. 3 (2014): 403–423.

García-Izquierdo, Mariano, Ríos-Risquez, Isabel M., Carrillo-García, Cesar, and Sabuco-Tebar, Emiliana. "The moderating role of resilience in the relationship between academic burnout and the perception of psychological health in nursing students." *Educational Psychology* 38, No. 8 (2015): 1068–1079.

Hobfoll, Stevan E. "Conservation of resources. A new attempt at conceptualizing stress." *American Psychologist* 44, No. 3 (1989): 513–524, doi:10.1037//0003-066x.44.3.513.

Jensen, Phyllis Marie, Trollope-Kumar, Karen, Waters, Heather, and Everson, Jennifer. "Building physician resilience." *Canadian Family Physician* 54, No. 5 (2008): 722–729.

Juillerat, Stephanie Lee. *Investigating a two-dimensional approach to the assessment of student satisfaction: Validation of the student satisfaction inventory* (Dissertation, Temple University, 1995).

Kamalpour, Somayeh, Azizzadeh-Forouzi, Mansoureh, and Tirgary, Batool. "A study of the relationship between resilience and academic burnout in nursing students." *Journal of Medical Education Development Center* 13, No.5 (2017): 476–487.

Kim, Boyoung, Lee, Minyoung, Kim, Keunhwa, Choi, Hyunju, and Lee, Sang. "Longitudinal analysis of academic burnout in Korean middle school students." *Stress Health* 31, No. 4 (2015): 281–289.

Kiuru, Noona, Aunola, Kaisa, Nurmi, Jari-Erik, Leskinen, Esko, and Salmela-Aro, Katariina. "Peer group influence and selection in adolescents' school burnout: A longitudinal study." *Merrill-Palmer Quarterly* 54, No. 1 (January 2008): 23–55.

Kotzé, Martina, and Kleynhans, Ronel. "Psychological well-being and resilience as predictors of first-year students' academic performance." *Journal of psychology in Africa* 23, No. 1 (2014): 37–41.

Luthans, Fred, Vogelgesang, Gretchen R., and Lester, Paul B. "Developing the psychological capital of resiliency." *Human Resource Development Review* 5, No.1 (2006): 25–44.

Masten, Ann, Herbers, Janette, Cutuli, J.J., Lafavor, Theresa. "Promoting competence and resilience in the school context." *Professional School Counseling* 12, No. 2 (2008), doi:10.1177/2156759X0801200.

May, Ross, Bauer, Kristina, and Fincham, Frank. "School burnout: Diminished academic and cognitive performance." *Learning and Individual Differences* 42 (2015): 126–131.

McNeely Clea A., Nonnemaker James M., and Blum Robert W. "Promoting school connectedness: Evidence

from the national longitudinal study of adolescent health." *Journal of School Health* 72, No. 4 (2002): 138–146, doi: 10.1111/j.1746-1561.2002.tb06533.x.

Parviainen, Milja, Aunola, Kaisa, Torppa, Minna, Lerkkanen, Marja-Kristiina, Poikkeus, Anna- Maja, and Vasalampi, Kati. "Early antecedents of school burnout in upper secondary education: A five-year longitudinal study." *Journal of Youth and Adolescence* 50 (2021): 231–245.

Pietrzak Robert, Johnson Douglas, Goldstein Marc, Malley James, Rivers Alison, Morgan Charles, and Southwick Steven. "Psychosocial buffers of traumatic stress, depressive symptoms, and psychosocial difficulties in veterans of Operations Enduring Freedom and Iraqi Freedom: The role of resilience, unit support, and postdeployment social support." *Journal of Affective Disorders* 120, No. 1-3 (2010): 188–192, doi: 10.1016/j.jad.2009.04.015.

Rahmati, Zeinab. "The study of academic burnout in students with high and low level of self-efficacy." *Procedia - Social and Behavioral Sciences* 171 (2015): 49–55.

Resnick, Michael D., Harris, L. James, Blum, Robert W. "The impact of caring and connectedness on adolescent health and well-being." *Journal of Paediatrics and Child Health* 29, No. 1 (1993): S3–S9, doi: 10.1111/j.1440-1754.1993.tb02257.x.

Romano, Luciano, Angelini, Giacomo, Consiglio, Piermarco, and Fiorilli, Caterina. "Academic Resilience and Engagement in High School Students: The Mediating Role of Perceived Teacher Emotional

Support." *European Journal of Investigation in Health, Psychology and Education* 11, No. 2 (2021): 334–344, doi: 10.3390/ejihpe11020025.

Romano, Luciano, Buonomo, Ilaria, Callea, Antonino, Fiorilli, Caterina, and Schenke, Katerina. "Teacher Emotional Support Scale on Italian High School Students: A contribution to validation." *The Open Psychology Journal* 13, No. 1 (2020): 123–132, doi: 10.2174/1874350102013010123.

Romano, Luciano, Tang, Xin, Hietajärvi, Lauri, Salmela-Aro, Katariina, and Fiorilli, Caterina. "Students' Trait Emotional Intelligence and Perceived Teacher Emotional Support in Preventing Burnout: The Moderating Role of Academic Anxiety." *International Journal of Environmental Research and Public Health* 17, No. 13 (2020): 4771, doi:10.3390/ijerph17134771

Russo, Claudia, Barni, Daniela, Zagrean, Ioana, Lulli, Maria, Vecchi, Giorgia, and Danioni, Francesca. "The Resilient Recovery from Substance Addiction: The Role of Self-transcendence Values and Hope." *Mediterranean Journal of Clinical Psychology* 9, No. 1 (2021).

Salmela-Aro Katariina, and Upadyaya Katja. "School burnout and engagement in the context of demands-resources model." *The British Journal of Educational Psychology* 84, No; 1 (2014):137–151.

Salmela-Aro, Katariina, Kiuru, Noona, Leskinen, Esko, and Nurmi, Jari-Erik. "School burnout inventory (SBI) reliability and validity." *European Journal of Psychological Assessment* 25, No. 1 (2009): 48–57.

Santhosh, Rajan Kareepadath, and James, Jimmy. "The effect of resilience on burnout among the blue collared employees in metal factories." *International Journal of Multidisciplinary Management Studies* 3, No. 6 (2013): 48–55.

Schaufeli Wilmar, Martinez, Isabel, Pinto, Alexander, Salanova, Marisa, and Bakker, Arnold. "Burnout and engagement in university students, a cross-national study." *Journal of Cross-Cultural Psychology* 33, No. 5 (2002): 464–481.

Smith, Bruce, Dalen, Jeanne, Wiggins, Kathryn, Tooley, Erin, Christopher, Paulette, and Bernard, Jennifer. "The brief resilience scale: assessing the ability to bounce back." *International Journal of Behavioral Medicine* 15 (2008): 194–200.

Young, Lauryn, Mulloy, Maura, Huckabee, Sloan, Landoll, Ryan, Miller, Elaine, Miller, Marissa, and Weist, Mark D. "Child and Adolescent Mental Health and the Schools." In *Transition of Youth and Young Adults; Advances in Learning and Behavioral Disabilities*, edited by Bryan G. Cook, Melody Tankersley, and Timothy J. Landrum, 197–224 (Bingley: Emerald Group Publishing, 2015.

Zhang, Xiaozhou, Klassen, Robert M., and Wang, Yun. "Academic burnout and motivation of Chinese secondary students." *International Journal of Social Science and Humanity* 3, No. 2 (2013): 134–138.

Chapter Four
Yearbooks and the cultural memory of education in Uganda

Joel Isabirye

Introduction

This study examines the use of Year Books in preserving a cultural memory of education in Uganda. A Year Book refers to a publication that captures images and relevant data about classes in particular schools across a given year. Yearbooks serve informative and cultural functions that have endeared them to many students, alumni, and institutions through the years.

Cultural memory signifies a process in which distant and collateral events are standardized in agreeable forms by different groups and societies. A cultural memory of education refers to a process in which educational experiences are remembered and commemorated by students and educational institutions.[1]

Since 2018, the Digital Yearbook project has documented different schools in Uganda. The project was founded by Dr. Ronnie Mich Egwang, a social entrepreneur in Uganda. The focus of the Year Book project has been to capture photography and video of the students who were in a specific class that completed school each year. The project has also integrated additional data that includes a panoramic documentation of the school, interviews with staff, students, parents, and communities in which the schools are situated. Through these activities, each yearbook presents invaluable memories of education as

[1] Martin Bommas, ed., *Cultural memory and identity in ancient societies*. Vol. 1 (New York: Bloomsbury Publishing, 2011).

a cultural practice through various institutions in Uganda. To digitize the yearbook, a web portal was created (www.thedigitalyearbook.com).

Structured as an archival historical project, the Year Book project lists the following outputs as central to its objectives: Year Books, Advanced Digital Web Portal (ADWP), AudioVisual Recordings, Exhibitions, Workshops and Seminars, Publications, and Institutional Courses.

Uganda's educational system as a cultural space

The educational sector in Uganda is one of the most important sectors in the country. Not only has education become an enterprise, but it has also evolved into a vibrant cultural space. Each beginning and closure of school terms, life comes to a standstill as parents embark on taking their children to or back from school.

Uganda's educational system dates to the pre-colonial era, when the Christian Missionaries arrived in the territory that was later to be constituted as Uganda. The Church Missionary Society (CMS) of Anglican missionaries reached Uganda in 1877 and two years later, the Catholic missionaries arrived. As part of their evangelical program, the missionaries introduced formal education that was initially meant to inculcate their values in the lives of their converts. Education was further established to train converts to perform roles that they had been assigned.

The first school set up by the Church Missionary Society (CMS) missionaries was Mengo School in 1895. Initially Mengo SS was an elementary school called Kayanja (because of its short distance away from the Kabaka's lake called Kayanja ka Kabaka). Between 1895 and the 1990s, several schools offered primary and secondary education to the public with many of the initial schools being formed by the Christian Missionaries although Nabisunsa Girls was founded by the Muslims (see Table 1). A wealth of historical knowledge accompanies this heritage, yet most of it remains undocumented.

No.	Heritage School	Year of Formation	Founder
1.	Mengo Senior School	1895	Church Missionary Society (CMS)
2.	Namilyango College	1902	Catholic Mill Hill Fathers (Bishop Henry Hanlon)
3.	Gayaza High School	1905	Church Missionary Society (CMS)
4.	Kings College Buddo	1906	Church Missionary Society (CMS) (Henry Walter Weatherhead)
5.	St. Mary's College Kisubi	1906	Catholic White Fathers (Reverend Raux Modeste)
6.	Mt. St. Mary's Namagunga	1942	Catholic Franciscan Sisters for Africa (Mother Mary Kevin)
7.	Trinity College Nabingo	1942	Catholic White Fathers
8.	Makerere College School	1945	Colonial Government
9.	Nabisunsa Girls	1954	Muslim Prince Badru Kakungulu

Source (field data)

Table 4-1: *Heritage schools in Uganda*

Snapshot of the education sector in Uganda

Over the years, with the rapid growth of the Ugandan population, and the lack of adequate resources on the part of government to expand the public school system, Uganda extensively liberalized the education sector. The 1990s saw sweeping liberalization of the sector, with many private educational institutions given licenses to operate. Further, in 1996, the Government of Uganda introduced Universal Primary Education (UPE) which changed the educational sector. Almost all families were able to send their children to primary school.

Subsequently, the government enacted Universal Secondary Education (USE). Having shifted priorities from mass funding of students in higher education, Uganda was able to grow early childhood literacy rates and create a mass culture of education. Since then, Uganda's educational landscape has grown leaps and bounds, with the most recent statistics from the Ministry of Education and Sports (MOES) (2019) estimating that there are 30,785 pre-primary, primary, secondary, and post-primary educational institutions in Uganda. There are 10,883,840 learners in these institutions. Today, the number of privately owned educational institutions exceeds by far, those owned by the Government of Uganda. Nonetheless, the statistical outlay of schools in Uganda is given below in Table 2:

No.	Category of Institution	Number of Institutions	Number of Students Enrolled
1.	Pre-Primary	7210	608,973
2.	Primary	20,305	8,840,589
3.	Secondary	2,995	1,370,583
4.	Post-Primary	275	63,695
	Total	***30,785***	***10,883,840***

Source: field data: Ministry of Education and Sports (MOES) (2019)

Table 4-2: *Number of schools and enrollment in Uganda*

Problem statement

Across the world, there is limited evidence of projects that document educational institutions specifically as a means of preservation of cultural memory. However, there is information to the effect that educational institutions tend to maintain archives to study other aspects of society through relevant materials included in such archives. Most of the archives of educational history are not focused on a cross-section of schools but are aimed at collecting materials related to either one or two schools or the education sectors in different countries. On the other hand, those that collect such information are national archives, which are created and sustained by government.

However, these tend to be focused on historical records of policies, and specific developments related to the educational sector in respective countries. As a result, the focus on educational institutions is not given priority. This deprives societies of good resources to study the evolution of education through the basic unit of the education section: the school system.

Education forms a central part of people's past, present and future experiences. The school system is a principal locality of socialization and culture, often leaving behind memories that people take away for a lifetime. In Uganda, education and the school system are an integral part of society. By March 2020, president Yoweri Museveni announced there were at least ten million Ugandans taking courses within the school system. Uganda also has thousands of pre-primaries, primary, secondary and tertiary institutions which indicate that the education sector is not only a vibrant industry, but also a cultural milieu in which 22.7% of the population is active.

Yet, although formal education has subsisted in Uganda, since the 1870s with the arrival of the Christian Missionaries, the preservation of this historical culture through modern and innovative ways has been lacking.

Recorded memories of the sphere of education during the period of Uganda's turbulent past (1971 to 1986) face extinction because they are largely in the hands of individual collectors and a few institutions. Recently, the digital era has come to pose a threat to the preservation of century old memories of education in Uganda. Not only that, physical materials such as artefacts, monuments, apparel, and curriculum amongst other elements of school culture that have lived over the years are being lost or scattered. The loss of historical memory can deprive the current and the next generation of critical resources that can be used for reflection, research and where need be continuity of time-tested values through the education system.

The urgency to document social change in the education sector is not only significant for institutional memory, but also an instrumental process of safeguarding/preserving individual memory and development. For example, the printed photography which was an essential item in households is long gone. Physical albums are no longer *en vogue*. This predicament makes efforts to document a cultural memory of education worth studying.

Objectives

The study has two objectives:

1. To examine the significance of the Year Book project in preserving the cultural memory of education in Uganda
2. To analyze the production of the Year Book project in preserving the cultural memory of education in Uganda

Research questions

The study seeks to answer two research questions:

1. What is the significance of the Year Book project in preserving the cultural memory of education in Uganda?
2. How is the Year Book project produced for preserving the cultural memory of education in Uganda?

Contribution to knowledge

The need to explore how the Year Book project has captured a multiplicity of voices and artifacts that embody cultural memory of education in Uganda is an important priority in this study. The erosion or distortion of this memory may lead to the erasure or absence of modern historical records that can be used for learning in theory and practice. Historical record tends to preserve or disseminate old age values and traditions.

This study of this project and particularly the project's digital resource is more necessary than ever before because of COVID-19 and its ramifications. In this era, online and remote access to learning materials has become a priority. In the context of COVID-19, there is need for more digital resources for learning which the digital aspects of the Year Book Project entails.

Literature review

The significance of preserving the cultural memory of education

Literature on the cultural memory of education let alone the significance of it is profoundly limited. To address this gap and locate the significance of preserving the cultural memory of education, related literature examining concepts that can applied to explain a cultural memory of education, have been explored. Because Year Books embody a large volume of photography, the role of photography in constructing and preserving Cultural memory is also examined.

Memory is a significant concept because it plays an important role in life (Savage, 2018). Savage explains that the importance of memory is that it reflects the past and helps us to connect it with the present and the future. Memory also helps us to use our experience of the past and tap it for the present. Finally, memory is a reflection of a person's previous experience. This reflection is active, subjective, and intelligent. It does not only reflect the past as the past, but it can also offer us the possibility of reusing all past and present experiences. Memory is an active, subjective, intelligent reflection of a person's previous experiences. Perhaps the most important aspect of memory we can all relate with is that it is connected to learning. What is learnt formally or informally, is stored in people's memories.

The role of memory in giving human beings their unique identities has been considered as the recollection or storage of information that people receive. It can then be estimated that the memories people have of the schools they went to provide them with an identity based on that school, its processes and communities. Our memory makes us who we are, and it is one of the most intimate parts of ourselves.[2]

Different disciplines approach the study of memory differently. Historians look at memory as a tool for people to make meaning from events. Thus, one's memory of something is just as important as what actually happened. It requires one to study the meaning made of an event and the event itself. In the humanities (which may include history), the focus is on the significance of how and what people remember. It is noted that memories can be unconsciously flawed. Different people may also have different or conflicting memories or recollections of the same event. This makes memory a complex process because it may be in a state of flux from one individual to another.

The construction of history is largely based on memory. After all the statement of historical fact depends on how a group of people collectively remember them. It has been argued further that memory is important in historical studies because it presents history with a flow and an emotional meaning and knowledge that is void in most basic historical documents. But it ensures that we understand a past on which basis we can understand the future.

Beyond the academic role and identity construction that some studies have implicated memory in, there is the particular significance it has to the individual. Liberman, Boehm, Lyubomirsky, and Ross[3] note that memories (past experiences) determine people's happiness and well-being. This however should be stated with a caveat that this only occurs with good memories.

---

[2] Gabriel A. Radvansky, "Event segmentation as a working memory process," *Journal of Applied Research in Memory and Cognition* 6, No. 2 (2017): 121–123.

[3] Liberman, V., Boehm, J. K., Lyubomirsky, S., and Ross, L. D.,"Happiness and memory: Affective significance of endowment and contrast," *Emotion* 9, No. 5 (2009), 666–680.

Cultural memory

Memory sites assume a particular cultural role.[4] German Egyptologist Jan Assman[5] coined the concept and term cultural memory which he applied to examine the textuality of the past. Cultural memory consists of individual storage of texts, images and rites that are meant for reuse related to various societies and epochs. In recent times there has been a growth of research and scholarship on cultural memory. These studies attempt to understand how peoples' memories function in cultural spheres. Therefore, they analyze the distinguishing features of memories. This covers how, where and when memory is produced. It also involves finding out how people make use of memory in their daily lives. Cultural memory research further reviews how personal or individual memory connects with shared, public forms of memory, and ultimately, how memory figures in, and even shapes the social body and social worlds.[6]

Cultural memory then is shared by a collective group of people. It is a shared and constructed understanding of the past that is transgenerational through text, oral traditions, monuments, rites, and other symbols. Like all forms of memory, cultural memory has important functions. For example, it crystallizes shared experiences. In doing so, cultural memory is helpful because it gives us an opportunity to understand the past. It also pronounces the values and norms of the group (or more accurately groups) to which we belong.

Cultural memory also creates a form of shared identity and a means of communicating this identity to new members. To some studies, cultural memory is an institution. It is exteriorized, objectified, and stored away

---

[4] Maurantonio, Nicole. "The Politics of Memory." In *The Oxford Handbook of Political Communication*, eds. Kate Kenski, and Kathleen Hall Jamieson (Oxford: Oxford University Press, 2014.), 1–17.

[5] Assman, Jan. "Communicative and Cultural Memory." In *Cultural Memory Studies. An International and Interdisciplinary Handbook*, eds. Astrid Eril, Ansgar Nunmig (Berlin and New York: de Gruyter, 2008), 109–118.

[6] Annette Kuhn, "Photography and cultural memory: A methodological exploration," *Visual studies* 22, No.3 (2007): 283–292.

in symbolic forms that, unlike the sounds of words or the sight of gestures, are stable and situation-transcendent: they may be transferred from one situation to another and transmitted from one generation to another.[7]

Education and cultural memory

The location of Cultural memory in education relates to the role of educational history or history education that focuses on how students learn about the past.[8] The mass media has been described as one of the instruments of shaping historical memory and which should be studied for its gradually increasing role.[9]

Photography and memory

One of the items that aids our understanding of Cultural memory is photography. Studying photographs can help us to decipher the connection between human memory and the photographs human beings take. Photographs store memory but also help to activate memory recall by identifying specific aspects of memory that trigger the mind.[10] This makes their role in documentation and evoking of time critical. Photography is regarded as a time machine in domestic culture. Specifically, because it stimulates the remembrance of particular moments in time.[11]

Photographs are therefore an invention and instrument of memory not a replacement of memory. Studying photography has proven a critical

---

[7] Assman, "Cultural Memory."

[8] Geerling, Judith, "Memory and Education – what is the role of education in preserving memory?," *euroclio.eu*, October 11, 2018, https://euroclio.eu/2018/10/11/memory-and-education-what-is-the-role-of-education-in-preserving-memory/.

[9] Kirik, Vladimir, Leshkevich, Tatiana, and Motozhanets, Anna. "Memory Culture as the Main Priority of the Modern Education Process." In *4th International Conference on Arts, Design and Contemporary Education (ICADCE 2018)*. Amsterdam: Atlantis Press, 2018.

[10] Sarinana, Joshua, "Memory, Photography, and the Human Brain," *joshuasarinana.com*, n.d., https://www.joshuasarinana.com/memory-photography-and-the-human-brain.

[11] David Bate, "The memory of photography," *Photographies* 3, No. 2 (2010): 243-257.

way of understanding cultural memory. This is because photographs play a significant role in the reconstruction of individual and collective memory and history.[12] For a lot of the emerging qualitative social research visual materials and methods, photographic self-image-self-portraits and portraits are instrumental in studying time and memory.[13]

At the individual level, beyond scholarship, photography, plays the important role of constructing family images and family memories. It also evokes a certain sense of belonging for the members towards their family.[14] It is valued by family memberships because it can "preserve" or capture memories for posterity.[15] Thus, the future can rely on photographs and memories to depict past events.

Despite the contestations over whether photographs are truthful representations of reality, people naturally rely on photographs (what they see) and what they remember.[16] In summary therefore, photography and the different manifestations of it (still or moving photography for example) record the personal history of people, for the purpose of reviving memories of specific encounters later. It therefore cannot be far-fetched to consider photography as part of memory itself. In cultural memory, and memory work, personal and family

---

[12] Tim Fawns, "Photography and the disruption of memory and meaning," *Ubiquity: The Journal of Pervasive Media* 3, No. 1-2 (2014): 3–14.

[13] Brian Roberts, "Photographic portraits: Narrative and memory," *Forum Qualitative Sozialforschung/Forum: Qualitative Social Research* 12, No. 2 (2011): doi.org/10.17169/fqs-12.2.1680.

[14] Erkonan, Şahika. "Photography and the construction of family and memory." In *Politics, Civil Society and Participation: Media and Communications in a Transforming Environment*, eds. Leif Kramp, Nico Carpentier, Andreas Hepp, Richard Kilborn, Risto Kunelius, Hannu Nieminen, Tobias Olsson, Pille Pruulmann-Vengerfeldt, Ilija Tomanić Trivundža, and Simone Tosoni (Bremen: edition lumière, 2016); 257–272.

[15] Shevchenko, Olga. "'The mirror with a memory': placing photography in memory studies." In *Routledge International Handbook of Memory Studies*, eds. Anna Lisa Tota, and Trever Hagen (London: Routledge, 2015), 294–309.

[16] Maria Theresa Moerman, *The Magic Mirror. Reflections on Photography as a memory* (Dissertation Fine Art Photography. Atlantic International University, 2012).

photographs offer a route for us to understand the social and cultural aspects of memory.[17]

Alumni's, Year Books and the cultural memory of education

Alumni and their associations exist because of the inherent benefits they accrue to their membership and the institutions they hail from. There is an enormous amount of public relations value that institutions get from their alumni. Alumni associations help to create, maintain, or modify relations between the institutions and their publics.[18] To this effect, the Malaysian Government, through its Ministry of Higher Education (MOHE) views alumni as one party to realize the goals of universities' internalization.[19] Alumni and alumni associations improve the image of their respective institutions because their successes are attached to a good foundation they secured at the institution (Singer and Hughey, 2002/2003).[20]

Therefore, it can be argued that the achievements of alumni are traced to their foundational institutions while the improvements in status and quality of the institutions impact positively on the status of alumni. This creates more brand recognition for the institution. Khanfar, Swaidan, and Mujtaba[21] point out the need for institutions to maintain a relationship with their alumni for outreach purposes and to obtain data for their decisions. Most importantly, through alumni associations,

---

[17] Kuhn, "Photography and cultural memory."

[18] Alfredo Arceo, "The role of student and alumni associations in the democratization process in Spain," *Higher Education in Europe* 28, No.4 (2003): 523–528.

[19] U. N. Saraih, Nor Irwani Abdul Rahman, Norshahrizan Noordin, Sayang Nurshahrizleen Ramlan, Razli Ahmad, Mohd Fo'ad Sakdan and M. Harith Amlus, "Modelling Students' Experience Towards the Development of Alumni Involvement and Alumni Loyalty," *MATEC Web of Conferences Volume 150, 2018, Malaysia Technical Universities Conference on Engineering and Technology (MUCET 2017)*: 05050, doi.org/10.1051/matecconf/201815005050.

[20] Tara S. Singer, and Aaron W. Hughey, "The role of the alumni association in student life," *New directions for student services* 100 (2002): 51–68.

[21] Nile M. Khanfar, Ziad Swaidan, and Bahaudin G. Mujtaba, "A Study in Relationship Orientation and Prioritization of Alumni Association Preferences with College Seniors in Higher Education," *Contemporary Issues in Education Research* 2, No. 3 (2009): 15–22.

alumni connect with their former classmates which creates for them an ongoing sense of community. In some instances, alumni might be an alternative source of income at universities as is the case in South Africa.[22]

Year Books are valuable items that form part of the rituals of schools. One historic school ritual of graduating—or simply finishing one grade and moving on to the next—has been getting a copy of the yearbook, and passing it around for friends to sign and scribble in. This historical ritual serves five different functions according to Stanley.[23] These functions are: they serve as memory books, history books, reference books, public relations tools, and educational experience. In essence, Year Books preserve memory, document memory, are points of reference, and serve as public relations tools for institutions, while embodying educational experiences. There are various concerns about the future of Year Books, especially with the digitization of published materials over the years. Smith[24] citing National Public Radio notes that there was a drop in the publications of Year Books in the United States from about 2,400 in 1995 to about 1,000 by 2010. Correspondingly, there is a shift in publication of Year Books to the digital space as they embrace new technology and ways of doing business.

Year Books are artifacts of Cultural memory of educational institutions and tie in with Alumni culture which is another process of constructing Cultural memories of these institutional communities. The review of literature has mainly borrowed ideas from studies that examine the notion of cultural memory and the significance of photography in the construction, preservation, and the remembrance of the past. The purpose of this approach is to establish how the Year Book, which is

---

[22] A. A. Braam Rust, "Challenges of alumni associations at universities: Income from alumni (donations and bequests) at South African Universities," *African Journal of Business Management* 6, No. 45 (2012): 11273–11280.

[23] Stanley Todd, 5 functions of a yearbook, *slideshare.net*, April 19, 2020, https://www.slideshare.net/Todd_Stanley/5-functions-of-a-yearbook.

[24] Susan Smith, "The Future of the Venerable Yearbook: Embracing New Technology, New Ways of Doing," *cmreview.org*, June 17, 2013, http://cmreview.org/Business.

essentially a photographic preservation project has assumed similar functions in the education sector in Uganda.

Methodology

The study is designed as a descriptive study. In this sense, the findings are presented in a descriptive form and the main approach in the collection and analysis of data is qualitative. Methods used in the study were content analysis and interviews were methods employed to collect data for the study.

Findings

Objective 1: To examine the significance of the Year Book project in preserving the cultural memory of education in Uganda

All of the respondents found the Year Book project beneficial to the preservation of cultural memory of education in Uganda, as given by their responses in the interviews conducted. More specifically unique responses related to the significance of Year Books in preserving a cultural memory of education were extracted from the interviews. The Year Book Project assists in the selective preservation of collective memory. It is selective in the sense that it picks interesting highlights of an educational institution's collective remembrance of its past. This is articulated by Ronnie Egwang as follows:

> The year book helps to keep the memories people have of their school in one piece. It does not collect everything because different people will always have different memories about different things. But it has many things that most of the people can remember. The purpose is to make sure that people collectively keep their memories about the education together. What are the interesting social moments that represent an era and capture it. Then we can compare (Ronnie Egwang, Interview).

Year Books have closed the gap where students were passing through institutions without the means of capturing their memories of their institutions. Elly Sentongo and Carol Achen Ocheng explain this further respectively:

> Many individuals have gone through various institutions and there is no structure in place to capture their memories and their times of study (Owekitibwa Elly Sentongo Interview).

> Without a doubt, there was a gap and we have already lost so much history as individuals, families, and institutions because of wars, lack of technology, and lack of systems/processes to share culture/memories. There would be a sincere concern about what legacy and heritage that we will pass on to our children if not in a beautifully packaged format (Carol Achen Oceng Interview).

Two senior officials at the Ministry of Education and Sports in the Republic of Uganda found the project to be an important endeavor that can be supported or built upon in future:

> It is important that they have already started this project and when someone sees the work and outputs, they may want to substantiate and say here I have information that I can give you or I have photos that we can share with you (Mary Ntete Gunteese Interview).

> It has a robust emotional impact (Patrick Muinda Interview).

The Digital Year Book has been described by one respondent as a tool for record keeping:

> The Digital Year Book is a critical project that is helping fill gaps for people like us who are really bad at record keeping. There is an immense amount of knowledge and information that is being misplaced and lost forever because we are not caretakers of content (Ben Mwine Interview).

One of the respondents who works with the Year Book Project explains why the Year Book was an important project for them. She highlights the pictorial element and conceives the project as significant for Uganda:

> Memories are captured most effectively using pictures and videos and that is what sets aside The Digital Year Book from other projects (Beneth Ampaire Interview).
>
> The Digital Year Book helps to keep memories for students and their days in school and their institutions (Desire Mukisa Interview).
>
> "The Digital Year Book keeps people connected and memories alive… It's a networking medium for former students staying in touch… And it's a marketing tool for schools to showcase and highlight the unique selling propositions of their institutions... It's a medium which shares accolades and what the institution has achieved…" (Qudrat Nankya Interview).
>
> The yearbook stores knowledge that if not archived today will be hard to collect in the future (Christopher Mutenyo Interview).

In addition to explaining how they thought the Year Book Project was significant not only as a cultural resource the different stakeholders offered perspectives on how it could be tapped for broader relevance. According to Elly Sentongo, the Year Book Project needed to look beyond the school and also cover the community around it:

> The history and background of the institutions are very important and should be catalogued in some sort of system. In addition, community relevance and their contribution to the area of influence should be highlighted i.e., socio-economic development of the area. The local and national impact of the

> institution should be highlighted for example in training of the youth, increasing accessibility of education to financially challenged, levels of the community, infrastructure development and more (Owekitibwa Elly Sentongo Interview).

At the Ministry of Education of Sports, they were of the view that the educational sector needed to become an integral part of the Year Book project as follows:

> I would also like it to have an educational outcome i.e. Can I track certain individuals and see where I went to school and what are they doing now? And how has going through the education system/that school impacted on their life? Can the Uganda Education Sector Strategic Plan be integrated into execution and implementation objectives of the project? (Patrick Muinda Interview).

> Can they profile current and past students from all institutions to see where they have come from and where they are now? Can they capture specific information about foundation bodies and individuals and the historical infrastructure of the institutions? Who set it up, community information, who gifted it to who, the missionaries, etc...? Can they also ensure the culture, language, history, archive information, etc... is also safeguarded because a lot of information is lot during movement and migration from analog to digital records? (Buye Abubaker Interview).

> Can they profile a section of the Ministry of Education as a pilot to showcase your capacity and possibly scale up slowly to generate buy in? Can they assist to enrich the content on the MOES website and digital content? Can they include the foundation bodies to ascertain the origin of the schools i.e. Catholic or Muslim, Buganda Kingdom, etc...? (Mary Ntete Gunteese Interview).

> There is an educational management system that does statistical research whom they can partner with in order to get information for content required. Can they ensure that information is kept in the cloud to prevent loss during movement or migration, strikes, fires, etc…? (Mary Ntete Gunteese Interview).

The responses from the three officials at the Ministry of Education of Sports (MOES) indicates that the policy makers have picked interest in the Year Book as an instrument of preservation of data in the sector. They are however conscious of the need to safeguard the preservation of these materials. Other respondents wanted a number of inclusions to the Year Book that could have a stronger impact in its attempt to preserve memories. One respondent wanted emphasis on the most impactful stories and events while others felt that the evolutionary nature of education should be attended to as show in their responses below.

> There are urban legends, stories, and personal recounts about events and activities that happened in the past and impacted the students, school, community and even the nation (Ben Mwine Interview).

> More emphasis needs to be placed on the evolution of school structures, culture, and history over the years and the institutions impact on the scholar's behavior. Can there be more focus on old/former students their contributions to the school during and after their education cycle and how they can influence and impact the growth and wellbeing of the students and the institution (Beneth Ampaire Interview).

There were two responses on cost and format of the Year Book. One respondent said that the book may be costly for parents, while another suggested that the hard copy format might be prone to wear and tear. These responses are given blow:

> The Year Book project is a cost to parents that maybe conflicted in the current times of Covid where parents will have to tradeoff between value, they get from saving memories and share of wallet for school fees and pocket money (Carol Achen Oceng Interview).
>
> The focus of the yearbook should be shifted from the hardcopy; more to the digital format which may be a greater resource for future generations than books that may wear and tear (Christopher Mutenyo Interview).

Some other respondents would like the Year Book Project to get the young generation to have a sense of ownership of the project.

> The Year Book should have aspects that motivate the kids to be excited about the project and helps them to understand the value of the project. Because currently it is mostly the elderly and senior citizens who see value in archiving (Desire Mukisa Interview).
>
> Why not get young people excited about archiving… knowledge management and valuing information…? Possibly initiating a "History Hunt" where groups of students go on a treasure hunt for old content… photos… stories… from old students/stories/ past teachers/communities and info from the past that can be added to the archive databank. It is important that the yearbook prioritizes the online/digital aspect of the project to ensure that there is increased access to information for a significant number of individuals (Qudrat Nankya Interview).

Objective 2: To analyze the production of the Year Book project in preserving the cultural memory of education in Uganda

The production of the Year Book follows specific activities and timelines as indicated in the excerpt of interview with one of the producers of the project:

> Production cycle is monthly and involves planning, production, outreach and stakeholder relations and research (Ronnie Egwang, Interview).

There are three main phases in capturing the cultural memory of a particular school in the Year Book. These phases in order of sequence are outreach, research and production. Findings from the interview data relating to this is presented below:

> Outreach involves talking to stakeholders to get buy in. The stakeholders are old student associations, board of directors, the administration, teachers, students, and parents. The purpose of the stakeholder engagement is to outline the benefits of the project to the organization, to the school, to the students and to the parents. We classify the stakeholders into three different layers: policy (old students, Parents Teachers Association (PTA), Board of Governors, and Head Teachers, and Students. Each stakeholder is engaged to show them the benefits of preserving the cultural memory of their school to them as individuals or institutions (Ronnie Egwang, Interview).

Outreach impacts on the next phase of research because it helps to identify data and material sources and cooperation from a wide range of people who are encouraged to volunteer to participate. The research process is extensive and forms phase two as described by another member of the Year Book Project Team:

> In the research phase, everything that we can get about the institution is captured. For example, photos of all the past head teachers, different people who have different materials and people to contact. So, we extract this information and triangulate or corroborate the facts to get a collective history and memory. The research is primary research. We talk to individuals who are recommended by stakeholders at the institution, and we go and find out from them. This is an important phase because without

> research the production will be very scanty (Ronnie Egwang, Interview).

The final phase, which is phase three, is the production phase. It is subdivided into two parts: shooting and editing. According to Egwang, this is the most taxing of the three phases although it may not be as important as the first two because without them, it cannot be adequately done.

> We plan the production in such a way as to capture an array of photographs. We capture the institution in three ways; first is videography of the entire school with a drone. Drone footage is a snapshot of everything, and it brings the project to life. Secondly, we also do photography of everything (infrastructure). Thirdly we photograph all the stakeholders, everyone from top to bottom at one point in time (Ronnie Egwang, Interview).

The stakeholders are a broad coalition of interest groups involved in the running of the school as Egwang states:

> These stakeholders include: the Board, Parent Teachers Association-PTA, Teachers, Old Students Association, every student, every non-teaching staff, headboy, headgirl, oldest teacher, student representatives, representatives of classes, clubs and associations, patrons of clubs and any other designation we can find that can generate content for that year. These are captured as pictures and interviews. We interview every single stakeholder; we interview every student and get articles from representatives. We are also keen on interviewing former (old) students because we know that it can inspire young students. After production we evaluate if the details are consistent. For example, if we were given a list of twenty-nine students for a given class and we have twenty-five pictures, we have to go back and capture the remaining four students (Ronnie Egwang, Interview).

At the production phase, there is a high possibility that material can be lost even before the project team leaves the institution. This has taught them the need to back up their resources in multiple formats and devices. Although it is possible to re-film what has been lost, rarely can the same expressions of memory be collected in repeated sessions.

> We back up everything after the production shoot. We do a backup of a backup. No one leaves a venue until there are three backups: cards, 3 computers and the hard drives (Ronnie Egwang, Interview).

Not only does losing the production of a particular film become a financial loss, it can be an insurmountable task to locate some of the sources of data and they might not be able to repeat the facts or recollections that were captured in the first production sessions. The editing phase of production is equally time consuming and painstaking. Ronnie Egwang describes the process which like the other phases is required to be completed within a specific time frame.

> This is a painstaking process. We take 10,000 to 15,000 pictures and editing one person takes 10 to 15 minutes. We edit 1,000 to 2,000 people. We clean up meta data such as the name, class and title then edit the videos and photos. After editing and clean of each photo, we do a lay out of the printed version of the Year Book. The design team lays out the book by designing where each material shall be apportioned. They align pictures with texts and deal with mundane elements such as pagination and table of contents. Here there is no room for error because the book will be a permanent record of a student, a class and an institution. At the layout stage we match primary data and secondary data and put together the book over 3 to 4 days with a ceiling of a week as the maximum duration we care supposed to do this (Ronnie Egwang, Interview).

The various processes of producing the Year Book may not follow a linear fashion although the three phases are sequential in arrangement:

> All these activities can overlap while others are part of a critical path. Then we review the look and feel of the year book before sending it for review and approval by the school and its stakeholders. We make one sample for this purpose. They usually make changes and comments then we do revisions and when they approve the final product and all the elements, we print the final version of the Year Book and upload the material to the digital version on the web portal. We create profile entries for the students for example: class of 1928, class of 1997 and so on. We create a whole Year Book page for the institutions (Ronnie Egwang, Interview).

The contents of different Year Books have a standard structure and some basic elements that differentiate them.

> We have a standardized structure. Certain schools have unique aspects which are unique for that school which makes it different from other. For example, at Namilyango, the Headmasters, those White Fathers used to keep detailed records which they passed on to the next Headmaster. These are stories that go through World Wars etc. Others had magazines from the 1980s which other institutions did not have. You must have detailed discussions with the institutions to find out which information do I need to have and that is what makes them differentiated (Ronnie Egwang, Interview).

Discussion

Objective 1: To examine the significance of the Year Book project in preserving the cultural memory of education in Uganda

From the qualitative interviews, it was determined that the Year Book project is an instrumental tool for the preservation of the cultural memory of education in Uganda. Its significance was manifested in the various explanations given by different stakeholders who rationalized its usefulness.

In essence, it was found that most of the educational institutions that feature or may feature in this project have been monumental institutions in the provision of education services to the country. For many people, they have either studied in these institutions, have relatives who have studied at these institutions or have heard about these institutions. This project serves as a museum of sorts. A central repository that is digitized, and which the public can utilize for different purposes, from time to time while the hard copy version is a tangible preservation of the cultural memory of schools.

The vibrancy of the school system in Uganda makes the project a frontline source of data gathering concerning cultural memory in the country. Uganda's turbulent and checkered past, mainly between 1971 and 1986 created a severe disruption of socio-cultural, economic, and political life. Subsequently, it affected a structured preservation of cultural memory. A lot of what is known in the school system about this period is only reflected in oral transmission and in few and rare collections of individuals and the institutions. There is no central repository that reflects this and other aspects of Uganda's educational heritage.

Officials from the Ministry of Education and Sports that have been grappling with ways of conserving data and historical moments of thousands of schools expressed the invaluable nature of the project. Thus, it is in the interest of government to have a documentation of Uganda's educational history. There are many lessons to be learnt from the changing face of education. At the same time, having a repository of schools in the education sector reflects how much the government could have contributed to the transformation of the education sector in the country. From a handful of schools at independence, Uganda now boasts of thousands of schools with millions in enrollment. The process has not been entirely smooth and some of the documented materials could support the government\s effort to spearhead reform where it is needed.

Some of the respondents thought the project offers a unique opportunity for researchers to source primary data on cultural memory through the school system in Uganda. The project is and shall further become a springboard for publications, workshops and seminars that could be produced out of these materials.

At a global level, the conservation of culture has been on the agenda of international agencies since the establishment of the United Nations in 1945. By and large, the respondents considered the project as being about the preservation of culture through creating a repository of information and photography/videography about the education sector. Both culture and education are foci of the United Nations Education Scientific and Cultural Organization-UNESCO. But most importantly, UNESCO is interested in preserving cultural heritage and historical sites across the world. Most of these are designated by Nation-States. While schools that have existed as much as these countries have existed or even existed before having not been catered for in the preservation project. This could be a first experiment that UNESCO and other agencies can replicate elsewhere.

In the view of some of the respondents, the Year Book project is a platform for collaboration and participation by all educational institutions. Each educational institution that is featured in this project will have an archival entity that can be purposeful for the institution and students who have gone through the school. It will be a centralized location for data preservation and retrieval for different institutions.

At the level of students, respondents interviewed indicated that current students and Alumni of the given institutions featured in the project shall find it relevant to preserve their cultural memories, and materials. They will also find that the repository is an important tool of historical record, that they and their relations can refer to when reflecting on their journey of passage at the school. Finally, one respondent looked at the value that creative producers could get from using the materials obtained from this project. In his view, producers of films and documentaries, who may want to adopt these materials for their productions can find it useful.

Objective 2: To analyze the production of the Year Book project in preserving the cultural memory of education in Uganda

Production of the Year Book is an elaborate and systematic process carried out within a strict deadline. It is structured into three broad phases of: outreach, research, and production. Outreach is a very important first phase that coordinates the participation of different stakeholders in the project. The goal of outreach is to get buy in for the project to be accepted and to get leads to data and materials. Outreach is also necessary for the project to be owned by the stakeholders. The main stakeholders are in three categories:

1. policy makers and influencers
2. teachers and parents
3. Students (current and alumni).

Stakeholder manager is crucial for cultural preservation projects. Each stakeholder brings and takes away something from the table. To manage all stakeholders, their interests should be represented in the project and their input and voices must be sought. The phase of research undergirds the success of this cultural preservation project. Most of the desired information and materials are not readily available. An extensive research process should be undertaken to access surface and hidden materials. The approach taken to the research process is integrated, holistic and conducted with an open mind. This is to create an atmosphere where anything available can be sourced. A critical path of this research process is using the multiple approach to verify, corroborate, and validate the different types of data being sourced. The combined approaches also result into a collective ownership of the process. Advanced technologies have been deployed to enhance efficiency in the implementation of the project. For example, drones are utilized to capture some of the images that cannot be easily captured with manual means. Drones helps to manage time and bring more accuracy in the collection of pictorial data. Robust preservation methods of the materials collected are employed. This is because any loss of gathered data is a loss of memory. The use of multiple backups is vital because loss of one collection of materials may call for redoing the entire project. Detailed editing of materials is also undertaken. The focus of materials to be collected reflects the culture of the respective institutions being documented. For example, clubs, motto, flags, symbols, slangs, and anthems These comprise the cultural fabric of these institutions through the years. The stakeholders and particular the school administration serve as gatekeepers of the cultural memory of the institution. They vet the content at the final stage by making comments on the project output. The producers of the Year Book require an approval from the school administration, which often requires that they revise the Year Book in line with comments from the school administrators. The adherence to strict deadlines is a mark of efficiency. Production of each project is planned for a maximum duration of 30 days. All projects need to be completed within a specific time frame for other projects to be implemented. The challenge with this aspect of the project is that the information and materials that are not collected within that time frame will be left out. This implies that over time follow up production on the different institutions will be necessary, if only to capture aspects of memory that could have been skipped or lost.

Conclusion

This chapter set out to examine Year Books and the Cultural Memory of Education in Uganda. The study had two objectives: first was to examine the significance of Year Books in the Cultural Memory of Education in Uganda and the second was to analyze the process of production of the Year Book in the Cultural Memory of Education in the country. Conclusively it was found that the Year Book Project is a significant tool for Cultural Memory of Education in Uganda. Various stakeholders expressed their views about its role in preserving individual and institutional memory. Some of the stakeholders visualized the project as an instrumental element in documenting the educational sector in Uganda. It was also concluded that the process of producing the Year Book is complex and needs a negotiation between multiple stakeholders with various interests and memories of particular institutions. Further, it was concluded that the technical aspects of producing the Year Book are astute and there are safeguards in place to ensure that the materials collected and the memories they collect are lost. Based on the findings, it is recommended that the Year Book Project takes into account the views of more stakeholders as they come and there is need to sensitize the young generation that is digitally savvy about the merits of the Year Book Project. The costs of production notwithstanding, the Year Book Project should endeavor to cover as many institutions as possible if it is to accomplish the goal of documenting a comprehensive Cultural Memory of Education in Uganda.

Bibliography

Arceo, Alfredo. "The role of student and alumni associations in the democratization process in Spain." *Higher Education in Europe* 28, No.4 (2003): 523–528.

Assman, Jan. "Communicative and Cultural Memory." In *Cultural Memory Studies. An International and Interdisciplinary Handbook*, edited by Astrid Eril, Ansgar Nunmig, 109-118 (Berlin and New York: de Gruyter, 2008).

Bate, David. "The memory of photography." *Photographies* 3, No. 2 (2010): 243–257.

Bommas, Martin. ed. 2011. Cultural Memory and Identity in Ancient Societies. London and New York: Bloomsbury Publishing.

Erkonan, Şahika. "Photography and the construction of family and memory." In *Politics, Civil Society and Participation: Media and Communications in a Transforming Environment*, eds. Leif Kramp, Nico Carpentier, Andreas Hepp, Richard Kilborn, Risto Kunelius, Hannu Nieminen, Tobias Olsson, Pille Pruulmann-Vengerfeldt, Ilija Tomanić Trivundža, and Simone Tosoni, 252–272 (Bremen: edition lumière, 2016).

Fawns, Tim. "Photography and the disruption of memory and meaning." *Ubiquity: The Journal of Pervasive Media* 3, No. 1-2 (2014): 3–14.

Geerling, Judith. "Memory and Education – what is the role of education in preserving memory?." *euroclio.eu*. October 11, 2018, https://euroclio.eu/2018/10/11/memory-and-education-what-is-the-role-of-education-in-preserving-memory/.

Khanfar, Nile M., Swaidan, Ziad, and Mujtaba, Bahaudin G. "A Study in Relationship Orientation and Prioritization of Alumni Association Preferences with College Seniors in Higher Education." *Contemporary Issues in Education Research* 2, No. 3 (2009): 15–22.

Kirik, Vladimir, Leshkevich, Tatiana, and Motozhanets, Anna. "Memory Culture as the Main Priority of the Modern Education Process." In *4th*

International Conference on Arts, Design and Contemporary Education (ICADCE 2018). Amsterdam: Atlantis Press, 2018.

Kuhn, Annette. "Photography and cultural memory: A methodological exploration." *Visual studies* 22, No.3 (2007): 283–292.

Liberman, V., Boehm, J. K., Lyubomirsky, S., and Ross, L. D. "Happiness and memory: Affective significance of endowment and contrast." *Emotion* 9, No. 5 (2009), 666–680, doi.org/10.1037/a0016816.

Maurantonio, Nicole. "The Politics of Memory." In *The Oxford Handbook of Political Communication*, edited by Kate Kenski, and Kathleen Hall Jamieson, 1-17 (Oxford: Oxford University Press, 2014).

Moerman, Maria Theresa. *The Magic Mirror. Reflections on Photography as a memory* (Dissertation Fine Art Photography, Atlantic International University, 2012).

Roberts, Brian. "Photographic portraits: Narrative and memory." *Forum Qualitative Sozialforschung/Forum: Qualitative Social Research* 12, No. 2 (2011), doi.org/10.17169/fqs-12.2.1680.

Saraih, U. N., Nor Irwani Abdul Rahman, Norshahrizan Noordin, Sayang Nurshahrizleen Ramlan, Razli Ahmad, Mohd Fo'ad Sakdan and M. Harith Amlus, "Modelling Students' Experience Towards the Development of Alumni Involvement and Alumni Loyalty," *MATEC Web of Conferences Volume 150, 2018, Malaysia Technical Universities Conference on Engineering and Technology (MUCET 2017)*: 05050, doi: 0.1051/matecconf/201815005050.

Sarinana, Joshua. "Memory, Photography, and the Human Brain." *joshuasarinana.com*, n.d., https://www.joshuasarinana.com/memory-photography-and-the-human-brain.

Shevchenko, Olga. "'The mirror with a memory': placing photography in memory studies." In *Routledge International Handbook of Memory Studies*, edited by Anna Lisa Tota, and Trever Hagen 249-304 (London: Routledge, 2015).

Singer, Tara S., and Hughey, Aaron W. "The role of the alumni association in student life." *New directions for student services* 100 (2002): 51–68.

Susan Smith. "The Future of the Venerable Yearbook: Embracing New Technology, New Ways of Doing." *cmreview.org*. June 17, 2013, http://cmreview.org/Business.

Stanley Todd. 5 functions of a yearbook. *slideshare.net*. April 19, 2020, https://www.slideshare.net/Todd_Stanley/5-functions-of-a-yearbook.

Radvansky, Gabriel A. "Event segmentation as a working memory process." *Journal of Applied Research in Memory and Cognition* 6, No. 2 (2017): 121–123. doi.org/10.1016/j.jarmac.2017.01.002.

Rust, A. A. Braam. "Challenges of alumni associations at universities: Income from alumni (donations and bequests) at South African Universities." *African Journal of Business Management* 6, No. 45 (2012): 11273–11280.

Chapter Five

The impact of social media use, religiosity, self-esteem, and anxiety on relationship satisfaction among young Ugandan couples

Ayodeji Awobamise, Yosra Jarrar, Gabriel E. Nweke

Introduction

People have sought ways to share their feelings, ideas, information, and many more through different media of communication. Perhaps one of the most enduring functions of communication is our ability to express how we feel to our partners, start new romantic and platonic relationships, and express our emotions. Traditionally, this required us to be in the same space with the individual we want to express ourselves to, but with time and the evolution of technology, humans found new ways to express and share emotions. Today, with the help of social media and the internet, people can interact with one another through time and space using telephones, the internet, and various platforms on the internet, often referred to as social networking sites.

Facebook, Twitter, and a growing list of online social networking sites have over the years tried to recreate human interactions in real life on social media. We can have a private conversation on social media with someone completely unknown to us, we can share emojis that properly explain how we feel about a person and the emotions we experience; we can interact with our friends and families and can share intimate and special moments on social media. This has allowed us to replicate a lot of our offline social interactions and even offline social groups online. With the click of a button, we are instantly connected and can stay connected for as long as we so desire.

One other aspect of social media interactions that has not been widely discussed is how social media is actively challenging traditional beliefs that are strongly rooted in religiosity. Morality and its definitions are evolving at such a rate that the modern-day Christian, Muslim, or Pagan might find difficult to keep up with. The relationship between social media usage and religion is increasingly becoming topical in the scholarly literature.

Pittman and Reich[1] surmised that social media is shaping religion's impact on life satisfaction. They explained that for 'religious' people, social media can have a negative impact on the quality of their life and social interactions. Verschoor-Kirss,[2] however, warned that this relationship is not always adversarial. He explained that technology can enhance the religious experience depending on how it is used. Technology, and by extension, social media can be beneficial to religion because of its capacity to enhance a sense of community. So, it is not surprising that religious groups and individuals are increasingly turning to social media for support and community.

Another aspect of social media usage that is often discussed is the issue of self-esteem and anxiety. Studies have shown that social comparison often leads to low body satisfaction and lower self-esteem as one is often comparing their lives, appearances and progress with their friends and influencers on social media. These comparisons can lead to deleterious effects on the psyche of individuals if they do not develop a healthy

---

[1] Matthew Pittman, and Brandon Reich, "Social media and loneliness: Why an Instagram picture may be worth more than a thousand Twitter words," *Computers in Human Behavior* 62 (2016): 155–167.

[2] Alex Verschoor-Kirss, "Even Satan gets likes on Facebook: The dynamic interplay of religion and technology in online social networks," *Journal of Religion & Society* 14, No. 1 (2012): 1–12.

social media use.[3] Furthermore, anxiety has also been linked to higher social media usage and lower self-esteem.[4]

So, understanding how religiosity, interacts with social media usage to influence relationship satisfaction and how these relationships differ between people with high and low levels of self-esteem and anxiety is worth studying. This is particularly relevant because not a lot of studies have examined how these different variables interact with one another to influence our offline romantic relationships.

Conceptualization of key variables

Social media can be defined as "a group of Internet-based applications that allow the creation and exchange of user-generated content."[5] Social networking on the other hand has been defined as "the use of Internet-based social media programs to make connections with friends, family, classmates, customers, and clients."[6]

Social media usage, according to Davis, can be either normative or pathological (also referred to as problematic and addictive usages).[7]

---

[3] Stephanie McKee, Heather J. Smith, Aubrey Koch, Rhonda Balzarini, Marissa Georges, and Matthew Paolucci Callahan, "Looking up and seeing green: Women's everyday experiences with physical appearance comparisons," *Psychology of Women Quarterly* 37, No. 3 (2013): 351–365; Alexandra F. Corning, Angela J. Krumm and Lora A. Smitham, "Differential social comparison processes in women with and without eating disorder symptoms," *Journal of Counseling Psychology*, Vol. 53, No. 3 (2006): 338–349; Helga Dittmar, and Sarah Howard. "Thin-ideal internalization and social comparison tendency as moderators of media models' impact on women's body-focused anxiety," *Journal of Social and Clinical Psychology* 23, No. 6 (2004): 768–791.

[4] Michael A. Jenkins-Guarnieri, Stephen L. Wright, and Brian Johnson. "Development and validation of a social media use integration scale." *Psychology of popular media culture* 2, No. 1 (2013): 38–50.

[5] Liu Yi Lin, Jaime E. Sidani, Ariel Shensa, Ana Radovic, Elizabeth Miller, Jason B. Colditz, Beth L. Hoffman, Leila M. Giles, and Brian A. Primack. "Association between social media use and depression among US young adults." *Depression and Anxiety* 33, No. 4 (2016): 323–331.

[6] Dollarhide, Maya, "Social Media: Sharing Ideas and Thoughts," Investopedia, February 8, 2022, https://www.investopedia.com/terms/s/social-media.asp.

[7] Richard A. Davis, "A cognitive-behavioral model of pathological Internet use," *Computers in Human Behavior* 17, No. 2 (2001): 187–195.

Davis proposed the term pathological internet usage to refer to a situation where someone addictively makes use of the internet and cannot do without it.[8] When social media came about, the focus was simply narrowed down to social media usage as against the general internet. Therefore, for the purpose of this study, social media usage shall be divided into two broad categories: normative usage and pathological usage.

Social anxiety is "the fear of interaction with other people that brings on self-consciousness, feelings of being negatively judged and evaluated…and leads to avoidance."[9] The definition of social anxiety instead of just general anxiety was adopted because this study focuses on relationships and how anxiety can impact romantic relationship satisfaction. Finally, religiosity can be defined as "the extent to which an individual believes in and venerates the founder, gods or goddesses of the relevant religion, practices the relevant teaching, and participates in the relevant activities."[10]

Theoretical perspective

This study is premised on the social identity theory, which describes self-concept and the feeling of self-worth which is derived from the perceived membership of a certain group or class within a given society.[11] Because social groups on social media are limitless, our capacity as individuals to build networks across different groups can lead to a form of psychological conflict as a result of the need to maintain a certain image across those social groups. This theory is particularly relevant to this study as it examines how social media,

---

[8] Davis, "A cognitive behavioral model."

[9] Richards, Thomas A., Social Anxiety Institute, 2017, https://socialanxietyinstitute.org.

[10] Anuradha, Iddagode, and H.H.D.N.P. Opatha, "Religiosity: Towards A Conceptualization and An Operationalization," *Sri Lankan Journal of Human Resource Management* 7, No. 1 (2017): 59–69.

[11] John C. Turner, and Penelope J. Oakes, "The significance of the social identity concept for social psychology with reference to individualism, interactionism and social influence," *British Journal of Social Psychology* 25, No. 3 (1986): 237–252.

social anxiety, religiosity, and self-esteem all impact romantic relationships.

Since the theory looks at how being a member of a certain group determines how we perceive ourselves, it is applicable to this study because religiosity in particular denotes acceptance into a certain social group. One-way religiosity manifests itself for social media users is in determining what groups are joined, which influencers to follow and what entertainment items to consume. The researchers therefore are of the opinion that the frequency of social media usage and level of religiosity can influence how individuals interact with their romantic partners offline. This relationship is further compounded by the levels of self-esteem and anxiety among social media users. Studies have shown that people with high levels of self-esteem and low levels of anxiety are less likely to be influenced on social media than their more anxious and low self-esteemed counterparts.[12]

Review of literature

Studies on the relationship between social media and relationships abound and have existed since technology started to evolve.[13] In the early days, scholars were intrigued by how newspapers, radio and then TV affected family dynamics and relationships. Verschoor-Kirss explained that since online social networks generally foster a sense of community, it is not inconceivable to assume that a lot of religious people will seek out groups that promote their ideals and enhance their faith on social media.[14] The author however continues to caution that the increasing dependency on online communities can erode physical

[12] Bree Gregory and Lorna Peters, "Changes in the self during cognitive behavioural therapy for social anxiety disorder: A systematic review," *Clinical Psychology Review* 52 (2017): 1–18.

[13] Michelle H. Lim, Thomas L. Rodebaugh, Michael J. Zyphur, and John F. M. Gleeson, "Loneliness over time: The crucial role of social anxiety," *Journal of Abnormal Psychology* 125, No. 5 (2016): 620–630.

[14] Verschoor-Kirss, "Even Satan."

and real-life interactions and community which can be detrimental to society.

Bobkowski and Pearce explained that religiosity entails individuals' willingness to self-disclose.[15] They go on to explain that people that are overly religious tend to manifest their faith through piety and in an expression of their religious beliefs on new media platforms such as YouTube and other platforms. Knowing this, a lot of churches have turned to social media to recruit members into their fold and encourage members to volunteer in church and other aspects of community. It is therefore worth noting that in a lot of ways, new media technologies are influencing social and religious interactions in different ways.

Many scholars view innovation in technology as highly disruptive since it changes the way humans interact with one another. This disruption is not always negative, some scholars have highlighted the positive influence of computer mediated communication (CMC). For instance, Whitty explained that CMC can be a more efficient way for people to interact and communicate with one another because they can shed all pretenses when they are online and thus be their true selves.[16] Whitty goes on to explain that this feeling can lead to a greater feeling of love and support since an individual can be more expressive online than offline.

Similarly, Bargh and McKenna explained that social media usage is more convenient and allows easy and more regular communication between individuals, which can strengthen relationships.[17] Based on the foregoing, the following hypothesis is proposed:

---

[15] Piotr S. Bobkowski, and Lisa D. Pearce, "Baring Their Souls in Online Profiles or Not? Religious Self Disclosure in Social Media," *Journal for the Scientific Study of Religion* 50, No. 4 (2011): 744–762.

[16] Monica T. Whitty, "Liberating or debilitating? An examination of romantic relationships, sexual relationships and friendships on the Net," *Computers in Human Behavior* 24, No. 5 (2008): 1837–1850.

[17] John A. Bargh, and Katelyn Y. A. McKenna, "The Internet and social life," Annual Review of Psychology Vol. 55 (2004): 573–590.

H1: *Religious individuals who spend a lot of time on social media have a healthier romantic relationship*

Apart from examining how religious individuals interact with social media and how this interaction can impact romantic relationships offline, some scholars have also looked at how issues of anxiety and self-esteem when combined with social media usage can impact romantic relationships of social media users.

Social anxiety is usually a result of personal evaluation of one's social situation; real or imagined.[18] Studies by Odeh showed that there is indeed a relationship between social anxiety and self-esteem.[19] He explained that the lower the level of social anxiety, the higher the level of self-esteem in an individual and vice versa. A study by Zoccolillo[20] almost three decades ago and long before the advent of modern-day social media platforms, found out that there is an inverse relationship between social anxiety and self-esteem, which again denotes that the higher the self-esteem, the lower the level of social anxiety. That means people that have a high level of self-esteem are significantly more likely to be able to interact better socially.

Social anxiety and self-esteem issues are psychological in nature and various studies have shown that social media usage can impact the psychological wellbeing of individuals either positively or negatively.[21] Studies by Pittman and Reich and Valenzuela, Park, and Kee, showed the negative impact of social media usage on the mental wellbeing of individuals, while studies by Verduyn et al. indicated that social media

---

[18] Barry R. Schlenker, and Mark R. Leary, "Social anxiety and self-presentation: A conceptualization model," *Psychological Bulletin* 92, No. 3 (1982): 641.

[19] Odeh Suleiman Murad, "Social Anxiety in Relation to Self-Esteem among University Students in Jordan," *International Education Studies* 13, No. 2 (2020): 96–103.

[20] Mark Zoccolillo, "Co-occurrence of conduct disorder and its adult outcomes with depressive and anxiety disorders: A review," *Journal of the American Academy of Child & Adolescent Psychiatry* 31, No. 3 (1992): 547–556.

[21] Emily B. O'Day, and Richard G. Heimberg, "Social media use, social anxiety, and loneliness: A systematic review," *Computers in Human Behavior Reports* 3 (2021): 100070.

usage has a negative impact on self-esteem.[22] They explained that the more people make use of social media, the more likely it is for their self-esteem to be eroded. Studies by Donnelly and Kuss, Lup, Trub, and Rosenthal, Rosen, Whaling, Rab, Carrier, and Cheever and Shensa et al. all showed that social media usage can lead to a greater level of negative social comparisons which can affect the mental health if social media usage if left unchecked.[23]

Previous studies showed that social comparison is linked to feelings of social anxiety.[24] Social comparison, as earlier explained, refers to people's natural inclination to evaluate and compare their situation, skills, identity and even performance with other people they think they compare with.[25] Both upward and downward comparisons have been shown to have a negative impact on the mental well-being of

---

22 Pittman and Reich, "Social media and loneliness"; Sebastián Valenzuela, Namsu Park, and Kerk F. Kee. "Is there social capital in a social network site?: Facebook use and college students' life satisfaction, trust, and participation," *Journal of computer-mediated communication* 14, No. 4 (2009): 875–901; Philippe Verduyn, Oscar Ybarra, Maxime Résibois, John Jonides, and Ethan Kross, "Do social network sites enhance or undermine subjective wellbeing? A critical review," *Social Issues and Policy Review* 11, No. 1 (2017): 274–302.

23 Ella Donnelly, and Daria Kuss, "Depression among users of social networking sites (SNSs): The role of SNS addiction and increased usage," *Journal of Addiction and Preventative Medicine* 1, No. 2 (2016): 107; Katerina Lup, Leora Trub, and Lisa Rosenthal, "Instagram# instasad?: exploring associations among instagram use, depressive symptoms, negative social comparison, and strangers followed," *Cyberpsychology, Behavior, and Social Networking* 18, No. 5 (2015): 247–252; Larry D. Rosen, Kate Whaling, Sam Rab, L. Mark Carrier, and Nancy A. Cheever, "Is Facebook creating 'iDisorders'? The link between clinical symptoms of psychiatric disorders and technology use, attitudes and anxiety," *Computers in Human Behavior* 29, No. 3 (2013): 1243–1254; Ariel Shensa, César G. Escobar-Viera, Jaime E. Sidani, Nicholas D. Bowman, Michael P. Marshal, and Brian A. Primack. "Problematic social media use and depressive symptoms among US young adults: A nationally-representative study." *Social Science & Medicine* 182 (2017): 150–157.

24 Shaohai Jiang, and Annabel Ngien, "The Effects of Instagram Use, Social Comparison, and Self-Esteem on Social Anxiety: A Survey Study in Singapore," *Social Media and Society* 6, No. 2 (2020): 1–10.

25 Leon Festinger, "A Theory of Social Comparison Processes," *Human Relations* 7, No. 2 (1954): 117–140.

individuals.[26] Antony et al. explained this by stating that people who compare themselves to others (either upward or downward comparisons) are significantly more likely to care about how others perceive them which can affect their mental wellbeing.[27] Since they tend to feel that they lack certain skills, those individuals may develop a fear of engaging in social interactions.[28]

Weeks et al. in their study on social comparison and social anxiety, using a survey, found out that social comparison was positively related to social anxiety, as well as an increased fear of public scrutiny.[29] In a similar study carried out by Mitchell and Schmidt, the findings suggested that there is indeed a causal relationship between social comparison and social interaction anxiety.[30] Also, Gregory and Peters[31] concluded that social comparison is a major predictor of social anxiety disorder.

In contemporary society, social media has become a tool that enables and even facilitates social comparison. People now have access to unlimited content and feedback mechanisms that help quantify one's social standing. Likes, followers, retweets, and comments all help to create an ecosystem that encourages social comparison. This readily available information makes it easier for people to form impressions and perceptions about other people very quickly. According to Appel

---

[26] Paul Gilbert, "The relationship of shame, social anxiety and depression: the role of the evaluation of social rank," *Clinical Psychology & Psychotherapy* 7, No. 3 (2000): 174–189; Dan J. Stein, "Social anxiety disorder and the psychobiology of self-consciousness," *Frontiers in Human Neuroscience* 9 (2015): 489.

[27] Martin M. Antony, Karen Rowa, Andrea Liss, Stephen R. Swallow, and Richard P. Swinson, "Social comparison processes in social phobia," *Behavior Therapy* 36, No. 1 (2005): 65–75.

[28] American Psychiatric Association, *Diagnostic and statistical manual of mental disorders* (Arlington: American Psychiatric Association, 2013.)

[29] Justin W. Weeks, Thomas L. Rodebaugh, Richard G. Heimberg, Peter J. Norton, and Tejal A. Jakatdar, "'To avoid evaluation, withdraw': Fears of evaluation and depressive cognitions lead to social anxiety and submissive withdrawal," *Cognitive Therapy and Research* 33, No. 4 (2009): 375–389.

[30] Melissa A. Mitchell, and Norman B. Schmidt, "An experimental manipulation of social comparison in social anxiety," *Cognitive Behaviour Therapy* 43, No. 3 (2014): 221–229.

[31] Gregory, and Peters, "Changes in the self."

et al.,[32] compared to offline settings, social comparison on social media is more visible.

Based on the above, it appears that there is a consensus on the impact of social media on mental health, however, there is a dearth of literature on how these factors impact the romantic relationship of social media users with particular reference to those that identify as religious. Based on the foregoing, the following hypothesis was developed:

H2: *There is a significant relationship between pathological social media usage, self-esteem, religiosity, anxiety and romantic relationship satisfaction.*

Methodology

Study design

The study made use of a cross sectional research design which is a type of observational design that investigates the outcome and exposures within the study participants at the same time. Questionnaires were distributed to study participants and their responses were analyzed and interpreted before arriving at a conclusion on the subject matter being investigated. Before filling the questionnaires, the respondents were informed about the study and confidentiality was assured.

Participant recruitment

This study population consisted of young adults between the ages of eighteen and twenty-five who live in Central Uganda, mainly in Kampala region. The decision to target this demographic of the population is because they are the most likely to have a social media account. This assumption is based on Facebook's analytics which show that over ninety percent of Ugandans that make use of social media live in Kampala and are between the ages of eighteen and twenty-five. These categories of individuals are expected to be venturing into new

---

[32] Helmut Appel, Alexander L. Gerlach, and Jan Crusius, "The interplay between Facebook use, social comparison, envy, and depression," *Current Opinion in Psychology* 9 (2016): 44–49.

relationships are in the early stages of romantic relationships. Considering the purpose of this study, this demographic is the most suitable to investigate.

Participants were required to be resident of Kampala district, between the ages of eighteen and twenty-five and to be aware of and make use of at least two different social media platforms. In total, 432 individuals participated in this study. Of this number, fifty-two percent are female, and forty-eight percent are male. The average age of the respondents is 22,4 years.

Measures

To collect pertinent data, the researchers opted to make use of a questionnaire that combines the following scales: the Rosenberg Self Esteem Scale (RSE),[33] Beck Anxiety Inventory, Relationship Assessment Scale and The Centrality of Religiosity Scale.[34] These scales were combined because they have been confirmed and validated to measure the variables measured in the current study.

Section One of the questionnaire collected demographic data like age, education level, income level, gender, and marital status. Also, section one highlighted the inclusion criteria question of social media usage. Respondents were required to confirm whether they make use of social media, the types of social media platforms they use and how frequently they are used.

---

[33] Morris Rosenberg Morris, *Society and the adolescent self-image* (Princeton: Princeton University Press, 1965).

[34] Maurice R. Friend, "Society and the Adolescent Self-Image: By Morris Rosenberg. Princeton: Princeton University Press, 1965. 326 pp." *Psychoanalytic Quarterly* 36 (1967): 452–453; Aaron T. Beck, Norman Epstein, Gary Brown, and Robert A. Steer, "An inventory for measuring clinical anxiety: psychometric properties," *Journal of Consulting and Clinical Psychology* 56, No. 6 (1988): 893–897; Susan S. Hendrick, Amy Dicke, and Clyde Hendrick. "The Relationship Assessment Scale," *Journal of Social and Personal Relationships* 15, No. 1 (1998): 137–142; Stefan Huber, and Odilo W. Huber, "The centrality of religiosity scale (CRS)," *Religions* 3, No. 3 (2012): 710–724.

Section Two of the questionnaire measured self-esteem. The Rosenberg Self Esteem Scale (RSE) was used in this section. The RSE is a ten-item scale that measures how people view themselves. It also makes use of a four-point Likert scale format with one being linked to strongly agree and four being attributed to strongly disagree.

Section Three of the questionnaire asked questions related to anxiety. This section adopted the Beck Anxiety Inventory by Beck et al.[35] Beck Anxiety Inventory is widely used to measure anxiety in both adolescents and adults and is accepted in both research and clinical settings. This section consisted of twenty-one questions which measure twenty-one different anxiety symptoms. Section Four of the questionnaire required the participants to answer questions related to respondent's general/romantic relationships. This section adopted the Relationship Assessment Scale by Hendrick[36] with seven questions being asked. A five-point Likert format was used.

Finally, section five of the questionnaire sought to collect data pertaining to the respondents' level of religiosity. In this section, The Centrality of Religiosity Scale was adopted. The Centrality of Religiosity Scale is a tool that is used to measure the importance and salience of religion to individuals or groups. This section consisted of fifteen questions broken down along five subscales, namely, ideology, intellect, experience, public and private practice.

Procedure

The researchers made use of stratified random sampling to ensure that the findings are generalizable to the entire youth population in Kampala. Kampala District is divided into five boroughs namely, Kampala central division, Kawempe division, Makindye division, Nakawa division and Rubaga division. So, the entire sample size of 432

[35] Beck et al., "An inventory."

[36] Hendrick, Dicke and Hendrick, "The Relationship Assessment Scale."

was divided proportionally. The breakdown of the distribution is as follows:

S/N	DIVISION	SAMPLE SIZE
1	Kampala central division	90
2	Kawempe division	80
3	Makindye division	112
4	Nakawa division	78
5	Rubaga division	72
Total		**432**

Table 5-1: *Sample size distribution*

Findings and discussion

To test the hypotheses of this study, multiple regression analysis, and slop estimates were carried out to explain the moderating role of social media usage on the relationship between religiosity and romantic relationship satisfaction. The multiple regression analysis sought to find out the impact of the relationship between social media usage, religiosity, and self-esteem on relationship satisfaction. The findings are presented and discussed below in line with the hypotheses.

H1: *Religious individuals who spend a lot of time on social media have a healthier romantic relationship*

Moderation Estimates

			95% Confidence Interval			
	Estimate	**SE**	**Lower**	**Upper**	**Z**	**p**
Religiosity	-0.01289	0.00736	-0.02731	0.00152	-1.75	0.080
Social media Use	-0.10086	0.03291	-0.16537	-0.03635	-3.06	0.002

Moderation Estimates

			95% Confidence Interval			
	Estimate	SE	Lower	Upper	Z	p
Religiosity * Social media Use	0.00852	0.00267	0.00328	0.01376	3.18	0.001

Hypothesis 1 was tested using *JAMOVI 1.8.4.0* software, which tests a model whereby social media use moderates the effect of religiosity on romantic relationship satisfaction. Social media use was found to moderate the impact of religiosity on romantic relationship satisfaction, b = .0085, 95% CI [0.0033, 0.14], t = 3.18, p < .001, indicating that the relationship between religiosity and romantic relationship satisfaction is moderated by social media use. It can therefore be concluded that Hypothesis 1 is accepted.

To further confirm this hypothesis, and to explain how social media usage moderates the relationship between religiosity and romantic relationship satisfaction, a test of simple slopes was carried out to show how the different levels of social media usage interact with the relationship between religiosity and romantic relationship satisfaction.

	Estimate	SE	Z	p
Average	-0.0129	0.00870	-1.482	0.138
Low (-1SD)	-0.0361	0.01196	-3.021	0.103
High (+1SD)	0.0503	0.04127	1.918	0.038

Note. shows the effect of the predictor (Religiosity) on the dependent variable (Relationship Satisfaction) at different levels of the moderator (Social media Use)

Tests of simple slopes showed a relationship between religiosity and relationship satisfaction on different levels of social media use. When social media usage is low, there is a negative relationship between religiosity and romantic relationship satisfaction, b = −0.036, t = −3.02, p = .103. When social media usage is high, there is a significant positive relationship between religiosity and romantic relationship satisfaction, b = 0.05, t = 1.92, p < .05. The slopes estimate showed a significant difference in relationship satisfaction for participants with high religiosity that spend more time on social media in comparison to participants with low religiosity and low social media use. These results revealed that participants with higher religiosity and higher level of social media use had healthier relationship satisfaction than those low in religiosity and low in social media use.

To explain this finding, the researchers surmise that social media usage creates an avenue for religious individuals to better express themselves as suggested by Bargh and McKenna who explained that social media makes it easy for people to communicate and therefore strengthen their relationships.[37] The current study supports this finding by showing that highly religious people characterized by piety and a willingness to self-disclose who spend a lot of time on social media tend to have a high level of romantic relationship satisfaction than their less pious colleagues.[38] The researchers posit that this is more likely a result of the choices highly religious people make in their social media interactions.

Bobkowski and Pearce showed that highly religious people are selective in things they expose themselves to on social media and therefore are less likely to be negatively impacted by social media.[39] Their findings showed that religious people seek out groups and online communities that help them strengthen their religious believes which are mostly rooted in piety. These attributes can be highly instrumental in fostering a healthy relationship as common issues that affect relationships like

---

[37] Bargh, and McKenna, "The Internet and social life."
[38] Verschoor-Kirss, "Even Satan gets likes on Facebook."
[39] Bobkowski, and Pearce, "Baring Their Souls."

abuse, cheating and lies might be less pronounced, thus strengthening the relationship.

Previous studies showed that social media can have a negative impact on anxiety levels, and self-esteem which can have a deleterious effect on the social relationships of individuals. Studies by Gregory and Peters have shown a relationship between social media usage and social anxiety.[40] They have explained that social comparison on social media can lead one to believe other relationships are better than theirs and start benchmarking the success of their relationship against the perceived success of other relationships on social media. However, the findings of this study have shown that religious people who spend a lot of time on social media are significantly less likely to have a low level of relationship satisfaction. This study lends credence to the social identity theory which explains that the feeling of self-worth is derived from the membership of certain groups or class within a given society.

In this context, the findings have shown that religious people seek out online communities, entertainment sources and online social groups that align with their religious beliefs and help them meet the expectations of their faith when it comes to social interactions. Based on the social media usage patterns of religious people in this study, it can be concluded that the social group one belongs to molds and influences how these individuals perceive themselves and how they interact with other people within that social group.

H2: *There is a significant relationship between social media usage, self-esteem, religiosity, anxiety, and romantic relationship satisfaction.*

---

[40] Gregory, and Peters, "Changes in the self."

Correlation Matrix

	Relationship Satisfaction	Social media Use	Anxiety	Self Esteem
Relationship Satisfaction	—			
Social media Use	-0.140 **	—		
Anxiety	-0.468 ***	0.136 **	—	
Self Esteem	0.200 ***	0.244 ***	-0.089	—
Religiosity	-0.130 **	0.327 ***	0.428 ***	-0.056

Note. * $p < .05$, ** $p < .01$, *** $p < .001$

Results of the Pearson correlation indicated that there was a significant positive association between self-esteem and relationship satisfaction, (r(430) = .200, p < .001) ; a significant negative relationship between social media use and relationship satisfaction, (r(430) = -.140, p < .01) ; a significant negative relationship between anxiety and relationship satisfaction, (r(430) = -.468, p < .001) and a significant negative relationship between religiosity and relationship satisfaction, (r(430) = -.130, p < .01).

Model Fit Measures

			Overall Model Test			
Model	R	R^2	F	df1	df2oo	p
1	0.524	0.275	40.5	4	427	< .001

Model Coefficients - Relationship Satisfaction

Predictor	Estimate	SE	t	p
Intercept	5.0849	0.28683	17.73	< .001
Social media Use	-0.1204	0.03185	-3.78	< .001
Anxiety	-0.6327	0.05916	-10.69	< .001
Self Esteem	0.2735	0.05686	4.81	< .001
Religiosity	0.0230	0.00753	3.05	0.002

Results of the multiple regression showed that there was a collective significant relationship between, social media usage, self-esteem, religiosity, anxiety and romantic relationship satisfaction, ($F(4, 427) = 40.5, p < .001, R^2 = .28$). The individual predictors were examined further and indicated that social media usage ($t = -3.78, < .001$); anxiety ($t = -10.69, < .001$); self-esteem ($t = 4.81, < .001$)); and religiosity ($t = 3.05, < .005$) were significant predictors in the model.

The result suggested that high social media use, and high anxiety negatively impacted relationship satisfaction while high self-esteem and high religiosity positively impacted relationship satisfaction. Therefore hypothesis 2, which states that 'There is a significant relationship between social media usage, self-esteem, religiosity, anxiety and romantic relationship satisfaction' is supported. The finding is a starting point into studies on the relationship between these variables.

It bridges an important gap in literature and empirical studies on the intersection between social media usage, religiosity, self-esteem, and relationship satisfaction since no study has considered this area of research. This is particularly relevant in the African context, because Africans tend to be highly religious and are an emerging social media audience and therefore understanding how social media usage affects them is important.

Conclusion and recommendations

This chapter has expanded the literature on the effects of social media usage on audience behavior and society in general. The study is particularly relevant because it specifically addresses how religiosity and social media usage impact social interactions offline, an area that has not been explored in academic literature yet. The findings show that religious people who spend a lot of time on social media but are not pathological social media users have a higher level of romantic relationship satisfaction than less religious people who spend less time on social media. Based on this finding, it is important that further studies seek to find out why this is the case and what factors make normative users of social media that are not religious less likely to have a high level of romantic relationship satisfaction.

The researchers posit that those people spending less time on social media tend to have a higher level of self-esteem and are usually more sociable than those that spend a lot of time on social media, and this might explain why they might be perceived to be less committed to their romantic relationships- which might explain the low level of relationship satisfaction suffered by this category of people. However, these assumptions need to be tested empirically in future studies. Furthermore, the study sought to find out the relationship between social media usage, self-esteem, social anxiety, religiosity, and romantic relationship satisfaction. The findings showed that social media usage, self-esteem, social anxiety, religiosity are predictors of romantic relationship satisfaction.

By including more variables in the model seeking to understand the predictors of romantic relationship satisfaction, the researchers have expanded discourse on the phenomenon of relationship satisfaction and the role social media plays in this model. It is however worth noting that there is a dearth of literature on this issue and very little, if any at all, research has been carried out using social media usage, self-esteem, social anxiety, and religiosity as predictors of romantic relationship satisfaction. It is therefore recommended that more studies are carried out especially in the African society and other uber-religious cultures to find out how social media usage can impact romantic relationship satisfaction.

Bibliography

American Psychiatric Association. 2013. *Diagnostic and statistical manual of mental disorders*. Arlington: American Psychiatric Publishing.

Antony, Martin, Rowa, Karen, Liss, Andrea, Swallow, Stephen, Swinson, Richard (2005). Social comparison processes in social phobia. *Behavior Therapy* 36, No. 1 (2005): 65–75, doi.org/10.1016/S0005-7894(05)80055-3.

Appel, Helmut, Gerlach, Alexander L., and Crusius, Jan. "The interplay between Facebook use, social comparison, envy, and depression," *Current Opinion in Psychology* 9 (2016): 44–49, doi.org/10.1016/j.copsyc.2015.10.006.

Bargh, John, and McKenna, Katelyn Y. A. (2004). "The Internet and social life." *Annual Review of Psychology* 55 (2004): 573–590, https://doi.org/10.1146/annurev.psych.55.090902.141922

Beck, Aaron T., Epstein, Norman, Brown, Gary, & Steer, Robert A. (1988). "An inventory for measuring clinical anxiety: psychometric properties." *Journal of Consulting and Clinical Psychology* 56, No. 6 (1988): 893–897, doi.org/10.1037/0022-006X.56.6.893.

Bobkowski, Piotr, and Pearce, Lisa. "Baring their souls in online profiles or not? Religious self-disclosure in social media." *Journal for the Scientific Study of Religion* 50, No. 4 (2011): 744–762, doi.org/10.1111/j.1468-5906.2011.01597.x.

Corning, Alexandra, Krumm, Angela, and Smitham, Lora. "Differential social comparison processes in women with and without eating disorder symptoms." *Journal of Counseling Psychology* 53, No. 3 (2006): 338–349, doi: /10.1037/0022-0167.53.3.338.

Dittmar, Helga, and Howard, Sarah. "Thin-ideal internalization and social comparison tendency as moderators of media models' impact on women's body-focused anxiety." *Journal of Social and Clinical Psychology* 23, No. 6 (2004): 768–791.

Donnelly, Ella, and Kuss, Daria. "Depression among users of social networking sites (SNSs): The role of SNS addiction and increased usage." *Journal of Addiction and Preventative Medicine* 1, No. 2 (2016): 107, doi.org/10.19104/japm.2016.107.

Festinger, Leon. "A theory of social comparison processes." *Human Relations* 7, No. 2 (1954): 117–140, doi.org/10.1177/001872675400700202.

Friend, Maurice, R. "Society and the Adolescent Self-Image: By Morris Rosenberg. Princeton: Princeton University Press, 1965. 326 pp." *Psychoanalytic Quarterly* 36 (1967): 452–453.

Gilbert, Paul. "The relationship of shame, social anxiety and depression: The role of the evaluation of social rank." *Clinical Psychology and Psychotherapy* 7, No. 3 (2000): 174–189.

Gregory, Bree, and Peters, Loma. "Changes in the self during cognitive behavioural therapy for social anxiety disorder: A systematic review." *Clinical Psychology Review* 52 (2017): 1–18.

Hendrick, Susan S, Dicke, Amy, and Hendrick, Clyde. "The Relationship Assessment Scale," *Journal of Social and Personal Relationships* 15, No. 1 (1998): 137-142, doi.org/10.2307/.

Huber, Stefan, and Huber, Odilo W. "The centrality of religiosity scale (CRS)." *Religions* 3, No. 3 (2012): 710–724, doi.org/10.3390/rel3030710.

Iddagode, Anuradha, and Opatha, H.H.D.N.P. (2017). Religiosity: Towards a conceptualization and an operationalization. *Sri Lankan Journal of Human Resource Management*, 7, No. 1 (2017): 59–69, doi.org/https://journals.sjp.ac.lk/index.php/sljhrm/article/view/3423.

Jenkins-Guarnieri Michael A., Wright, Stephen L., and Johnson, Brian. "Development and validation of a social media use integration scale." *Psychology of Popular Media Culture* 2, No. 1 (2013): 38–50.

Jiang, Shaohai, and Ngien, Annabel. "The Effects of Instagram Use, Social Comparison, and Self-Esteem on Social Anxiety: A Survey Study in Singapore." *Social Media and Society* 6, No. 2 (2020): 1–10, doi.org/10.1177/2056305120912488.

Lim, Michelle, Rodebaugh, Thomas L., Zyphur, Michael J., and Gleeson, John F. M. "Loneliness over time: The crucial role of social anxiety." Journal of Abnormal Psychology 125, No. 5 (2016): 620–630, doi: /10.1037/abn0000162.

Lin, Liu Yi, Sidani, Jaime, Shensa, Ariel, Radovic, Ana, Miller, Elizabeth, Colditz, Jason, Hoffman, Beth., Giles, Leila, and Primack, Brian.

"Association between social media use and depression among U.S. young adults." *Depression and Anxiety* 33, No; 4 (2016): 323–331. doi: 10.1002/da.22466.

Lup, Katerina, Trub, Leora, and Rosenthal, Lisa. "Instagram #instasad? Exploring associations among Instagram use, depressive symptoms, negative social comparison, and strangers followed." *Cyberpsychology, Behavior, and Social Networking* 18, No. 5 (2015): 247–252, doi.org/10.1089/cyber.2014.0560.

McKee, Stephanie, Smith, Heather, Koch, Aubrey, Balzarini, Rhonda, Georges, Marissa, and Callahan, Matthew Paolucci (2013). "Looking up and seeing green: Women's everyday experiences with physical appearance comparisons." *Psychology of Women Quarterly* 37, No. 3 (2013): 351–365, doi: /10.1177/0361684312469792.

Mitchell, Melissa A., and Schmidt, Norman B. "An experimental manipulation of social comparison in social anxiety." *Cognitive Behaviour Therapy* 43, No. 3 (2014): 221–229, doi.org/10.1080/16506073.2014.914078.

O'Day, Emily B., and Heimberg, Richard. "Social media use, social anxiety, and loneliness: A systematic review." *Computers in Human Behaviour Reports* 3, (2021): 100070.

Murad, Odeh Suleiman. (2020). "Social anxiety in relation to self-esteem among university students in Jordan." *International Education Studies* 13, No. 2 (2020): 96–103.

Pittman, Matthew, and Reich, Brandon. "Social media and loneliness: Why an Instagram picture may be worth more than a thousand Twitter words." *Computers in Human Behavior* 62 (2016): 155–167, doi: /10.1016/j.chb.2016.03.084.

Richards Thomas A. (2017, February 3). Social Anxiety Institute. February 3, 2017, https://socialanxietyinstitute.org/.

Rosen, Larry D., Whaling, Kelly, Rab, Sam, Carrier, L. Mark, and Cheever, Nancy. "Is Facebook creating 'iDisorders'? The link between clinical symptoms of psychiatric disorders and technology use, attitudes and anxiety." *Computers in Human Behavior* 29, No. 3 (2013): 1243–1254. doi.org/10.1016/j.chb.2012.11.012.

Schlenker, Barry, and Leary, Mark (1982). "Social anxiety and self-presentation: A conceptualization model." *Psychological Bulletin* 92 (1982): 641–669.

Shensa, Ariel, Escobar-Viera, Cesar G., Sidani; Jaime E., Bowman; Nicholas D., Marshal Michael P., and Primack, Brian A. "Problematic social media use and depressive symptoms among U.S. Young adults: A nationally representative study." *Social Science & Medicine* 182 (2017): 150–157, doi.org/10.1016/j.socscimed.2017.03.061.

Stein, Dan J. "Social anxiety disorder and the psychobiology of self-consciousness." *Frontiers in Human Neuroscience 9*, (2015): 489, doi.org/10.3389/fnhum.2015.00489.

Turner, John & Oakes, Penelope (1986). "The significance of the social identity concept for social psychology with reference to individualism, interactionism and social influence." *British Journal of Social Psychology* 25, No. 3 (1986), 237–252, doi.org/10.1111/j.2044-8309.1986.tb00732.x.

Valenzuela, Sebastian, Park, Namsu, and Kee, Kerk (2009). "Is there social capital in a social network site?: Facebook use and college students' life satisfaction, trust, and participation." *Journal of Computer-Mediated Communication* 14, No. 4 (2009): 875–901, doi.org/10.1111/j.1083-6101.2009.01474.x.

Verduyn, Philippe, Ybarra, Oscar, Resibois, Maxime, Jonides, John, and Kross, Ethan. "Do social network sites enhance or undermine subjective well-being? A critical review." *Social Issues and Policy Review* 11, No. 1 (2017): 274–302, doi.org/10.1111/sipr.12033.

Verschoor-Kirss Alex. "Even Satan gets likes on Facebook: The dynamic interplay of religion and technology in online social networks." *Journal of Religion & Society* 14, No. 1 (2012): 1–12.

Weeks, Justin W., Rodebaugh, Thomas L., Heimberg, Richard G., Norton, Peter J., and Jakatdar, Tejal A. "To avoid evaluation, withdraw: Fears of evaluation and depressive cognitions lead to social anxiety and submissive withdrawal. *Cognitive Therapy and Research* 33, No. 4 (2009): 375–389, doi.org/10.1007/s10608-008-9203-0.

Whitty, Monica T. "Liberating or debilitating? An examination of romantic relationships, sexual relationships and friendships on the Net." *Computers in Human Behavior* 24, No. 5 (2008): 1837–1850, doi.org/10.1016/j.chb.2008.02.009.

Zoccolillo Mark (1992). Co-occurrence of conduct disorder and its adult outcomes with depressive and anxiety disorders: A review. *Journal of the American Academy of Child and Adolescent Psychiatry, 31*(3), 547–556, doi.org/10.1097/00004583-199205000-00024.

Chapter Six
Black Crescent: Afro-Turks, slavery, and early Black American Islam

Ayman Kole, Martin A. M. Gansinger
Emre Daghan Tokgoz

Introduction

This chapter provides an insight into the descendants of enslaved Africans, their ties to Islamic culture and religion. This will mainly be achieved by shedding light on specific experiences of Africans during the Ottoman Empire and in modern-day Turkey, as well as including the influence of religion on post-slavery identity struggles among Black Americans. As such, the missing incorporation of undesirable past experiences into school curriculums and their consistent media coverage alike bears the potential to cause problematic social and personal identity conceptions among young Turks of African descent.

The African continent, located along geo-strategic trade routes and is home to the world's important civilizations, has historically been an area of action over power struggles at various stages. In the twenty-first century, the African continent has become a political and military address of influence with its rich underground and aboveground inventory concerning the energy and production needs of global actors, as well as its population potential and capacity to thrive.

Equally important, the significance of the African continent in relation to Turkey is also increasing as global actors try to build areas of influence and friendship with different motivations and methods behind these moves.[1] In this context, Turkey, which claims to be a regional power, has involved itself in the geopolitical struggle on the continent in line with the decidedly multidimensional foreign policy it has pursued in recent years running parallel with the increasing pre-eminence of the African continent, which was one of the regions neglected in Turkey's foreign policy for many years.[2]

Early slavery

The fifteenth and sixteenth century largely marked the beginning of the slave trade between Africa and Europe which led to the depopulation and devastation of Africa, but on the other hand, resulted in the prosperity and growth of Europe.[3] Indeed, it is acknowledged that Portugal, in particular, began abducting individuals or groups of people from the west coast of Africa and transporting them to Europe as slaves.[4] Furthermore, by the early sixteenth century it was believed that up to ten percent of Lisbon's population was actually of African heritage.[5] Following the discovery of the American continent by Europeans, the demand for African labor reached incredible heights, as American and European sources of labor proved to be unsatisfactory in terms of sufficiency and, of course, capacity.

---

[1] Mehmet Ozkan, "*Turkey Discovers Africa: Implications and Prospects.* SETA Foundation for Political, Economic and Social Research," *Policy Brief* 22 (2008).

[2] János Besenyő, and Péter Oláh, "One of the new competitors in Africa: Turkey. Academic and Applied Research," *Public Management Science* 11, No. 1 (2012): 135–148.

[3] Etienne Félix Berlioux, *The Slave-Trade in Africa in 1872. Pricipally Carried on for the supply of Turkey, Egypt, Persia, and Zanzibar* (London: Edward Marsh, 1872).

[4] Ana Lucia Araujo, "Dahomey, Portugal and Bahia: King Adandozan and the Atlantic Slave Trade," *Slavery & Abolition A Journal of Slave and Post-Slave Studies* 33, No. 1 (2012): 1–19; Ferreira, Roquinaldo, and Silva, Pablo Miguel Sierra. "Portugal, Spain, and the transatlantic slave trade." In *The Iberian World 1450-1820*, eds. Fernando Bouza, Pedro Cardim, and Antonio Feros (London: Routledge, 2019), 375–392.

[5] Adi, Hakim, "Africa and the Transatlantic Slave Trade," *BBC*, May 10, 2012, https://www.bbc.co.uk/history/british/abolition/africa_article_01.shtml.

Ottoman period

Colonial activities justified by claims such as missionaryism, racial diversity and civilization, not only left deep scars on the continent in the past but also played a large role in the main causes of the crises the continent is experiencing in the present. On the other hand, new countries such as Turkey, who have not pressingly had a negative or traumatic colonial past linked to the African inhabitants, are now setting out to develop fresh ties in a bid to increase their visibility on the continent, have appeared to be more sympathetic, and this, in turn, has had a positive effect on the relations with·African countries.

The Ottoman period is important in Turkey's relations with the African continent, as the Republic of Turkey is somewhat considered to be the heir to the Ottoman Empire in light of its past roles in the region. In Ottoman-African relations, a partnership-axis integration rather than an exploitative relationship had been practiced.[6] Contrary to the assimilation policies of European powers during the reign of the Ottoman Empire, the religious beliefs of the peoples in Africa were preserved and fair policies were put in motion.[7]

Indeed, during various periods of the Ottoman Empire, people of African descent from Niger, Saudi Arabia, Libya, Kenya and Sudan were appointed to the state offical positions, and there existed no racial hostilities hindering Africans from assuming such important roles. Moreover, these individuals, after their retirement, settled in the Aegean and Mediterranean regions with the support of the state. The Ottomans were the only independent state that stood against the Europeans' attempts to obtain African people and different kinds of wealth of the region by ruthless exploitation and violence. European great powers, which became increasingly common in the middle of the

---

[6] Frederick Millingen, "On the Negro Slaves in Turkey," *Journal of the Anthropological Society of London* 8 (1870 - 1871): ixxxv-xcvi.

[7] Orakçı, Serhat, "Turkey-Africa relations: Historical process, Approaches and Expectations," INSAMER, IHH Humanitarian and Social Research Center Humanitarian and Social Research Center, 2018.

nineteenth century and colonized all but a few countries of the earth at the beginning of the twentieth century, were most influenced by the Roman colonial organization and the use of military force in history.

The Europeans, just like Roman colonialism, not only confiscated the facilities of the locals, but treated them as slaves. What ultimately stood out in European colonialism was the principle that the law created by the strong applied. That this was also partly the case in the rule of law in Islamic administrations eventually led to a different sense of justice emerging with the two being carried out side by side. However, contrary to the "divide, bash in, swallow" ideology of European colonialism, the Ottoman era replaced this with the "conquer, preserve, live and develop" administration mindset.

After the 1884 Berlin Conference, considered the beginning of modern colonialism, Africa was made dependent on Europe, while the Ottoman Empire, undergoing a phase of decline, was reliant on Europe. Due to imperialist occupations during the First World War, the Ottomans began acting out of concern for their existence. In the era of the First World War, the Ottoman Empire's struggle against imperialism played an important role in the development of the idea of independence, which would later lead to the emergence of the nation-state model.[8] The employment of Afro-Turks in Western Anatolia in the Ottoman lands was not due to the slave trade, but to the measures taken against slavery.[9]

Manumissions in the Ottoman Empire was enforced religiously and culturally. Furthermore, the system promoted that after roughly ten years of service the slaves were to be set free, as Islam encouraged liberation. However, most of the time former slaves chose to continue living with the family members who had enslaved them. Also, since most of these slaves were domestic slaves, their workload and

---

[8] Mustafa Aksakal, *The Ottoman road to war in 1914: the Ottoman Empire and the First World War* (Cambridge: Cambridge University Press, 2008).

[9] Yusuf Erdem, *Slavery in the Ottoman Empire and its Demise 1800-1909* (Berlin: Springer, 1996).

experiences were not really comparable to the slavery conditions their unfortunate relatives underwent in America.[10] As a matter of fact, Africans in the Ottoman Empire were more or less treated as foster children rather than as slaves. In other words, their slavery was limited.

Despite the fact that slavery cannot be justified under any circumstance, history must be examined through the lens of its peculiar historical period. It must be noted that despite being slaves, these individuals found employment throughout the Ottoman Empire as guards, lackeys, porters, agricultural workers, masons, scribes and musicians among other professions. Of course, most of them worked in households, undertaking the roles of maids, cooks, and laundresses. Therefore, it must be emphasized that the population of enslaved people did not differ substantially from that of freed people and women in major cities. Individual defiances and rebellions were rare, and significant numbers of slaves who were committed were not only elected to be heirs of their former masters and mistresses, but also had greater social standing and material conditions than most freeborn contemporaries.[11]

Some examples of celebrated Afro-Turk personalities are:

Arab Ahmet

Ahmet Ali Bey was born in 1883 as the children of Ali Bey of Nigerian descent and Emine Hanım, who were Ottoman citizens living in Izmir. Mr. Ahmet Ali's grandmother was taken from Nigeria's Borno emirate in Africa by slave traffickers in the 1830s and brought to Istanbul as a maid.[12] Ahmet Ali, the eldest child of the family, entered the Navy

---

[10] Antoinette T. Jackson, "Shattering Slave Life Portrayals: Uncovering Subjugated Knowledge in U.S. Plantation Sites in South Carolina and Florida," *American Anthropologist* 113, No. 3 (2011): 448–462.

[11] Madeline C. Zilfi, *Women and slavery in the late Ottoman Empire: The design of difference* (Cambridge: Cambridge University Press, 2012).

[12] Atar, Mesut, "Ahmet Ali," *havacilar.com*, October 17, 2011, http://www.havacilar.com/ahmetali.html.

Machinery School in 1904.[13] In addition to mechanical technical training, students at this school were trained in language and military systems. Ahmet Ali Bey started his career in the Ottoman army in 1908 with the registration number 1394.[14]

After graduating from the Navy Machinery School in 1908, Mr. Ahmet Ali was assigned to the Damascus Ferry to perform his ship mission. He served on the Damascus Ferry and on navigational missions in the Bahr-i Ahmer (Red Sea) and African coasts. In 1910, he served in the Masoudite armory during the Tripoli and Balkan Wars. Most importantly, Ahmet Ali (Celikten), became the world's first black pilot in November 1916.

Safiye Ayla

She is the daughter of Egyptian Hijazîzade Hafiz Abdullah Bey.[15] Mr. Abdullah passed away before Safiye Ayla was born. Safiye Ayla, who lost her mother when she was only three years old, was given to the Caglayan Hospice in Kagithane at the time she was orphaned. Ayla graduated from school and was appointed as an elementary school teacher in Beyoglu. There, Ayla, took music lessons from Eyyubi Mustafa Sunar and left teaching. She benefited further from the musical knowledge of Yesari Asim Arsoy, Hafiz Ahmet Irsoy, Selahattin Pinar, Saadettin Kaynak and Udi Nevres Bey. In 1932, at an invitation at the home of Nuri Bey, deputy governor of Istanbul, she sang for the first time in the presence of Ataturk and became one of his favorite voices. In 1950, she married the composer Sharif Muhittin Targan. She has performed numerous concerts on Turkish radio stations and released more than five hundred records.[16]

---

[13] CDA, ZB Zaptiye, 314-64-R- Hijri, 19-01-1325. Prime Ministery of Turkey, Ottoman Archives.

[14] CDA, BEO-004180-313427-001-002. Prime Ministery of Turkey, Ottoman Archives.

[15] Arslanbenzar, Hakan, "Safiye Ayla: Queen of classic Turkish music, pride of Afro-Turks," *Daily Sabah*, January 29, 2021, https://www.dailysabah.com/arts/portrait/safiye-ayla-queen-of-classic-turkish-music-pride-of-afro-turks.

[16] Ibid.

Esmeray

Esmeray was born in Istanbul in 1949 and traces her ancestry back to Morocco.[17] The Ottoman Empire had overseen a migration movement in the 19th century that brought her forefathers to Turkey. As a black woman, she became a messenger of equality in Turkey. Esmeray began her career as a stage performer in 1960, when she was just eleven years old. Until 1974, she performed in several famous theatres as a child actor at Istanbul City Theatres.

In 1970, she joined the choir of Neriman Altindag Tufekci and began singing in films. She made her singing debut three years later when she became a soloist for "Kim Bunlar" (Who Are They), a musical society, singing the song "100 Kere 1000 Kere" (100 times 1000 times). In the same year, she married Semi Diriker. In 1974, Esmeray won TRT's Toplu Igne Composition Contest award for the song "Unutama Beni" (Do Not Forget Me) written by her husband, but sung by her.

Zenci Musa

He was born in Crete in 1880, but was originally from Sudan. Upon his father's death, he moved to Cairo with his grandfather and grew up in a Turkish neighborhood where he became fluent in Turkish. He and his grandfather voluntarily participated in the battle of Tripoli in 1911. Meanwhile, he met Ashraf, an esteemed Ottoman secret service agent, who came to Libya to organize the indigenous people against the Italians. After the end of the Battle of Tripoli, Musa participated in the Balkan Wars, the Sinai-Palestine Front during World War I, the Hejaz-Yemen Front, the Dardanelles War and the First Channel Movement. According to Turkish historian Cemal Kutay, during the invasion of Istanbul, General Harington of the British Army offered gold to draw Musa to the British side, but Musa refused. In the wars he participated

---

[17] "Meet Esmeray: the black music diva of Turkey and icon of diversity," *TRT World*, June 10, 2020, https://www.trtworld.com/magazine/meet-esmeray-the-black-music-diva-of-turkey-and-icon-of-diversity-37161.

in, he not only carried out armed struggle, but also played pivotal roles in intelligence activities.[18]

Republic of Turkey

During this period, the newly established Republic of Turkey was more concerned with pursuing westernization goals, and such policies were the reason for keeping relations with the African continent at a minimum level.[19] It was not until 1998 - as a result of revisionist policies implemented against the foreign policy after 1960 - that the Africa Expansion Action Plan was announced. The Plan itself included visions and principles for Africa in line with the more contemporary mindset holding political power in Turkey at that point. Despite all this, the reason for the failure of the action plan, which had been planned at an extensive range, can be better explained by Turkey's internal dynamics.

In 2002, when the Justice and Development Party (AKP) came to power, Turkey-Africa relations reached a turning point and perceptions of Africa began to change in the Turkish public. Steadily, interest in the African continent, which had sadly been neglected for a long time in Turkish foreign policy, started to increase with the Africa Action Plan announced in 1998. Turkey's Africa policy, which started on a humanitarian level in its first years, has also gained intense attention in media and academia circles in line with the steps taken to improve political and commercial relations. Significant changes in both intellectual, social and institutional planes related to the continent may contribute to the development of Turkey-Africa relations. Also

[18] Ilhan Zengin, "Turkey-Sudan Relations from Past to Present," Master Thesis, T.C Kırıkkale University Institute of Social Sciences, Department of Republic History, Kırıkkale, 2013.

[19] Tarik Oğuzlu, "The future of Turkey's westernization: a security perspective," *Insight Turkey* 9, No. 3 (2007): 48–58.

noteworthy, in recent years there has been an increase in the number of written and visual materials on this relationship.[20]

The president of African Solidarity Association, Mustafa Olpak, claims that the Afro-Turks are now searching for their ancestors and examining their pasts. Although the first African Slaves in Turkey largely ignored their origins, some members of today's generation are beginning to question their ancestry and the places that they were brought to. The Afro-Turks, especially those who live collectively in Izmir and nearby towns, were relocated from sub-Saharan Africa, from the region widely called Sudan, and African kingdoms such as Kanem, Borno, Bagirmi, and lesser numbers brought from West Africa.

The majority of these people live today in Cimentepe, Eşrefpaşa, İkiçeşmelik, Yapıcıoğlu, Karabağlar, Balçova, Bornova, Basmane, Yurtoğlu and other surrounding towns of Izmir (except those who married regular Turks and later were totally assimilated). The towns of Antalya are also home to a few Afro-Turks. Additionally, a minority of these people have migrated to Turkish metropolitan cities. Of course, most Afro-Turks today regard themselves as both Turks and Muslims. In general, Afro-Turks are not very interested in their ancestral origins, except for some members of the new generation.

Early Black Islam in the United States

The nexus between Turkey and its Muslim tradition and Black Americans of African descent bears yet another interesting blossom. As a reaction to the atrocities inflicted upon dislocated and enslaved inhabitants of the African continent under the tolerating and justifying Christian ideology of salvation in the afterlife,[21] Islam was introduced

---

20 Orakçı, Serhat, "Turkey-Africa relations: Historical process, Approaches and Expectations," INSAMER, IHH Humanitarian and Social Research Center Humanitarian and Social Research Center, 2018.

21 Dan Shepherd, "Teaching about American slavery and its connections to Christianity and
the Bible," *Social Studies Research and Practice* 14, No. 2 (2019): 225–237.

to Black Americans as a welcome counterpart in the early nineteenth century.[22] Although for many of the forcefully re-educated and culturally disenfranchised Africans this might have been as well a return to their native religion, the political symbolism and equally distributed focus of the Muslim religion on affairs of the mundane world as well as the hereafter alike provided a promising sphere of projection for the aspirations of those among the many victims of the slave trade who were tired of turning the other cheek in hope for a postponed redemption.[23]

By looking at the phenomenon of the Moorish Science Temple,[24] it becomes evident that the theatrically invoked grandeur and majesty of its founder Timothy Drew, better known as the silk clothes and feathered-turban-wearing Noble Drew Ali, served as a literal balm of Gilead for the systematically attacked self-image and evaluation on the descendants of the unfortunate captives. While the central proposition of Drew Ali to provide a focal point of identification for Blacks in the United States that reached way back and beyond their current conditions in their imposed destination of forced immigration by establishing a link with the royal past and present of the North-African Moors, there is more to this than practical empowerment.

Although the attire and appearance of Ali and hence the regalia of the Moors is heavily modeled after its Moroccan originals, recognizable from the typical fez as a headgear, which has also been adopted by the Ottomans, to the use of the five-pointed star on their insignia; the movement incorporates more than the clever instrumentalization of a political nod towards their Maghrebian brothers endowed with the

---

22 Edward E. Curtis IV., *Islam in Black America: identity, liberation, and difference in African-American Islamic thought* (Albany: SUNY Press, 2012).

23 Dimitris J. Kyrtatas, "Slavery as progress: pagan and Christian views of slavery as moral training," *International Sociology* 10, No. 2 (1995): 219–234.

24 Herbert Berg, "Mythmaking in the African American Muslim context: The Moorish Science Temple, the Nation of Islam, and the American Society of Muslims," *Journal of the American Academy of Religion* 73, No. 3 (2005): 685–703.

freedom and independence that seemed so far out of reach in the US at that time.

There is more than one evidence that Drew Ali's Moorish Science Temple carried a similarly strong message of religious nature that often goes unseen in the socio-political discussions of the phenomenon. This is even more important to consider, as that the Moorish Science Temple served as the original blueprint for highly influential offsprings such as the Nation of Islam or the Five Percent Nation/Nation of the Gods and Earth, often referred to by the simplified term of the Black Muslim movements.[25]

As a matter of fact, it has been claimed that Drew Ali's parents had actually been followers of a certain Sufi shaykh and that their son had long been trained and prepared for his mission. Other sources claim ties to the Iranian scholar and reformer Jamāl al-Dīn al Afghani.[26] Bowen[27] even claims that Ali was in possession of documents handed to him by the Caliph of Egypt and the Sultan of Mecca that made him the first person officially authorized to teach the Muslim religion in the West.

In any case, and despite its title, Drew Ali's fundamental written artifact, the *Circle 7 Koran*[28] mainly represents an obscure compilation of esoteric texts, namely "The Aquarian Gospel of Jesus the Christ"[29] and a mysterious work of unknown origin titled "The Economy of Human

---

[25] Berg, "Mythmaking."

[26] Salomon, Noah, and Dew, Spencer, "Theologies of American Exceptionalism: Ali and Khomeini. Secularism, religion, and the public sphere," *The Immanent Frame,* March 1, 2017, https://tif.ssrc.org/2017/03/01/ali-and-khomeini/.

[27] Patrick D. Bowen, "Abdul Hamid Suleiman and the origins of the Moorish Science Temple," *Journal of Race, Ethnicity, and Religion* 2, No. 13 (2011): 31–51.

[28] Drew Ali, *The Holy Koran of the Moorish Science Temple of America*, ed. Dr. C. S. Moore (Clifton: African Studies African Tree Press. 2014. [1927]).

[29] Levi H. Dowling, *The Aquarian Gospel of Jesus the Christ* (Camarillo: DeVorss, 2020 [1907]).

Life" or "Infinite Wisdom"[30], which also gained high popularity among Rosicrucians,[31] rather than references to orthodox Islam.

However, at certain occasions, Ali's compilation featured passages from the authentic holy book of the Muslim faith as well. As pointed out by Clark,[32] there is evidence that it was of considerable relevance for Ali to assert that the teachings of the Moorish Science Temple are very much in line with orthodox Islam, at least with how he understood and defined it. Hence, the *Moorish Guide*, the first newspaper of the movement, regularly featured editorials in which the authors were "demanding due credit for their ancestors' cultural work, affirming their Moslem traditions, and explaining Ali's view on Islam,[33] as well as promoting restrictions in diet that "reflected Islamic *halal* restrictions of pork, as well as alcohol and other intoxicants.[34]

Clark furthermore notes that the affix of *Bey* that many of the Moorish Science Temple members added to their names, directly relates back to the Ottoman Empire, where it was used as "an Ottoman courtesy title used for chieftains and other leaders"[35]. This may not have happened without consideration of its practical advantages, however. Many Black Americans thankfully embraced their new identity that would bestow upon the dignity and self-esteem of their North-African and Middle-Eastern kinfolk under the guise of a cultural interpretation of the Muslim religion.[36] Slave names got traded for exotic Muslim names, and identity cards provided by the Moorish Science Temple confronted

---

[30] Muhammed Al-Ahari, *The Second Moorish Akashic Record: An annotated edition of Infinite Wisdom. Source documentation of the revelations to the Lost-Found Moorish Nation of Northwest-Amexem* (Chicago: Magribine Press, 2011).

[31] Sri Ramatherio, *Unto Thee I Grant* (San Jose: Supreme Grand Lodge of A.M.O.R.C., 1995 [1968]).

[32] Emily Suzanne Clark, "Noble Drew Ali's 'Clean and Pure Nation': The Moorish Science Temple, Identity, and Healing," *Nova Religio: The Journal of Alternative and Emergent Religions* 16, No. 3 (2013): 35.

[33] Clark, "Clean and Pure Nation," 35.

[34] Clark, "Clean and Pure Nation," 36.

[35] Clark, "Clean and Pure Nation," 45.

[36] Christopher. W. Chase, "Prophetics in the Key of Allah: Towards an Understanding of Islam in Jazz," *Jazz Perspectives* 4, No. 2 (2010): 157–181.

bouncers executing a segregationist agenda with the tough decision to estimate if they are denying entry to a racially discriminated second-class citizen or rather an Arabian prince instead.

Bowen even suggested that Ali might have been a former follower of Abdul Hamid Suleiman, a self-declared masonic Muslim who founded the *Mecca Medina Temple of Ancient Free and Operative Masons from 1 to 96 degrees* in 1910.[37] Again, the name of its founder, which relates to the Ottoman/Turkish transliteration of the originally Arab words, as well as his decoratively embroidered fez hint towards the Turkish influence on the aesthetics and stylistics of early Black American Islam. This is furthermore supported by Bowen's mention of the fez as the chosen headgear among Ahmadis, the Shriners, or lesser known groups such as the Fahamme Temples of Islam and Culture. Even more direct significance to Turkish rather than Arabic ties in early Black American Islam can be attributed to statements of Abdel Hamid Suleiman, in which he declares that "he is bringing into closer religious harmony the Negro, Turkish and Syrian Moslems"[38].

Conclusion

As illustrated, the experience of enslaved Africans in the Ottoman empire considerably differs from the one of their kinship on the plantations of the United States. This circumstance can be seen as a reflection of Ottoman political strategies to counter the European imperialist agenda out of concern for the survival of the empire. Hence, in prolongation of the display of tolerance towards religious or cultural identities and traditions attributed to populations of territory conquered by the Ottoman army, those individuals obtained for labor during the Ottoman era were granted the right to maintain their native beliefs and practices.

---

[37] Bowen, "Abdul Hamid Suleiman."

[38] "Mahometans Will Try to Convert Negroes," *New York Age*, July 21, 1923.

This marks a strong difference to the harsh and systematic suppression of every aspect of African identity among victims of the slave trade in the United States, which also included the prohibition of native languages and artistic expression. In accordance with Islamic law, many Africans got freed after a period of time and were considered as extended family members or even obtained high-ranking positions in the Ottoman empire. The

specific identity of these Afro-Turks, who fully embraced the culture and traditions of their new environment has been discussed via a handful of case studies that provide historical information on the integration of these individuals into Turkish society.

The instrumentalization of Muslim culture and religion as a strategy of empowerment and liberation in the United States could not be more different in that regard. The Moorish Science Temple's recursion toward Ottoman pomp and aesthetics, as well as to the kingdoms of North Africa, especially Morocco, provided a cultural link to a past that was long made lost and forgotten among Black Americans. On the other hand, it also represented a perfect opposition to the cruelties and crimes committed by Christian slave owners, justified by Christian theology and its postponing of justice and liberation to the hereafter, tolerated by religious and governmental institutions alike.

Bibliography

Adi, Hakim, "Africa and the Transatlantic Slave Trade," *BBC*, May 10, 2012, https://www.bbc.co.uk/history/british/abolition/africa_article_01.shtml.

Aksakal, Mustafa. 2008. *The Ottoman road to war in 1914: the Ottoman Empire and the First World War*. Cambridge: Cambridge University Press.

Al-Ahari, Muhammed. 2011. *The Second Moorish Akashic Record: An annotated edition of Infinite Wisdom. Source documentation of the revelations to the Lost-Found Moorish Nation of Northwest-Amexem*. Chicago: Magribine Press,

Ali, Drew. 2014. [1927]. *The Holy Koran of the Moorish Science Temple of America*, ed. Dr. C. S. Moore. Clifton: African Studies African Tree Press.

Araujo, Ana Lucia. "Dahomey, Portugal and Bahia: King Adandozan and the Atlantic Slave Trade." *Slavery & Abolition A Journal of Slave and Post-Slave Studies* 33, No. 1 (2012): 1–19.

Arslanbenzar, Hakan. "Safiye Ayla: Queen of classic Turkish music, pride of Afro-Turks." *Daily Sabah*. January 29, 2021, https://www.dailysabah.com/arts/portrait/safiye-ayla-queen-of-classic-turkish-music-pride-of-afro-turks.

Atar, Mesut. "Ahmet Ali." *havacilar.com*. October 17, 2011, ttp://www.havacilar.com/ahmetali.html.

Berg, Herbert. "Mythmaking in the African American Muslim context: The Moorish Science Temple, the Nation of Islam, and the American Society of Muslims." *Journal of the American Academy of Religion* 73, No. 3 (2005): 685–703.

Besenyő, János, and Oláh, Péter. "One of the new competitors in Africa: Turkey. Academic and Applied Research." *Public Management Science* 11, No. 1 (2012): 135–148.

Berlioux, Etienne Félix. 1872. *The Slave-Trade in Africa in 1872. Principally Carried on for the supply of Turkey, Egypt, Persia, and Zanzibar*. London: Edward Marsh.

Bowen, Patrick D. "Abdul Hamid Suleiman and the origins of the Moorish Science Temple." *Journal of Race, Ethnicity, and Religion* 2, No. 13 (2011): 31–51.

Clark, Emily Suzanne. "Noble Drew Ali's 'Clean and Pure Nation': The Moorish Science Temple, Identity, and Healing." *Nova Religio: The Journal of Alternative and Emergent Religions* 16, No. 3 (2013): 31–51.

Curtis IV, Edward. E. 2012. *Islam in Black America: identity, liberation, and difference in African-American Islamic thought*. Albany: Suny Press.

Dowling, Levi H. 2020 [1907]. *The Aquarian Gospel of Jesus the Christ*. Camarillo: DeVorss.

Erdem, Yusuf. 1996. *Slavery in the Ottoman Empire and its Demise 1800-1909*. Berlin: Springer.

Ferreira, Roquinaldo, and Silva, Pablo Miguel Sierra. "Portugal, Spain, and the transatlantic slave trade." In *The Iberian World 1450-1820*, edited by Fernando Bouza, Pedro Cardim, and Antonio Feros, 375–392. (London: Routledge, 2019).

Jackson, Antoinette T., "Shattering Slave Life Portrayals: Uncovering Subjugated Knowledge in U.S. Plantation Sites in South Carolina and Florida," *American Anthropologist* 113, No. 3 (2011): 448–462. https://doi.org/10.1111/j.1548-1433.2011.01353.x.

Kyrtatas, Dimitris J. "Slavery as progress: pagan and Christian views of slavery as moral Training." *International Sociology* 10, No. 2 (1995): 219-234.

"Mahometans Will Try to Convert Negroes," *New York Age*, July 21, 1923.

"Meet Esmeray: the black music diva of Turkey and icon of diversity," *TRT World*, June 10, 2020, https://www.trtworld.com/magazine/meet-esmeray-the-black-music-diva-of-turkey-and-icon-of-diversity-37161.

Millingen, Frederick. "On the Negro Slaves in Turkey." *Journal of the Anthropological Society of London* 8 (1870 - 1871): ixxxv-xcvi.

Oğuzlu, Tarik. "The future of Turkey's westernization: a security perspective." *Insight Turkey* 9, No. 3 (2007): 48–58.

Orakçı, Serhat. "Turkey-Africa relations: Historical process, Approaches and Expectations." INSAMER, IHH Humanitarian and Social Research Center Humanitarian and Social Research Center, 2018.

Ramatherio, Sri. 1995 [1968]. *Unto Thee I Grant* (San Jose: Supreme Grand Lodge of A.M.O.R.C.

Salomon, Noah, and Dew, Spencer, "Theologies of American Exceptionalism: Ali and Khomeini. Secularism, religion, and the public sphere," *The Immanent Frame*, March 1, 2017, https://tif.ssrc.org/2017/03/01/ali-and-khomeini/.

Shepherd, Dan. "Teaching about American slavery and its connections to Christianity and the Bible." *Social Studies Research and Practice* 14, No. 2 (2019): 225–237.

Zengin, Ilhan. 2013. "Turkey-Sudan Relations from Past to Present." Master Thesis, T.C Kırıkkale University Institute of Social Sciences, Department of Republic History, Kırıkkale.

Zilfi, Madeline C. 2012. *Women and slavery in the late Ottoman Empire: The design of difference*. Cambridge: Cambridge University Press.

Chapter Seven
The discourse of exile in poetry: Mahmoud Darwish's poem "Contrapuntal"

Tamara Khlefat, Shahla Ujayli

Introduction

This chapter aims to juxtapose the poem of "Contrapuntal"[1] by Mahmoud Darwish with the concept of contrapuntal, which means "Tebaq" in Arabic, as it was developed by Edward Said. The chapter also investigates the multifarious aspects of this approach and the reasons that have led Said to adopt this type of analysis in his critique, as well as his enthusiasm to write his autobiography telling his own story. Additionally, it explores the concept of exile as represented in the Palestinian discourse and reviews the way Darwish employed this vision in his poem of the same title.

The objectives of this research are mainly to probe some aspects related to the theme of exile through exploring the thoughts and the emotions of two famous Palestinian writers, in addition to other aspects of exile that contribute to the discourse that contemporary readers can view. The chapter examines the way each one of the two writers faced the dilemmas of existence like occupation, home, literary writing, exile, identity, and illness, and presents literary techniques that enabled them to change these suffering into a poetical themes and artistic experience. The chapter explores the motifs of the history of the relationship between the colonizers and the colonized through scanning the history from Babylonians and Jews to redskins until the moment of modernity

[1] Mahmoud Darwish, "Contrapuntal," trans. Julie Stoker, *Le Monde Diplomatique,* January 15, 2005, https://mondediplo.com/2005/01/15said.

of the skyscrapers in New York, and how the poetry could transfer this wide history of colonialism into dense and deep metaphors just in one poem through the thought of (contrapuntal) that Edward Said used to extract the voices of the victims from the voice of the torturers.

Historical context

14th of May1948 marks the day when Israel was established and is known by Palestinians as the day of *Al-Nakba* (The catastrophe)[2] as many Palestinians were forced to leave their homeland. This event is considered to constitute the very core of their distinct national identity as Palestinians. The developments led to many Palestinian writers being displaced and exiled from their homes and caused them to go through an ongoing state of homelessness.

Before *Al-Nakba* took place, the residents of these lands were Arabs who had deep historical roots. However, within months the area was populated by a Jewish society. It all started when the League of Nations broke the Ottoman Empire into different territories that were under the authority of different European colonial powers. The land of Palestine was under the colonialism of Britain (The League of Nations previously). It must be mentioned that Britain made a promise to the Zionist movement to make a "national home for the Jewish people" in 1917. The Belfour declaration defined the Palestinians as a non-Jewish nation with religious and civil rights. However, there was nothing mentioned about the political rights of these people.

In 1967, tension was drastically increasing in the Arab region; Israel exploited the waters of the Jordan River, the Kinneret طبرية lake, which escalated the events and caused military clashes referred to as *Al-Naksa* (setback or defeat).[3] The 1967 War, or June War, represented the

---

[2] Ibish, Hussein, "A 'Catastrophe' That Defines Palestinian Identity," *The Atlantic*, May 14, 2018, https://www.theatlantic.com/international/archive/2018/05/the-meaning-of-nakba-israel-palestine-1948-gaza/560294/.

[3] Asser, Martin, "Obstacles to Arab-Israeli peace: Water," *BBC News*, January 20, 2021, https://www.bbc.com/news/world.

culmination of a number of causes, starting with the Egyptian and the Syrian pact which the Jordanian forces participated to later on.[4] As such, the straw that broke the camel's back was the closure that was conducted by Egypt of the Straits of Tiran to the shipping of Israel. Thus, the conflict mainly occurred over the shared waters between Israel and some Arab neighbouring countries. After Israel failed in getting international support, they launched their pre-emptive aerial strike on the 5th of June 1967, and the war ended with the victory of Israel. All of this led to the invasion of invading more territory, such as the Golan mountains or the Jordan Valley (currently the West bank), in addition to the river of Litany in Lebanon.

This represented a great loss for the Arab countries which caused much devastation to the Arab nation and led to more pessimism about the future. The *Naksa* has deepened the concept of exile and has caused a great number of people to turn into refugees. It strongly underlined the impossibility to return, and that has made the exile dilemma a prominent element in the Palestinian literary works.

The Oslo Agreement of peace which was signed by the Palestinians Liberation Organization and Israel on 13th of September 1993, in the era of Clinton's presidency.[5] The agreement entailed that the Palestine Liberation Organization would have to commit to the right of Israel to live in peace and find a solution for all the problems which occurred. This was supposed to be the beginning of an era without violence and fights, and the beginning of solving problems through negotiations; the Palestinian side stated that such an agreement would prevent terrorism and other violent acts and the Israeli side decided to consider the Palestine Liberation Organization as the representative of Palestine and as such begin negotiations with the latter.

---

[4] "Events leading to the Six Day War (1967)," *Israel Ministry of Foreign Affairs*, https://www.gov.il/en/departments/general/events-leading-to-the-six-day-war
[5] Lustick, Ian, "The Oslo Agreement as an Obstacle to Peace," *Journal of Palestine Studies* 27, No. 1 (1997): 61-66.

This agreement has led to a lot of changes in the context of the Palestinians identity, mainly due to the acknowledgement of Israel's right on the territory and the consideration of revolutionary acts as terrorism. These are two main themes in the Palestinian discourse and the Palestinians identity, and each of these poets have stood against the oppression that the Palestinians Liberation Organization committed after this agreement. Yasser Arafat who was the only one responsible for the political decisions had disabled the Palestinian national committee which Darwish and Said was part of. Said expressed his feeling about those events in "Oslo 2 Peace without a Land"[6], and declared that he was against those acts and the way that the Palestinians Liberation Organization was negotiating with the Israelis.

For a consideration of the Palestinian discourse and narrative, one needs to turn to Foucault's discussion of the terms.[7] The philosopher questioned the truth in the discourses produced by certain political systems. According to him, such truths or meanings gained status because of their presence in the texts. On the other hand, there would be other discourses that happened to be marginalized. He stated that there is no such a definitive structure of identity or social practices; it rather needs to be considered as a socially determined construct.[8]

The Palestinian narrative evolves around the story of dispossession, exile, and discrimination.[9] It faces a systematic effort that attempts to empty it from its significance and purpose by making it a habitual account of a "normal situation." In addition to that, on a cultural and global level, the world literature contributes to this misrepresentation of history, geography, and identity of Palestinians. This context includes the language that is used in international organizations and

---

[6] Edward Said, *Oslo 2 "Peace without a Land"* (Cairo: Dar Al Mustaqbal Al Arabi, 1995).

[7] Michele Foucault, *Ḥafrīyāt Alma'refah. [Archaeology of Knowledge]*, (Beirut: Almarkaz al thaqāfī al 'arabī, 1987): 181.

[8] Carol Bacchi, "The Turn to Problematization: Political Implications of Contrasting Interpretive and Post structural Adaptations," *Open Journal of Political Science* 5, No. 1 (2015): 1–12.

[9] Hilal, Jami, "Reclaiming the Palestinian Narrative," *Al Shabaka*, January 6, 2013, https://al-shabaka.org/commentaries/reclaiming-the-palestinian-narrative/.

even by the United Nations and the international mass media. Another significant misrepresentation consists in considering the borders of Palestine to only involve the West bank area, East Jerusalem, and Gaza district. Israel is also attempting to present the history of the area since the year 1967 as if the country has not been going through any event before the year of 1967.

History is a main factor for defining identity, and to examine the identity of Palestine, there are many things to consider. Palestinians are the ones who were living in the Palestinian lands, and it was a home for many ethnic groups, races, and nations.[10] There were many nations that invaded the Palestinian lands and the one that influenced the Palestinian history the most was the Roman invasion, but that invasion did not convert the Palestinian people into Romans, for instance. These events were followed by the Crusades. Many Palestinians fled

from their homeland and Damascus was their destination at those times. Nevertheless, even during these events, most of the places in Palestine remained Arab, including the villages (the Christian and the Muslim ones).

After the crusades, the Islamic conquests started to reach Palestine, and if one were to examine the geographic position of Palestine in modern time, one would only find the map that is basically the geographic definition under the British mandatory of the borders of the country, which in the times of the Bronze and the Iron ages was called the land of Canaan. The borders that were created by Britain were not created based on the demographic, ethnic, or historical and cultural concepts, but they were sensitive to the needs of the Palestinian people as it was a part of "Belad Al-Sham," which included Jordan, Palestine, Syria, and Lebanon.

---

[10] Nazmi Al-Ju'beh, *Palestinian Identity and Cultural Heritage* (Beirut: Presses de l'Ifpo, 2008).

The result of drawing such a border between those countries was taking away their unity and creating division between them. In addition to that, the borders helped Britain in building the new Jewish territory in the Palestinian lands. The origins of the Palestinian people come from the Canaanites, the Assyrians, the Egyptians, the Byzantines, and many other nations that settled in the land of Palestine. In the fourth century, Palestine had gone through an Arabization process, mainly due to the Arab-Islamic conquests.

The Israeli and the Palestinian narratives regarding the territory differ a lot. For instance, the Israeli narrative about the origins of the Jewish people in the world is that they are a race descending from Eretz Yisrael whose origin is in Israelites. Hence, Jews derive their right for inheritance of the land from religious claims and race, stating that the Jewish people have always prayed towards the direction of Jerusalem.

On the other hand, the Palestinian narrative considers Jews as a people of the region with revelation and faith just like Christians and Muslims. According to the Palestinian narrative, the Jews were mainly few people who do not constitute a united single race, and that the Israelites' presence in the land of Palestine existed for a short period of time compared to the Palestinian history of the land. Palestinians are considered as descendants from the native nation that lived in Palestine since old ages of time, and that the Arab rule was the longest one in the region.

The Israeli narrative puts a strong focus on the Babylonian captivity.[11] This is one of the most essential and important events in the history of Jews as this caused them to face diaspora, where they scattered all around the world and were prohibited from going back to Judah. This event has turned from being an ideological explanation which illustrates the Jews as victims, and as evidence of their presence in Palestine into a cultural symbol which is used in order to face the other

---

[11] Spitzer, Jeffrey, "Babylonian Exile," *My Jewish Learning*, https://www.myjewishlearning.com/article/babylonian-exile/.

side. While Palestinians consider this explanation inaccurate, Israelis would use it to justify them taking over the territory. Darwish has used this symbol in several his poems such as "The Trip of Al-Motanabi to Egypt," and "Tebaq"[12]. He also uses the symbol of Sodom and Gomorra to indicate the nations that are doomed because of the sins they committed on earth, and he indicates that this would be the ending of Israel because of its oppressive acts. Sodom and Gomorrah are one of the most prominent elements in the Quran and the Old Testament, telling the story of a nation which used to live in the Dead Sea area, doomed because of their sinful acts.[13]

Definition of terms

In "Reflections on Exile,"[14] Said describes exile as a concept that is compelling to think about and adds that it is a terrible thing to experience. He says that the sadness that comes from it is something that can never be surmounted.

Said argues that the western culture is a huge part of the exiled writers' works, and that the literature of the United States is a result of the pain of the refugees that ran away from fascism, communism, and regimes that oppress its people. Literature that represents exile usually expresses the anguish that the exiled writers feel, which is a feeling that not everybody goes through. He denies that literature produced by the exiled is merely historical and horrendous and he argues that it is like death but missing the ultimate mercy of the latter.

Exile is highly present in Said's and Darwish's literary works, and especially through the writings of Said, the reader is able to see his avocation for the plural outlooks in the colonized and the other

---

[12] Mas'ūd, Meqdād, "'dwārd Sa'īd men khelāli Mahmūd Darwīsh Fī qaṣīdet Ṭebāq" [Edward Said Through Mahmoud Darwish in Tibaq Poem], *alnaked-aliraqi.net*, August 29, 2017, https://www.alnaked-aliraqi.net/article/45474.php.

[13] Ryan Juza, "Echoes of Sodom and Gomorrah on the Day of the Lord: Intertextuality and Tradition in 2 Peter 3:7–13," *Bulletin for Biblical Research* 24, No. 2 (2014): 227–245.

[14] Edward Said. *Reflections on Exile: And Other Literary and Cultural Essays* (New York: Granta Books, 2001).

(colonizer).[15] Many critics stated that Said's experience of exile and alienation was a physical and a linguistic one as being disconnected from his own homeland, and it gave him the encouragement to question the socio-political systems that are unfair.

As for Mahmoud Darwish, the Oslo accords permitted him from entering the Israeli territories because of his PLO membership. He lived in exile for twenty-five years and travelled to many places (like Edward Said), including Egypt, the Soviet Union, Beirut, Tunisia, and Paris. Darwish had given a special expression for his people's ordinary needs and desires as "the eye towards the beautiful."

Just like Mahmoud Darwish since the Nakba of 1948, Said was not settled. He travelled a lot; he was displaced even at his own homeland as he was Protestant and most of the Palestinian Christians were Catholic. Hence, he developed certain feelings about his own identity and the place where he belongs. Said stated that "it is geography—especially in the displaced form of departures, arrivals, farewells, exile, nostalgia, homesickness, belonging, and travel itself—that is at the core of my memories of those early years." And that indicates how lost he was away from his own homeland and how it influenced him.

He furthermore noted that he believes in the ontological instability of both concepts of the east or orient, and the concept of the west, and that the reason for such belief is because both of them are a definition of what he called "the other." This quotation represents the western side and how it looks at any oriental culture in general (at least in the point of view of Said), it shows the idea that the centre and the other in this context are the non-western people or the orientalist people.

This is the main idea of Orientalism which has led Said to the idea of antithesis later on, as the existence of one's self should depend on

---

[15] Rehnuma Sazzad, *Edward Said's Concept of Exile: Identity and Cultural Migration in the Middle East* (London and New York: Bloomsbury Publishing, 2017).

something else, and this includes the existence of the colonized and the colonizer in parallel with the exile and the homeland.[16]

The misconception that exile is the essential element that makes this type of literature an advanced one in the human sense is an insult to the concept itself, and to the people who are suffering and living in the diaspora. In fact, exile is mainly a topic that is directly related to the historical background of the matter, and it is caused by

humans to other fellow humans through banishing these people from their own heritage, geography,. and family. In Said's view, exile is a harsh experience that a human should not go through in life, and in this point, Said gets his aesthetic experience through representing the exile as "ugly."

The place in Said's memoir is Palestine and his story is a metaphor for all the Palestinian people's stories, and in his memoir, he clearly expressed how his departure from his mother tongue and how his early life has influenced his feelings towards his identity as someone always being out of place. He mentioned Aunt Nabeeha and how that woman changed his ideas about his homeland and helped him discover Palestine through her. Said moved to the United States when he was fifteen years old, he graduated from Harvard University and started teaching at Colombia University, he was the voice of Palestine for the American people.

When it comes to the two writers' point of view about their own identity, it is noticeable that both have the belief that their identity is dynamic, and that it is changing day by day, and they both believe that an individual's identity has multiple dimensions. Darwish has stated that his identity is still being written, and it can be said that a lot of Arab modern critics such as Amin Malouf share the same view as them.

---

[16] Edward Said. *Orientalism* (New York: Pantheon Books, 1978).

When it comes to their Arab identity, both identified themselves as Arabs since they share the same language and the same heritage. It can be noticed that they are not just concerned with the Palestinian cause, but they are concerned with other issues faced by Arabs, and they produced many texts that discuss a lot of Arab causes such as "Write down I am an Arab" by Mahmoud Darwish, and "Covering Islam" by Edward Said.

Darwish had a great interest in Arab literature, and he stated that he highly believes in Eliot's definition of the literary piece as the feeling of the poet or the writer of his own ancestors and his connection with them. As such, innovation does not mean that the writer or the poet would have to be separated from the works and the movements that occurred in previous times.

Darwish has stated that he believes that renewing the Arabic language cannot be conducted unless it was through depending on the Arab heritage and ancient literature which was written by his own Arab ancestors. But a true revolution of the language would mean that the writer must be aware of the language and what his ancestors have done, and to come up with a new form of that base that he has. He mentioned that breaking the old traditions cannot be conducted unless new traditions were innovated to take their place.

The poet must know the historical background when it comes to his own nation in order to be able to function it in a certain content, and to be able to discuss modern and current causes. And this is what we can view in his poems, which make use of a lot of cultural symbols and historical events. This has enabled him to represent both, the Palestinian and the Israeli through his own poetry.

In Orientalism, Said has criticized the way that the west is presenting the east, and how it is performing its image for the western audience. He has defended his Arab identity through using the method of Foucault in defining the identity of the colonizer which is a result of the propaganda and the racism that is rooted in that colonizer's thought.

Darwish has also adopted this point of view which is mainly concerned with fighting imperialism and oppression.

Another form of identity that both Said and Darwish belonged to is a global or international identity in a broader sense. Said stated that he prefers the concept of global orientalism over globalization, as globalization originally derived from American ideas and American ideologies.

He suggested the concept of hybridity, and used it in his well-known work, "Culture and Imperialism," as did Homi Bhabha in "The Location of Culture,"[17] as he stated that the identity today is not being introduced to the reader through biographical and historical stories, but it is conducted through the borders that are set up by cultural differences. This hybridity of identity is viewed as a result of the imperial experience, but it led to making a number of writers go back to their mother language and reformulate the identity concept into an aesthetic status, which is positioned against the imperialist experience and addresses the oppression acts of these imperial powers as oppressive acts. As a matter of fact, this is exactly what Said has said about Darwish's works.

The identity should not be a fatal one, but it should be one that gives the poet and the reader the feeling of being alive, and this is what makes an experience that is worth living as Malouf has indicated in his book "In the Name of Identity." Darwish focused on the role of hybridity in Said's identity and turns it into an aesthetics situation. He says: I come from that place. I come from here, and I am neither here nor there. I have two names that come together but pull apart. I have two languages, but I have forgotten which is the language of my dreams. I have the English language with its accommodating vocabulary to write in. And another tongue drawn from celestial conversations with Jerusalem. It has a silvery resonance, but rebels against my

---

[17] Homi Bhabha, *The Location of Culture* (London: Routledge, 1994).

imagination." He also discusses the concept of identity as defined through a relationship between the colonizer and the colonized:

Tebaq

Mahmoud Darwish starts this poem by addressing the place and the time (the setting), where he is writing this piece, which is New York, November. Throughout the poem, the reader is being made aware that the work was written in 2002, which would turn the question of the poet in the first stanza have the shape of an answer rather than a question. After that, the poet recalls the time that he met Edward Said, thirty years before this piece was written.[18]

Darwish moves from "write down I am an Arab" to questioning the identity in this poem, and especially after Oslo, as the identity has been shaped by a political decision. It should be mentioned that the two poets did not have the same beliefs about their own identities, as Said used to present himself as a Palestinian American, which is why he used to introduce himself in his works as an outsider. For the same reason he titled his memoir "Out of Place." Darwish on the other hand used to present himself as a Palestinian that expresses the feelings of all Palestinians, and that is why he stated "who am I without exile?"— a way for him to express his existential dilemma.

The word *Tebaq* itself in Arabic means "contradiction," and that is why Darwish was talking about the contradictions and dualities that exist in American society, such as speaking two languages just as in the case of Said, and having two different cultures, and even two identities, a thing common among intellectuals in the United

States. It should be mentioned that Darwish does not follow the traditional ways of writing, as he follows a form that makes all his poems special and indicate that they belong to the same poet. This can

---

[18] Dwīkat, Jamīl, "Multaqa Bullatah yunaqesh qaṣīdet Ṭebāq [The Gathering of Balata Discussing the Poem of Mahmoud Darwish Lamenting Edward Said], *alwatanvoice.com*, September 15, 2004, https://pulpit.alwatanvoice.com/articles/2004/09/15/9813.html.

be observed in a lot of his statements such as "Rita and the Rifle" and "The ending of this night would be a day." The whole poem focused on the concept of antithetical reading, which is a concept that was developed by Edward Said as it was mentioned above, and this is something that Darwish has emphasized in the poem.

Literature review

Antithetical analysis is an approach where reading the text is dependent on the historical background and perspectives, and this approach has been developed by Edward Said. It is mainly used in interpreting postcolonial texts and it is considered an important method for generating contextuality in the novel or the text. Interpreting the text using contrapuntal methods is mainly based on interpreting different methods simultaneously to examine how the text interacts with itself and with the historical and the biological contexts of the author.[19]

It is important for the reader or the critic to have full awareness of the metropolitan history of narration and the representation of "the other." The reader also needs to take into consideration the small plot lines that are extremely important in contrapuntal reading, as well as the focus on the phrases. For example, when an author illustrates the sugar plantation in one of his novels and portrays it as one of the essential things in maintaining the lifestyle in London at a period, and when antithetical analysis is applied, the author must take into consideration both, the colonial side, and its opposing resistance.

The colonial empire has considered the mission of civilizing the barbarians as one of its essential duties through looking at other nations or races as inferior ones who need the supervision of an empire, such as the British Empire which took the burden of such a mission to control and colonize other nations based on this colonial point of view. The reason for applying antithetical reading to the text here is to explain

---

[19] Pinar Bilgin, ""Contrapuntal Reading" as a Method, an Ethos, and a Metaphor for Global IR," *International Studies Review* 18, No. 1 (2016): 134–146.

differences between the experience of the colonized and the experience of the colonizer in literature. Surprisingly, many of the well-known English writers, such as Rudyard Kipling and Jane Austin have contributed to spreading this perspective, this what made people like Edward Said develop a way of reading texts which suggested that literature and imperialism can be viewed together simultaneously.

According to archaeology of knowledge, discourse is not related to the exterior aspect of the language in the text, and it is not necessarily related to linguistics, but it is really connected and homogenous. The huge interest in discourse and the way it is practiced have enabled scholars like Foucault to ignore the authority for one's self whether it belongs to an individual or a whole society, or whether it was objective or subjective.20 It is mainly the exclusion of the curious consciousness. Thus, discourse is not something that can be determined by pure individualism, but it is mainly a group of individuals' activities and sayings.

Thus, discourse as applied by Darwish in his poem belongs to the historical and social contexts for the exile. Regarding the Palestinian and the Israeli experiences, it is not an individual discourse, it is a discourse that

concerns a whole nation such as the post-colonial and the colonial discourse, and the discourse which entails the poetic of exile. So, discourse can also be characterized as a series of defined events, and as a result, the content must have a point, a resource, and a reason behind it, in addition to its embedded historical background.

In his published essay "Eloquent, elegant Arabic,"21 Said narrates that the Arabic language was taught to him controversially in the United States and he stated that this was for ideological purposes. He discusses the idea that the Arabic language was always linked to violence and

[20] Michele Foucault, *Neẓām Al kheṭāb* (Beirut: Al Tanwīr, 2007): 32.

[21] Said, Edward, "Eloquent, elegant Arabic," *Le Monde Diplomatique*, August 11, 2004, https://mondediplo.com/2004/08/11said.

blood-curdling, suggesting that Hollywood movies have a role in this phenomenon. Said discusses the development of the Arabic language and goes back to the Abbasi period, mentioning the contributions of that era such as Al-Jahiz and Al-Jurjani, and how those writers have developed schemes that were considered as diverse and complex, bearing resemblance to a lot of modern characteristics. Said states that the Quran constitutes the origin of classical written literary works in the Arabic language and the Quran served as a model for every Arabic literary work that came after it. Said furthermore explains the development of colloquial Arabic and how it was formed.

Thus, the linguistic aspect that Said has focused on stemmed from his own exile and identity disorder, and that made Darwish mention it in "Tebaq,"22 as Darwish can speak and write in Arabic eloquently, unlike Said who had problems expressing himself in the language. "I have two names that come together but pull apart. I have two languages, but I have forgotten which is the language of my dreams. I have the English language with its accommodating vocabulary to write in. And another tongue drawn from celestial conversations with Jerusalem. It has a silvery resonance, but rebels against my imagination."

Poetics

As Aristotle[23] suggested, all kinds of poetry are having an inquiry into the structure to create a good poem. Aristotle argues that all forms of poetry are sources of imitation, but the thing that makes them different from each other is the medium, the objects, the manner, and the mode of imitation. This imitation is mainly produced by the rhyme, the language, and the harmony and they are all combined.

There are multiple types of poetics, such as the minor poetics which have been present in the Arabic 20th century poetry, influenced by

---

[22] Taysīr, Naẓmī, *Ṭebāq Khuṭūṭo ttalāqī wa lefterāq [The Strings of Attachment and Parting in Tebaq]*, *wata.cc*, December 19, 2007, http://www.wata.cc/forums/showthread.php?20483-.

[23] Aristotle, *Poetics*, Translated by Malcom Heath (London: Penguin Classics, 1996).

symbolism and surrealism. One of the types of minor poetics is the poetics of revolution, which has been mainly present in the works of poets that were influenced by the realists following the Marxist and the communist approaches. The texts that use the implications of revolution poetics usually deal with various topics, such as oppression, discrimination, colonialism, and many others, and those texts encourage the reader to reconsider and question those perspectives. Such texts also serve to describe the revolution or criticize it in some cases.

To sum it up, this poetic is mainly about oppressed people, and it includes elegizing themes, such as mourning the martyrs who died in the battles or on the lost homeland. It typically comes with a revolutionary context, but it is also considered to be romantic at the same time, which creates the impression of romanticism with a touch of a realist context. This realist context was the dominant characteristic of Arabic poetry in the second half of the twentieth century. This kind of poetics can be found in the early works of Darwish which have taken a traditional form such as "Write Down I am an Arab," but when it comes to contrapuntal style, he used another type of poetics which was mainly concerned with hybridity, exile, and contrapuntal, as the Palestinian narrative cannot be full without the Israeli one and vice versa. At the same time, there are the poetics of the cause, and here we will go back to the reason why the poem was written in the first place. We would find that Mahmoud has written this poem under certain circumstances, and these circumstances were the same circumstances that every Palestinian around the world is facing.

Nostalgia in Darwish's works and in "Tebaq"

Mahmoud Darwish stated that "Nostalgic is a scar in the heart, and the fingerprint of a country on the body." There is another statement where he notes that "as long as my soul is alive no one can smother my feeling of nostalgia for my country which I still consider as Palestine." It can be noticed that Darwish has focused on his feeling of longing to his motherland Palestine throughout most of his well-known poems such as "On this Earth," and there is a kind of anxiety that can be noticed throughout the lines in all his poems. The nostalgic feeling in the poems of Mahmoud Darwish comes from his homesickness, and the anxiety in his poems is constituted by feelings shared with all Palestinians. It is noticeable that the past is really disturbing for Darwish as it draws the illusion of the Palestinian lands being lost forever.

The aesthetics of illness

There are many narratives and writings which are mainly concerned with the suffering of the ill one, and these writings usually would concern encountering medicine and hospitals. Such narratives provide the reader with analytics of the communicative body and provide the reader with the opportunity to establish a relationship with the writer. These works are likely to provide the reader with more than intellectual acknowledgement of the writer's feeling. These types of works do more than portraying the suffering and the events that revolve around the author, but they also document the author as the main character in the story. The main difference in this case is that the thought bearing witness to their sickness experience fabricate a world of illness in a form of exemplification which has been proposed.

It must be mentioned that Mahmoud Darwish has suffered from heart disease since he was young, and he had other health problems which led to his death. He had a first heart attack in the eighties and another one in the late nineties, leading to a near death experience. In the period that he was recovering from his second heart attack, he wrote his well-known poem "The mural," which is mainly a reflection on the concepts of life and death.

The well-known autobiographical book "Out of Place" was written in his illness period.[24] This narrative can be described as what augments the writer's identity crisis of exile. The story of the book is mainly a

[24] Shadi Neimneh, and Marwan Obeidat, "Narrativising Illness: Edward Said's Out of Place and the Postcolonial Confessional/Indisposed Self," *Arab World English Journal (AWEJ) Special Issue on Literature* 3 (2015): 18–28.

confessional narrative of confusion between the identity and the cultural dissonance represented by the illness of the author. It is a postcolonial narrative instrumentalizing the illness aesthetics and narrative.[25] Throughout the book, Said is obliged to write about his experience of the "out of place," and as a confessional narrative, his illness is presented as the factor that compels him to tell his story of living in the Arab world in his early life until he went to the United States to continue his studies.

According to Lezard, this whole memoir was mainly written to recover his early life (Said's) after being diagnosed with leukemia, as he tells stories about his own family that went through the experience that all Palestinians have been exposed to, and his description can be described as a frank one, which makes the book a special one in the world of literature.

"Out of place" can be described as a book that delivered the exile while coping with the illness at the same time and Said himself described his own life as a series of farewells and goodbyes, and such feelings were arguably intensified by illness. In his book, he described the chemotherapy and the pain that accompanies it as something that intensified the feeling of homesickness that he had, and the identity crisis that he went through, therefore, we can conclude that the illness phase was highly influential in Said's literary works.

This suffering he shared with Darwish was the reason why both have adopted the form of a testament, as both of them had good reason to fear death at any moment, and this is what gave the text a great poetic value in a metaphysical sense.

---

25 Alan Radley, "The aesthetics of illness: narrative, horror and the sublime," *Sociology of Health and Illness* 21, No. 6. (2001): 778–796.

Post-colonialism

Colonialism and post-colonialism are essential theories that both influenced the two thinkers. While many of the emerging countries were free from direct colonization, Palestine was still directly colonized, and they both belonged to the post-colonialism period. Said was not the first one to criticize the policy of the colonizer and how it deludes the public. There were previous efforts by writers such as the Indian thinker Hommi Bhabha, as his works were the pillars of the post-colonial theory, and they were highly influential in Said's works as well. Bhabha indicated hybridity and exile as things that would lead to an identity disorder.

When it comes to Mahmoud Darwish, it must be mentioned that most of his works are significant in post-colonial literature. In his output, he described all types of oppression and how it is used against people. The context of "Tebaq" is presenting the reader with two narratives, an Israeli and a Palestinian one. The people that have been colonized would not be able to survive and avoid being a victim. Darwish indicates that the experience of Orientalism that Said came up with was a part of this antithesis.

Conclusion

It can be concluded that both writers differed from each other in a lot of aspects. But they both belonged to the same cause, having the same objectives of using their poetry for letting the world know about the oppression that they are suffering from as exiled people that have been banished from their own homeland. Both writers had a very unique way of telling their own suffering as an exiled individual, and their methods and concepts differ due to the different circumstances that they both have experienced during their lifetime.

It is noticed that Darwish has a great belief in what Eliot has suggested about the importance of the roots of the language and the roots of the literature, and that knowing the heritage is a must in order to be able to innovate and create new concepts and ideas. Examining one of the most significant figures in the Palestinian literature such as Said and Darwish would help in understanding the literature of the oppressed, and to understand the alienation that they are suffering from.

It is highly important to look at each of their own works considering the poetics and the significance of their works as individual writers. As writers who belong to the Palestinian cause, they both defended their own case using their writings as a tool, in addition to incorporating their historical memory, which is the most important weapon that an oppressed person can have in his hands. The thoughts of the poet can be viewed through his own literary works, and this is how this chapter has been able to illustrate the thoughts and the beliefs of both of Darwish and Said, as their works were mainly targeted towards communicating their suffering and to let the world know the oppression that was done against them and against all Palestinians around the world, whether they were inside Palestine or scattered around the world.

They emphasized that it is important to have a definitive expression for the concept of identity and the pain that comes with it, which is deeply rooted in one's self, as the narrative cannot be separated from other narratives. This is the reason why the poem was named "Antithesis," in reference to the theory Said developed. It is highly important to read the works of these writers to understand their experiences of oppression that they were going through while being away from home. The thoughts of Said and Darwish have influenced a lot of following works that were concerned with the same cause, and it must be mentioned that there are interrelations with other works, such as the ones of Hommi Bhabha and other postcolonial writers. It also needs to be mentioned that Darwish has strongly been influenced by his own culture and by the ancient Arabic language, which for him provided a framework to be creative and to develop a new form of poetry.

The language was the part that differentiated them the most, as Said faced limitations regarding the Arabic language. Darwish was an Arab poet that wrote in Arabic, and this has created a kind of distinction between both of them regarding their works, thought, and way of thinking. The poem describes the "Tebaq" or "antithesis" that Said came up with as a concept as Darwish mourned his old friend in this piece of work, talking about making the impossible happening, mentioning all of the historical events, such as the captivity of Jews, Sodom and Gomorra as a symbol expressing his own oppression as a Palestinians and stating that this oppression is one which was conducted by another person that used to be oppressed at a time.

Throughout the poem, Darwish mentions a lot of images from his own memory, such as the image of the blood stain everywhere, and that assures the significance of the memory as it keeps the rage and the enthusiasm towards defending the case, and towards making the impossible come true, as Darwish has said to Said in the poem.[26] Darwish also mentions details about his relationship with Edward Said, as they share the same thing which is the same cause, "the impossible," as he expresses it in the poem, and both had a strong belief in that impossible as it was in their own imagination. They both believed that if the past was an experience, then the future and the present times shall be the time of believing in the dream and making it come true.

To study the poem, history needs to be known and acknowledged, and to analyse and to understand what both Said and Darwish meant by their words, their backgrounds and thoughts need to be examined and observed. Such is essential in order to know the feelings that they are trying to portray through their writings. The Palestinian narrative is told by such people that have lived the suffer of exile and alienation and that is why Darwish's and Said's works are more important and essential than more typical literary works that talk about oppression.

[26] Mas'ūd, Meqdād, "'dwārd Sa'īd men khelāli Mahmūd Darwīsh Fī qaṣīdet Ṭebāq" [Edward Said Through Mahmoud Darwish in Tibaq Poem], *alnaked-aliraqi.net*, August 29, 2017, https://www.alnaked-aliraqi.net/article/45474.php.

Bibliography

Al-Ju'beh, Nazmi. *Palestinian Identity and Cultural Heritage* (Beirut: Presses de l'Ifpo, 2008).

Aristotle, Poetics, Translated by Malcom Heath, (London: Penguin Classics, 1996).

Asser, Martin. "Obstacles to Arab-Israeli peace: Water." *BBC News*. January 20, 2021, https://www.bbc.com/news/world.4.

Bacchi, Carol. "The Turn to Problematization: Political Implications of Contrasting Interpretive and Post structural Adaptations." *Open Journal of Political Science* 5, No. 1 (2015): 1–12.

Bhabha, Hommi. 1994. *The Location of Culture*. London: Routledge.

Bilgin, Pinar. ""Contrapuntal Reading" as a Method, an Ethos, and a Metaphor for Global IR." *International Studies Review* 18, No. 1 (2016): 134–146.

Darwish, Mahmoud. "Contrapuntal." trans. Julie Stoker. *Le Monde Diplomatique* January 15, 2005, https://mondediplo.com/2005/01/15said.

Dwīkat, Jamīl, "Multaqa Bullatah yunaqesh qaṣīdet Ṭebāq [The Gathering of Balata Discussing the Poem of Mahmoud Darwish Lamenting Edward Said], *alwatanvoice.com*, September 15, 2004, https://pulpit.alwatanvoice.com/articles/2004/09/15/9813.html.

"Events leading to the Six Day War (1967), Israel Ministry of Foreign Affairs. https://www.mfa.gov.il/mfa/aboutisrael/maps/pages/events%20leading%20to%20the%20six%20day%20war%201967.aspx#:~:text=The%20immediate%20causes%20for%20the,forces%20there%2C%20and%20finally%20the

Foucault, Michele. 1987. *Ḥafrīyāt Alma'refah. [Archaeology of Knowledge]*. Beirut: Almarkaz al thaqāfī al 'arabī.

Foucault, Michele. 2007. *Neẓām Al kheṭāb*. Beirut: Al Tanwīr.

Hilal, Jami. "Reclaiming the Palestinian Narrative." *Al Shabaka*. January 6, 2013, https://al-shabaka.org/commentaries/reclaiming-the-palestinian-narrative/.

Ibish, Hussein. "A 'Catastrophe' That Defines Palestinian Identity." *The Atlantic*. May 14, 2018, https://www.theatlantic.com/international/archive/2018/05/the-meaning-of-nakba-israel-palestine-1948-gaza/560294/.

Juza, Ryan. "Echoes of Sodom and Gomorrah on the Day of the Lord: Intertextuality and Tradition in 2 Peter 3:7–13." *Bulletin for Biblical Research* 24, No. 2 (2014): 227–245.

Lustick, Ian. "The Oslo Agreement as an Obstacle to Peace." *Journal of Palestine Studies* 27, No. 1 (1997): 61–66.

Mas'ūd, Meqdād. "'dwārd Sa'īd men khelāli Mahmūd Darwīsh Fī qaṣīdet Ṭebāq" [Edward Said Through Mahmoud Darwish in Tibaq Poem]. *alnaked-aliraqi.net*. August 29, 2017, https://www.alnaked-aliraqi.net/article/45474.php.

Naẓmī, Taysīr. *Ṭebāq Khuṭūṭo ttalāqī wa lefterāq [The Strings of Attachment and Parting in Tebaq]*. *wata.cc*. December 19, 2007, http://www.wata.cc/forums/showthread.php?20483-.

Neimneh, Shadi, and Obeidat, Marwan. "Narrativising Illness: Edward Said's Out of Place and the Postcolonial Confessional/Indisposed Self." *Arab World English Journal (AWEJ) Special Issue on Literature* 3 (2015): 18–28.

Radley, Alan. "The aesthetics of illness: narrative, horror and the sublime." *Sociology of Health and Illness* 21, No. 6. (2001): 778–796.

Said, Edward. 1978. *Orientalism*. New York: Pantheon Books.

Said, Edward. 1995. *Oslo 2 "Peace without a Land."* Cairo: Dar Al Mustaqbal Al Arabi.

Said, Edward. "Eloquent, elegant Arabic." *Le Monde Diplomatique*. August 11, 2004, https://mondediplo.com/2004/08/11said.

Said, Edward. 2001. *Reflections on Exile: And Other Literary and Cultural Essays*. New York: Granta Books.

Spitzer, Jeffrey. "Babylonian Exile." *My Jewish Learning*, https://www.myjewishlearning.com/article/babylonian-exile/.

Sazzad, Rehnuma. 2017. *Edward Said's Concept of Exile: Identity and Cultural Migration in the Middle East*. London and New York: Bloomsbury Publishing.

Chapter Eight
Video games as cultural artifacts: How players' morality and ethics are challenged in video games

Ayman Kole, Othmane Blidry

Introduction

How are video games able to pose moral demands on players and how do they encourage them to reflect on their behavior regarding ethical issues? This chapter will put the spotlight on how some ethically notable games managed to provide opportunities through various narrative and gameplay aspects that encourage players to reflect on their choices through ethical and moral reasoning.

This analysis will highlight the core role of moral dilemmas in the creation of ethically notable games. It will discuss the various ways these dilemmas are implemented and structured, for example by placing gamers in a context where their understanding of the ethical and moral system is challenged, or by simply creating a sort of tension between the goal of the player, the narrative, and the gameplay.

Furthermore, the chapter will discuss the different requirements and problems that arise when games try to handle such complex topics. These stem from a need for consistency in the story to ensure that the dilemma is a moral one. It further needs to be ensured that the player is the one facing the ethical challenge, rather than their video game characters. Hence, the analysis will explore how games have succeeded in investing the player in the story.

It has been argued that certain aspects of video games can offer valuable chances as learning tools, since they are a unique medium of entertainment, due to their ability to introduce a new form of persuasive rhetoric. The discussion will feature examples that document the early implementation of this concept as a moral learning tool.

What is an ethically notable game?

The ethically notable game typically refers to games that provide the opportunity for ethical reasoning and reflection. This may be achieved by their allowance for an emotionally moving and compelling experience driven by the narrative, designed to transport the player in the direction of a moral dilemma.[1]

The confrontation of audiences with moral dilemmas has been a central topic of philosophical discussion, as well as the substance of creative and expressive work through various media such as theatre, literature, and film. Much of the strength of drama relies on putting the characters through morally ambiguous and seemingly irresolvable moral situations. In this regard, while employing different rhetorical devices and strategies, the viewers, spectators or readers, witness the emotional agitation and turmoil of the characters. Without a doubt, these constitute major factors to get them thoroughly invested in the narrative.

Of course, such media formats making use of moral dilemmas can be seen as a kind of useful testing ground for reflection and reasoning, since the involvement of the audience is not limited to an intellectual level, but also features a strong emotional involvement. Equally important, when aiming to discuss ethics and gaming, the surrounding themes such as the morality of a game become more noteworthy. For

---

1 Christopher W. Gowans, ed., *Moral Dilemmas* (New York: Oxford University Press, 1987).

example, one might want to consider the ethical value of a specific game as a cultural artifact.

Reynolds,[2] for instance, raised the question of whether "Grand Theft Auto 3" (GTA 3) is to be viewed as good or bad in a moral sense, arguing that maybe GTA 3 is a bad game since it features depictions of violence and crime, displaying a negative portrayal of society. Likewise, he suggests it may be considered as a good game, since its design provides pleasure to those who play it. Reynolds' reflections underline the distinction between considering a game outside of its frame as a product designed to entertain audiences, and in its dimension as an ethical artifact.

Should, then, the act of playing a game inherently trivialize the myriad of controversial, dark, or emotional topics that perhaps are not usually discussed in other forms of entertainment media? And would that automatically make the game unethical? This chapter will provide a discussion of how video games, when considered as cultural artifacts, can be of great moral and ethical value, and how the evolution of video game technology and narrative design serve to support this perspective.

Modern video game design has evolved from mindlessly pressing buttons to investing the player in rich and engaging narratives that require a more complex understanding of the relationship between characters, problem-solving strategies, and also demonstrates a mastery of the underlying mechanics that the game is using. It should be noted that tools such as narrative symbols and the rules of the game constitute an ideological framework of a simulated environment the players find themselves immersed in.

Generally, video games provide clear orientation regarding the reward and compensation attributed to certain actions and behaviors, and

---

[2] Reynolds, Ren, "Playing a "Good" Game: A Philosophical Approach to Understanding the Morality of Games," International Game Developers Association, 2002, 1–12.

those to be avoided. Encouraged actions are being considered good, while the opposite is evaluated as bad (however, there are exceptions to this rule). A video game can represent a consistent ethical framework embedded in the specific narrative that contextualizes options of possible actions.

One such example is the fantasy role-playing video game "Fable" that was released for the Xbox in 2004.[3] The narrative has the player beginning his journey as a child in a fantasy village. In need of money to buy a birthday gift for his sister, the character is confronted with conflicting situations and forced to position himself accordingly. To illustrate, the player needs to decide whether to use this opportunity to generate money or to tell the truth to the husband's wife when offered a bribe to remain quiet by the husband engaging in adultery who has been caught by the character. Hence, "Fable" provides a clear ethical system that depicts the red line between "evil" discouraged behavior and "good" actions to be rewarded.

However, in some other games, like "Metal Gear Solid 2," the narrative context does not allow for a clear and transparent ethical vision and obvious ramifications concerning the players actions. The narrative design rather leaves the moral evaluation of actions to the gamer. Similarly, other games might not provide the player with sufficient information to distinctly contextualize his or her decisions.

Pohl[4] points out two forms of emotional involvement that characterize video games: the instantaneous (playing to win), and the spontaneous (playing to relate and identify with the story). All the narrative frame

---

[3] Peter Edward Rauch, "Playing with good and evil: Videogames and moral philosophy," Dissertation, Massachusetts Institute of Technology, 2007.

[4] Pohl, Kirsten. "Ethical reflection and emotional involvement in computer games." In Conference proceedings of The Philosophy of Computer Games 2008, eds. Stephan Günzel, Michael Liebe, Dieter Mersch (Potsdam: Universitätsverlag Potsdam, 2008), 92–107.

does is to push the player forward, make them invest in the game characters and relate to their concerns.

Although other media such as theatre, film, and literature can present troubled characters facing tricky situations and thereby emotionally invest their viewers in the story, video games in particular seem to be best suited for this purpose. Compared to passive audiences, video game players are heavily invested in the choices and moral decisions since they are influencing the storyline to some extent. In the following, three different games that successfully invest players in their stories through various intricate narrative tools and gameplay features will be discussed in detail.

Persona 5: video games as cultural artifacts

"Persona 5" was released in Japan by Altus, a subsidiary company of Sega in the year of 2016 and was quickly localized and translated for the western market the following year to critical acclaim. It is a spinoff of the highly successful "Shin Megami Tensei" franchise and has sold over 2.7 million copies. In addition to this, "Persona 5" has received outstanding reviews in both Japan and the West.

Its story unfolds around a group of high school student misfits who enter the metaverse, a supernatural realm inhabited by malevolent manifestations of society's subconscious desires (shadows) to change society by holding corrupt adults accountable for their actions. The game is set-in modern-day Japan, specifically Tokyo, and it highlights the different social issues that are affecting young people in Japanese society by enacting them in the game's narrative and mechanics.

The message of the game is crystal clear: the teenage characters controlled by the gamers act responsibly regarding their friends and society, by tackling the corruptions of adults in positions of power. The game displays and explores the different ramifications of intense societal pressure on Japanese youth, especially high schoolers, and young women. As such, the main cast of characters includes Ann

Takamaki, a victim of abuse by the school's physical education teacher, as well as a highly introverted Hikikomori Futaba Sakura who isolated herself after the death of her mother. The narrative presents the main cast and the phantom thieves (their identity when they explore the metaverse) as heroes, vigilantes, and brave liberators.

Other similar aspects presented in the core game mechanics play into the narrative theme to construct a kind of ludo narrative dissonance[5] that scales up a damnatory and strong criticism of the pressures on young people in Japanese society. Gregory and Walford[6] suggest that any kind of text allows for interpretations about the background of its author, and as such, video games as a more recent form of artistic expression similarly reflect the identity of its creators and the society that birthed them.

Although the term "culture "is as broad as it gets, there are some ways to frame it in the current case: Through the material object that form the environment (in this case Tokyo and Shibuya, the most popular district in Tokyo, or simply the geo localization of the game), its popular and artistic tradition (every reference to Japanese tradition in the game, from school uniforms to the architecture of the city), and through the values attitudes and beliefs (for example the *tatemae* and *honne* that are going to be explored later on in this chapter). Yet, regarding Japan and the game, the term culture mainly refers to a two-faced society where people act according to their social status, typically corresponding to social norms than honesty.

Therefore, the study of an artistic text or artifact can elucidate not only the intention of the creator, but also serve as a mirror for the subtle societal influence. Making any general statement about a certain culture, or when addressing a particular society, is a delicate matter and

---

[5] Seraphine, Frederic. "The Rhetoric of Undertale. Ludonarrative Dissonance and Symbolism." *Proceedings of the 8th Conference of the Digital Games Research Association Japan 2018.*

[6] Derek Gregory, and Rex Walford, *Horizons in Human Geography* (London: Barnes and Noble, 1989).

one of the most frustrating societies to address in this regard is probably Japan. Japanese society is constituted by robust social structures that consider the benefit of others over the individual, which led to the *wakamono mondai* (youth issues) that our main cast suffers from, and which is used to characterize an entire generation.

The Japanese proverb *deru kugi wa utareru* (the nail that sticks out gets hammered down) underlines why Japan is attributed to homogeneity, while western societies value self-interest over conformity and give credence to traits that reinforce self-direction such as assertiveness and independence.[7] Japan is widely different in this regard as it values conformity and the interest of the group over the individual, even as early as preschool education, where the children are encouraged to consider how their behavior will affect/influence the whole group rather than themselves.

This pattern remains consistent throughout a person's whole lifetime. For example, employees who leave earlier than their coworkers will apologize for doing so as their behavior is seen as letting the team down. Simple rituals like saying *itadakimasu* (I will humbly accept it) before eating or saying *gochishouma deshita* (Thank you for the wonderful meal, it was a great feast) may seem inconsequential, but they all add up concerning the Japanese identity. A pattern or ramification of this social structure is that most Asian cultures are deeply concerned with dignity and "saving face."

In Japan, a person is expected to interact with their environment using two different faces: the *tatemae* (the outside face) and the *honne* (true face). This change in attitude may be compared to acting a role and playing a part rather than faking emotions or presenting a false idea of who you are. These mechanisms are part of the group-oriented function of a general conformist approach, and while they helped to create

---

[7] Alan Miller, *Order by Accident: The Origins and Consequences of Group Conformity in Contemporary Japan* (New York: Routledge, 2018).

harmony on the surface of Japanese society it led to a fair share of underlying problems as well.

When globalization started to bring new ideas and beliefs to Japan around the mid-nineties, rapid changes were occurring. Many social problems resulted from a large generational gap between the youth and Japanese ageing population. Therefore, more and more youngsters are struggling with growing up in such a conformist society that severely rejects their identity and individuality. The following section will cover the game "Persona 5" from a narratological point of view by discussing the overall tone and argument of the game itself, explain how it reflects the different problems that Japanese youth suffers from, and elaborate on how this distinguished the game as a cultural artifact rather than a simple entertainment experience.

JRPGs (Japanese role-playing games) tend to instrumentalize the realms of fantasy science fiction and the supernatural to draw the players out of their comfort zone, seemingly liberating them from the invisible constrains of their real life. As such, this makes it easier to contemplate oneself and facilitates self-reflection. Therefore, "Persona 5" constitutes a harmonious balance between the literal and figurative as the game is set in the "real world" Tokyo with all the different elements that anyone would be familiar with if they ever set foot in modern-day Japan.

The main characters have a daily routine of going to school, getting part-time jobs, and doing their homework like any normal high schooler. The catch here is that they are normal, and as such, the perspective proposed by the narration provides a good base to build an argument regarding Japanese society, since the story line is neither too fantastic to be detached from reality, nor too grounded to offend or provoke feelings of unease or discomfort among the Japanese population.

Jung's consideration of the term "persona"[8] as "the mask of the soul"[9] is almost interchangeable with the concept of *tatemae* and *honne* previously mentioned and is explored rigorously in the persona games. Throughout the narrative, several members of the main cast, the "phantom thieves," come face-to-face with their "cognitive copies," an identical form of themselves, but one that conveys everything that they are ashamed of, or that which is socially perceived as negative.

For instance, when the "Joker" character is ridiculed by Kamoshida for being unable to help Ryuji, he comes to terms with his previous morally right and just actions, which resulted in him being branded as a criminal. This resolve bestows upon him the strength to face his doubts: he tears away his mask from his face, awakening his persona Arsène, which allows him to escape from Kamoshida.

This act of ripping off the mask is visceral, as you can see the character clearly screaming and struggling in agony, with his mask appearing to be a part of his flesh before he succeeds in his task with a rush of blood. Thus, awakening to their "true self" and being visibly liberated from the chains that held them back, the changes to the characters are evident, as many of them grin, standing tall and ardent with confidence. This theme of teenage characters liberated from the chains of society they feel trapped in by embracing their otherness and shedding the shame that has been heaped upon them is consistent throughout the game.

In line with this narrative, the virtual location of the "Velvet Room" changes its architecture according to the different characters of the game, depending on the psyche of the protagonist. For instance, it takes on the shape of a prison where the main character finds himself jailed. In addition, the high school attended by the characters is called *shujin* academy, with *shujin* being a synonym for prisoner. This clearly is a

[8] Stefan Bolea, "The persona and the shadow in analytic psychology and existentialist philosophy," *Philobiblon* 21, No. 1 (2016): 84–94.

[9] Bolea, "The persona," 84.

direct reference and a counterargument to the consensus and conformity often portrayed as the positive forces behind the "harmonious" aspects of Japanese society, and it is significant in this game, specifically because there is no proposed compromise between *tatemae* and *honne*.

The *tatemae* as the public face is clearly being portrayed as something of a burden, or at least a negative aspect impacting one's true self. The character in the game hence fits the description of Ruti[10] as "a subject who is willing to destroy itself in a vehement act of 'subjective destitution'—an act that presents an absolute break with the dominant establishment"[11] and who "attains the heroic status of someone who is ready to sacrifice his or her social viability for the sake of a larger cause."[12]

The metaverse in "Persona 5" allows the character to achieve singularity or rather their true self, disregarding all the social rules and norms, and completely leaving the *tatemae* behind. In this regard, Ruti stated the following:[13]

> In a certain way, we are constantly compelled to negotiate the inevitable tension between being a subject (in the sense of being subjected to social norms) and being a singular creature (in the sense of having a distinctive character and destiny). Most times, we are both at once, but arguably it is only as singular creatures that we are fully awake.

The removal of the mask and the ownership of control of the persona represents the characters becoming a singular creature, no longer bound between two personalities. While past persona games were advocating for a more conservative approach and negotiating between

---

[10] Mari Ruti, *The Singularity of Being: Lacan and the Immortal Within* (New York: Fordham University Press, 2012).

[11] Ruti, "The Singularity," 5.

[12] Ibid.

[13] Ruti, "The Singularity," 35.

being a subject and a singular creature, "Persona 5" pushes the idea further in that it suggests that authenticity can only be achieved through complete sacrifice of the *tatema*.

This thought is consistent with Sartre's idea of living in "bad faith," that is, "denying our freedom...to rid ourselves of the irksome obligation to act and take responsibility for our choices."[14] The challenge of living in good faith as depicted in "Persona 5" is the difficulty and the painful act of physically ripping off the mask. As soon as the characters come to terms with themselves in the metaverse, they become "phantom thieves" and are regarded as deviants and rebels for their independent spirit. Further, "Mementos" is one of the dungeons that the "phantom thieves" explore in the metaverse. It represents society's collective unconscious and is also considered to be the palace of Apathy.

As revealed eventually, when the "phantom thieves" reach higher levels, people would rather believe in obvious lies than challenge social and societal structures. This clearly alludes to the pressure to conform in Japanese society and its destructive potential or tendencies.

The design of the different characters underlines a "deviant as hero" message as most of the personas draw inspiration from fictional rogue representations. Game director Katsura Hashino said he was inspired by the picaresque, a genre that generally deals with a roguish hero, and his characters clearly reflect this with references to fictional rogue heroes such as Arsène Lupin, Captain Kidd, and Zorro. Parallels can be drawn with the "phantom thieves" who act as heroes outside of the law but for a greater good and are targeting the elite as an act of rebellion.

Consequently, "Persona 5" challenges the traditional structure of the Japanese hegemonic model by highlighting a subtle critique of the pressure put on the main cast, be it male or female; Video games bear the potential to argue for change in their structured mechanics, and in

---

[14] David Detmer, *Sartre Explained. From Bad Faith to Authenticity* (Chicago: Open Court, 2008), 75.

their narrative. Therefore, they may, in their innate construction, be persuasive and "make claims about how real-world processes do, could, or should work."[15]

"Persona 5" instrumentalizes the way players can interact within the game world to reinforce and strengthen its narrative argument. It also displays mechanics that deliberately deny player agency, which is discordant with the game narrative. It has been suggested that game developers may consciously subvert the narrative with the game mechanics in what is known as ludo narrative dissonance[16] "to create complex narratives of trauma and suffering."[17]

Accordingly, the subsequent section will explore the core mechanics of "Persona 5" and how they play a major role in the construction of the narrative. A central feature in this regard is the integrated confident system that measures the different relationships with other game characters by a sort of social credit system. The players can level up by spending time with other characters in the game and if they get far enough, they are able to unlock hidden special dialogue options, effectively providing the player with more information about that character, as well as their backstory, upgrades, and bonus gameplay.

In "Persona 5," gaming time is a resource that should be spent wisely, players are presented with various choices and must prioritize a balance between beneficial social links and taking care of other aspects of their in-game life. After a typical playthrough, the game will end with some characters' backstories left unexplored due to lack of time. However, there is a "perfect" way to play the game in which the player

---

[15] Ian Bogost. "The Rhetoric of Video Games." In The ecology of video games: connecting youth, games, and learning, ed. Katie Salen (Cambridge: MIT Press, 2008), 57.

[16] Seraphine, "Ethics at play."

[17] Evgeniya Kuznetsova, "Trauma in Games: Narrativizing Denied Agency, Ludonarrative Dissonance and Empathy Play," Master Thesis, University of Alberta, 2017, iii.

manages to increase all the social links to their maximum while also completing the regular tasks required to be performed in the game.

This procedure requires a lot of skills and optimization, since to achieve a perfect run, specific actions are supposed to be performed in a specific order to benefit from the different bonus effects such as exploring the metaverse only on rainy days. These options similarly apply to past person games, as developers always made sure that there was a "perfect" way to finish the game, but the main point is that it is almost impossible to do it without previous knowledge of game mechanics or guides. Most players would prefer to play the game "blindly" to enjoy the game the way that developers intended it to be experienced.

However, the views of specific guides amount to 90,000, which demonstrates that there is a demand in achieving a "perfect playthrough." This option for a perfect run could have been left out by the developers but they opted to include it. As a matter of fact, they included a twist at the very end of the game where it is revealed that the protagonist has been manipulated by a Yadabaoth, a god of control, throughout the entire narrative, revealing that all the actions of the 'phantom thieves' have been engineered from the start.

At this point, it is shown that the metaverse, mementos, and the "Velvet Room" are all under his control and that the protagonist's efforts were all in vain as he loses the game. But the character refuses to be executed and fully awakens, the prison door that once held him back in the "Velvet Room" disappears and the "phantom thieves" banish the god under the condition that all their achievements up until this point go unnoticed by society.

Here, the player is presented with the choice to either agree to the condition or choose to live in self-deceit and illusion. This final decision draws the player closer to the character he chose to play, as they both want to get rid of the evil god. The dilemma created by the developers is directly linked to the core message of the narrative: the only way to win the game is to give up on everything that made you feel powerful and unique. Hence, the game involves the player as being complicit in the choice of the character and this makes the whole argument more convincing and significantly strengthens the main plot. However, if the player decides to keep up their level of fame and social recognition, the game will result in a bad ending. This option contrasts the "happy end," that leaves the "phantom thieves"' achievements unacknowledged by society.

When the player opts to set up his character for a failure despite the many hours that they have spent to build and strengthen them, "Persona 5" offers a brilliant way to experience the frustration and constraint occurring in a flawed and corrupt system. This move can be interpreted as a clever and relatable expression of criticism regarding Japan's ever-present social norms and those who blindly abide to it, highlighting that the game was rigged from the very beginning.

With its bright colorful anime style and teenage-driven protagonists, it would be very easy to dismiss "Persona 5" and consider it as a cliché without significant academic relevance. Such a perspective relates to a bigger conception that tends to regard "fun" and "meaningful" as mutually exclusive regarding video games. Nevertheless, while "Persona 5," like most video games, is made and designed for entertainment purposes, it should not be disregarded as a cultural artefact and its significance as a reflection of societal norms and regulations.

There is a potential in video games that is unique to the medium, in this case the outstanding degree of player investment in narration and the successful way of encapsulating the significant shift in society (in this case modern Japan). "Persona 5" makes a strong statement in providing the player with the experience of the suffering of a whole generation, trapped by the expectations of the previous and the remains of a once booming economy.

NieR: Automata and the Metal Gear Solid Serie

This section will focus on moral dilemmas and how games are able to grant a certain weight to the player's decisions by using different narrative, game play and agency tools to facilitate immersion. For example, at the end of Metal Gear Solid 4, Snake, the main protagonist, must go through a scorching microwave tunnel to save the world. In this scene, the player does not dispose of the regular control schemes, but rather the game offers QTE (quick time event).

This means that the player needs to repeatedly tap one button; during this scene the screen is split into two, with the lower part depicting Snake crawling in the tunnel and the upper half showing his allies getting overwhelmed by enemy forces. The decision to make use of QTE is essential for the involvement of the player into the narrative, as the scene depicts Snake slowly crawling while he is getting roasted alive. If the game would not offer restricted gameplay in the form of QTE for this scene, the player would be able to get to the end of the tunnel quickly and save his comrades. This would have ruined the tension and the narrative moment, the use of QTE is crucial, as it prolongs the scenario.

Pressing the same button repeatedly becomes tiring and exhausting, which creates an overlapping experience for the player and the character. The game encourages the player to endure and move on, just like Snake is getting tortured by the heat, moving on through the tunnel. This creates an experience where both the player and the character share a sense of relief when reaching the other end of that tunnel. In short, the player feels that their repeated taps are meaningful to the mission, in fact pressing the button in a particularly faster way does not make the scene pass quicker, as one would be able to skip the enduring of Snake's pain.

In another game named "Papers, Please," the gamer takes on the role of an immigration officer who is responsible for checking immigrants' legal documents for a dystopian country, and they need to decide if they are allowed to enter the country or not. The player gets rewarded for each legal immigrant that he allows to enter the country in order to support their family. However, if the latter allows immigrants with either illegal or outdated documentation, he will obtain a citation. A certain number of citations may lead to a decrease in pay or even putting a family member in danger. The goal of the game is to keep their family alive and relatively healthy, as the "game over" screen is triggered when a member of the player's family dies.

However, the player is sometimes faced with moral dilemmas and complex ethical choices, for example, when a woman enters the immigration office and provides the player with an ad to a local brothel. She notes that a person named Dari Ludim is involved in the trafficking of women and forces women to work in the brothel and asks the player's character to deny the person entry in order to protect these women. Later, Dari Ludim will try to enter the country with perfectly legal documents, implying the right choice here to win the game is to let him enter, since he is in possession of legal documents and denying entry will result in negative impacts for the player. However, despite that, many players found themselves inclined to deny his entry.

NieR: Automata

Yoko Taro, the main writer for the NieR series has been known for his creative writing, drastically different premises across the different NieR games, and philosophic implications and undertones. In the original NieR game, the protagonist is trying to find a cure for his sister who has contracted a disease that is slowly destroying and eradicating humanity. NieR: Automata on the contrary is set in a post-apocalyptic setting around a conflict between two robots and androids, each of them representing their masters. Both games discuss major themes of death and are set in dark and grim environments. However, a consistent pattern in Taro's games are the different, not necessarily alternative possible endings, which add extra depth to the narrative.

NieR: Automata was released on March 7, 2017, in North America and a few days later in Europe. The story takes place in the year 11945, way before the events of the game, approximatively 6000 years before aliens invaded earth and humans fled to the moon. There they established the council of humanity and started building an army of androids to free earth from its invaders, the machines created by the aliens—an elite android army called YoRHa. This situation had lasted for millennia without any traces from the aliens or the council of humanity, as they only broadcasted short messages. Throughout the game, the player can control three different androids: 2B, 9S, and A2. 2B is the main protagonist the player starts the game with. The B refers to "battle," in relation to its primary mode as a YoRHa combat android.

2B is depicted as a cold-hearted, efficient, and professional female character, strictly focused on the goal of her mission. 9S accompanies her as a YoRHa scanner android, whose job is to gather information and intel and unlike 2B it was programmed to be curious and kind. A2 as the third protagonist rebelled against the order of YoRHa, which turns her into an enemy of the 2B and 9S characters.

As stated before, NieR: Automata closes with five major endings. However, these are not alternative endings, as for example ending A and B are predetermined by corresponding routes but not the entire plot, as the story resumes afterwards in ending C.

In the playthrough of the game (route A), the player controls 2B exclusively, while in another route the same events unfold from the perspective of 9S. The story begins in the middle of a ward between androids and machines, when 2B is assigned on a mission to defeat a goliath-class machine (a very large machine unite that has been abandoned in a factory), which the character comments as follows:

> Everything that lives is designed to end. We are perpetually trapped in a never-ending spiral of life and death. Is this a curse? Or some kind of punishment? I often think about the god who

> blessed us with this cryptic puzzle...and wonder if we'll ever get the chance to kill him.

This quote's value and ramification cannot be fully understood if taken at face value, but rather needs to be contextualized in the narrative frame. Androids and machines do not have a single physical body, but rather their personality and memory are stored in a black box that is kept in a database; in the case of 2B and 9S, in the YoRHa headquarter. They upload what they have learned into the database, and this explains the respawn system in the game.

The machines' equivalent of the black box is a mechanical core. Although machines are contrasted as mindless living weapons as compared to the androids who resemble humans' sentience, both were created from organic creatures, aliens and humans. Although androids can be built without a black box, they will lose all their previous experience and memories in this case. The quote is still unclear for new players but after finishing the game this statement becomes much clearer implying, she was referring to partaking in useless violence in addition to having to kill her friend repeatedly throughout the different endings.

The first minutes of the route A showcase the main characters 2B and 9S, highlighting 2B's straightforward methods of dealing with enemies by overwhelming them with strength. In contrast, route B starts with the perspective of 9S watching a machine trying to activate another machine referring to it as "brother" until 9S is called to help the incoming 2B to assist in her mission. As mentioned before, 9S is not designed for combat, so he assists 2B via a hacking mechanic introduced in the game. While hacking is used for fighting and weakening enemies, it is sometimes also employed for narrative purposes, like when 9S explores YoRHa's database.

Soon after their introduction, 9S arrives to help 2B to defeat the goliath unit. They exchange information before going their separate way to find an easier method to defeat the unit. An interesting difference between the two routes is that the camera is angled differently depending on the route, magnifying the routes' purpose to provide an alternative perspective. Another aspect of outlining the character of 2B is introduced by their discussion via radio contact. 9S tells 2B that he is glad to work with her, as usually scanner units work alone, and after describing it to be a fun experience 2B rejects him by saying that emotions are prohibited.

Even though 2B is presented as an unemotional android when talking to 9S, she is shown acting on emotions when alone. When 9S is not present, for example, 2B is accompanied by a robot called Pod 042, who gives strategic support, but also works as a range weapon for the player.

Eventually they regroup and fight the goliath unit, 9S gets damaged and 2B tells Pod 042 to help her repair 9S but he disagrees, as he tells her that 9S's vital signals are too low and that he will surely die. She interrupts him and orders him to do it anyway, 9S wakes up and tells 2B to leave him which she refuses. 9S states that they are soldiers and they should be proud of their service, 2B leaves 9S to recover and goes to fight the machine. While getting repaired, 9S finds a weakness and informs 2B that he is trying to hack her enemy. 2Bs only tells him to shut up. 2B deals the final blow to the goliath unit and stabs it with her sword.

However, various goliath units appear after this and 9S suggests 2B to use their self-destruct mechanism to obliterate the remaining goliath units while assuring her that he has uploaded her current black box data to a server.

2B and 9S suicide bomb themselves and appear in the YorHa headquarters. 9S congratulates 2B to the successful mission, but 2B interrupts and thanks him for uploading her memory. 9S replies that he has no recollection of the mission, since he was not able to upload his own memory into the bunker. After 9S walks away, 2B's clenching fist is shown on the screen.

There are over twenty-six possible endings in NieR: Automate, and throughout the adventures of 9S, 2B, and A2, the player must go through a frustrating number of hours to clear all the endings. These detailed descriptions of the characters have been added with the intention to provide an insight into the unusually complex narration achieved through perspective writing. While the whole premise of the game deserves its own paper, the following section will discuss how this relates to exposing players to moral dilemmas and challenges.

Ending three is located after the death of 9S or A2, with protagonists that are being introduced later in the story, Pod 042, and Pod 153. They confirm that all YoRHa units were destroyed, and it is also revealed that the main purpose of the Pods is to look after the progress of YoRHa. At this point, they are expected to delete all its data. However, as the credits roll, Pod 153 notices leaks in the data check and chooses to stop the credits and reset them. Pod 042 comments on how the protagonists' personal data is leaking out and Pod 153 tells him to ignore it and delete all data. However, Pod 042 refuses and comments that he cannot accept this resolution, as he wishes to keep it intact. Pod 153 agrees to his concern for the characters to survive. However, Pod 153 warns him that salvaging the data can be dangerous and asks Pod 042 if he still wishes for them to survive. If the player opts for yes, they unlock ending E: the [E]nd of YoRHa.

The game surprises with a definitive final shooting section that has the player facing one last enemy: the credits. The first name to appear is writer Yoko Taro's, others follow. In the midst of all this, the Pods discuss their creation and how they were not able to develop any kind of emotion, but they were connecting by exchanging information between "the six of us," most likely referring to the player as the sixth person, completing the cast of two Pods and three androids. In case the player dies in this battle, the game asks if he accepts defeat, and the screen goes black until a quote appears.

The quote stems from other players who have completed ending E and left a message for future players. If the player dies again, the game tells him "Whatever, this is all pointless," with even more quotes and support from other players being shared. After the third death, the game asks the player if they think games are just silly things, after the fourth time "Do you admit, there is no meaning to this world?," with the screen being flooded with player quotes. After the fifth death, if the player is still insisting on not quitting, they get a help offer from other players. Upon accepting the offer, the ship of the player is backed up by other gamers who provide more damage and firepower and help the player to defeat the credits.

After the final cutscene where the Pods are trying to revive the protagonists, the Pods directly speak to the gamer, addressing him as "the player." Pod 153 asks if the player wishes to leave a message for other players who were stuck in ending three and "who are suffering because they cannot finish NieR: Automata." If the player opts for yes, a menu offers different statements to be displayed to other players who are struggling, including their account name and country. Thus, it is revealed that the messages that were displayed to the player stem from other gamers. A dialogue is initiated when picking an encouraging message? And Pod 042 addresses the player:

> Please respond to this quarry. You have faced crushing hardship and suffered greatly because of it. Do you have interest in helping the weak? Selecting this option enables you to save someone somewhere in the world. However, in exchange, you will lose all of your save data. Do you still wish to rescue someone–a total stranger–in spite of this? The person you save will be selected at random. As a result, this person who cries out for help even as we speak may be someone you intensely dislike. Do you still wish to help? Pod 042: You worked so hard to unlock Debug Mode and Chapter Select but they will no longer be available to you. Do you…still wish to help? You may not receive thanks for your efforts. Some say that your efforts are purely for show. Do you still wish to help? Are you truly–TRULY–sure about this? Very

> well. In exchange for your data, I will convey your will to this world.

Then the game takes the player to the menu where they can observe that all their saved weapons and items are deleted one by one. The Pods deliver one last message:

> And so, we must say goodbye. I feel a slight amount…of sadness. To all of you who spent time with this game…Thank you for playing.

Ending E demonstrates a perfect usage of video game tools, gameplay, and narrative story line that powerfully underlines what the medium is capable of. The team of Platinum Games and Yoko Taro managed to truly invest the player and succeeded in making them care about the different choices they had to make.

Metal Gear

This final section is dedicated to the implementation of different moral dilemmas in the Metal Gear series that had previously been mentioned briefly. Developer Hideo Kojima is known for Metal Gear Solid, a highly popular contemporary Japanese video game. He is also known for his love of American cinema. Kojima started his career working for Konami, developing titles like Snatcher (1992), and Policenauts (1994).

The reason why the "Metal Gear" core design is so different to its contemporaries according to Kojima, is that it was made to be a "fighting game about war,"[18] made for the Microsoft's graphically limited MSX2 system. By encouraging stealth mechanics and non-violent gameplay, Kojima was able to produce a special combination of gameplay and narrative that set the stage for a bigger and much larger concept. According to Kojima, the most notable example for this is his original vision for "Metal Gear," where players could explore the entire

---

[18] Denis Brusseaux, Nicolas Courcier, and Mehdi El-Kanafi, *Metal Gear Solid: Hideo Kojima's Magnum Opus* (Toulouse: Third Editions, 2019), 23.

map, identify possible objectives, decide where to go, and then approach the mission from various points of entry, a vision he finally accomplished with games like "Peace Walker" and "The Phantom Pain."[19]

Professionals who worked closely with Kojima, such as David Hayter, the voice actor of Snake, described him as a visionary and as an exception in the industry, as rarely does he follow the rules of what video games should be:[20]

> When he takes a game and turns it into a so-called cinematic experience, he doesn't turn it into what he thinks a movie should be either; I think he creates a perfect kind of hybrid.

The main plot of "Metal Gear" revolves around the orders the game's hero Solid Snake is given by his commander Big Boss. The aim is to get into Outer Heaven, a giant fortress-nation near South Africa, where nuclear weapons have supposedly been developed. The goal is to sneak past numerous enemies the player encounters in his mission, with a plot twist in the end, revealing that Big Boss has been leading a rebellion all along, using a massive nuclear equipped bipedal tank called a Metal Gear to threaten the world. Snake seemingly defeats Big Boss and escapes Outer Heaven before the fortress explodes.

"Metal Gear 2: Solid Snake" (1990), the sequel to "Metal Gear," has a retired Snake being forced to help a scientist responsible for creating an infinite energy source for Big Boss and his new military nation called Zanzibarland. Interestingly, this was the first time that gameplay mechanics such as crawling, or using the environment to hide were added.

---

[19] DidYouKnowGaming?, "Hideo Kojima: From Metal Gear to Death Stranding - Did You Know Gaming? Feat. Furst," *YouTube,* accessed April 9, 2023, https://www.youtube.com/watch?v=LDqvzhPOSqA.

[20] DidYouKnowGaming?, "Hideo Kojima."

"Metal Gear Solid" (1998), the first 3D entry, follows Solid Snake as he infiltrates an Alaskan nuclear disposal site named Shadow Moses, where Liquid Snake, his former comrade, is the chief of an enormous uprising against the US government. "Metal Gear Solid 2: Sons of Liberty" (2001) introduces new protagonist Raiden, a novice FOXHOUND member.

"Metal Gear Solid 3: Snake Eater" (2004) gives players the chance to experience the series narrative by telling the original story of Big Boss on his first mission in the jungles of Russia in the 1960s. "Metal Gear Solid 4: Guns of the Patriots" (2008) implies the death of Snake at the end of the game but shows him metaphorically and literally defeating the bad guy character Revolver Ocelot. In "Metal Gear Solid: Peace Walker" (2010), Big Boss stops a nuclear equipped Metal Gear at the coast of Costa Rica and starts to build his private army.

"Metal Gear Solid 5" is split into two parts, "Ground Zeroes" (2014), where Big Boss fails the rescue mission at a CIA black site in Cuba and faces the destruction of his private army, and "The Phantom Pain" (2015), which focuses on Venom Snake's mission to act out his revenge as Big Boss's doppelganger.

"Metal Gear Solid 3: Snake Eater" is a PlayStation 2 stealth action game set in Cold War Russia. The game follows Naked Snake, a former Green Beret who currently works for the CIA, sent on his first infiltration mission to extract Dr. Nikolai Sokolov, a soviet scientist in possession of critical information concerning a top-secret program. After a short briefing about "virtuous missions" parameters, the player takes control of Snake and guides him throughout his mission, engaging with soviet soldiers along the way. Actually, the player has choices related to the manner the enemy is dealt with. This selection process constitutes a small moral dilemma, as there is always the option to avoid the enemy or use non-lethal tactics such as tranquilizers, throws or choke holds.

However, this option is easily overlooked, due to the number of enemies crossing the player's way. Scrupulous gamers can choose to capture and interrogate enemies to extract useful information such as patrol routes and radio frequencies that can be used to trigger alerts. All the necessary tools are explained on the radio call with the commander (Major Zero) during the route to find Sokolov, and these tools are essential in understanding Kojima's philosophy of stealth and nonviolence. As David Hayter said:[21]

> Theoretically, I believe, you can get through the whole game without killing anybody except for the bosses, the six main people who you're gunning to get, so I thought that was interesting from a gameplay perspective. But I also thought it was interesting from…a morality perspective.

After meeting Sokolov at the rendezvous point, the scientist explains the broad strokes of the situation surrounding Colonel Volgin, the commander of Soviet intelligentsia (GRU) and how this war machine, the Shagohod, fits into the grand scheme. Snake leads Sokolov out of the area only to meet with his mentor, The Boss, who informs him about personal defect intentions to the Soviet Union before throwing Snake into a nearby river. The Boss and Volgin depart after blowing up the weapons facility with a nuclear tipped recoilless rocket to make it appear as though the US has attacked the USSR. Snake finds himself on an embankment down the river and is extracted by a protype of the Fulton recovery system. This point marks the commencement of the main narrative: "Operation: Snake Eater."

After recovering from his injuries, in a bid to preserve international relations, Snake is instructed to return to Russia and kill The Boss, or otherwise be labeled a traitor. From this stage, a reinstated Snake meets Eva, one of two undercover Soviet operatives. Eva instructs Snake to go to Graniny Gorky, a nearby lab where she thinks Sokolov is being held captive. Concerning the infiltration of the facility, players have the following three options: firstly, in the bloodiest way possible, by choosing to kill everybody in the facility; and secondly, by sneaking

---

[21] DidYouKnowGaming?, "Hideo Kojima."

past different security systems without being detected. The third option is to enter the facility disguised as one of the lab scientists, which by far seems like the safest preference.

This choice provides an opportunity for the player to reflect on their actions and to also consider their approach in handling this mission. For example, embarking on a murder spree may not be the best option, since it is very costly in terms of equipment and health, and more importantly, the situation raises the question of whether violence is morally justifiable when other non-violent methods exist.

Indeed, there are arguments that refer to this aspect of morality in video games. To demonstrate, Schulzke[22] states that since video game characters lack essential human qualities such as consciousness or the ability to feel pain and internal biological similarities, their relationship to the gamer is ultimately superficial. Because everything is happening in the virtual world, where attacking avatars do not cause any real harm, the player should feel indifferent to the suffering taking place in the virtual world.

However, rather than finding Sokolo at Graniny Gorki, Snake meets Aleksandr Granin, who decides to aid Snake by sharing the location of the Shagohod. Continuing his mission, Snake heads to the mountain camp where he encounters two members of the Cobra Unit: The Fear and The End. In particular, The End presents one of the most interesting moral dilemmas for players.

There are several ways to kill this venerable sniper such as the option to face him head-on while making use of different environmental clues and tools to determine his location like the reflection from his scope. Of course, those players who prefer a more non-violent tactic or are possibly seeking a more challenging experience may opt to track the sniper's footprints to first sneak up on and then subdue him. However,

---

22 Marcus Schulzke, "Defending the morality of violent video games," *Ethics and Information Technology* 12 (2010): 127–138.

there exists two other methods that may be considered more morally ambiguous.

The first consists of simply not playing the game, if the player avoids the game for two weeks (or sets the game system clock ahead two weeks) The End will die of old age. The third method is to kill The End on the docks on the way to Graniny Gorky, where he can be seen sitting in a wheelchair in a cutscene featuring Volgin, preventing the sniper duel from ever happening.

This fight is commonly claimed as one of the best Boss fights to ever occur in the series (if not in gaming history). The moral implication of letting the legendary sniper die of old age is clear here, and in contrast, there are those players who are willing to shoot and old man sleeping in a wheelchair. Nevertheless, the battle with the End provides an opportunity to the player to reflect about their actions and their implications.

After defeating both Cobra Unit agents, Snake arrives at the summit of the mountain, where he meets Eva for more information about Shagohod. After going down the mountain and defeating the last member of the Cobra Unit, the furious Snake sneaks up to Groznyi Grad where he finds Sokolov. However, he is promptly captured by Volgin, tortured for information about his mission, and thrown in the Groznyi Grad Brig.

Alas, Snake escapes trough the sewer system while being chased by Ocelot Revolver and his guards. He escapes into a below waterway and finds himself unconscious and in a half-dead state. Snake encounters the spirit of The Sorrow, a psychic, and the final member of the Cobra Unit.

This scene is also providing an interesting view on the moral dilemmas that the player must go through, demonstrating that the battle with the Cobra Unit is different from all the others. Acting as a "dodge the incoming object" style of play, Snake must avoid the spirits of the men he killed up to this point. Here, the game rewards players who have been pacifist in their playthrough, while the more lethal they acted, the harder this part becomes.

Once The Sorrow notices that Snake is not dead, he compels him to return to the real world. Soon after, Snake meets with Eva, and they discuss a plan to destroy Shagohod. Snake infiltrates Groznyi Grad and carries out the plan, but he is again confronted by Volgin, who captures Eva while she was searching for the 'philosophers' legacy.' Snake is then challenged to hand-to-hand combat.

Snake defeats Volgin and escapes with Eva on her motorcycle. The Boss is waiting for them by the lake to explain the intricacies of his whole idea of creating a united world without the need for conflict, the suffering and pain of his experiences, but more importantly the ramifications of battles to come, and in his own words:

> I raised you. I loved you. I've given you weapons taught you techniques, endowed you with knowledge. There is nothing for me to give to you. All that's left is for you to take me by your own hand. One must die and one must live…it is our destiny…the one who survives will inherit the title of "Boss," and the one who inherits the title of 'Boss' will face an existence of endless battle.

Although the battle is difficult and there are tricks to gain advantages in the fight, the moral complication comes after Snake has won the battle. Once the player defeats The Boss, a final blow needs to be delivered as he lies dying on the ground. While the game does not leave the player with the option to spare The Boss, it does allow them, however, to take their time and does not force the player to pull the trigger.

This allows the player to sit down and reflect on the events of the game. The scene has been listed as one of the most compelling moments of the series, generally noted for its incredible significance of learning that The Boss is not a traitor. The act of killing The Boss, while sad, tragic, and painful, is necessary, as it acts as a device to convey the underlying themes and philosophy of the game.

MGS 5: Phantom Pain

Similarly, to other games, in MGS 5, players can choose to lethally or non-lethally eliminate enemies. However, the major point of this specific game is the DPS, the demon point system.

> In MGS5 there are different implications to your actions, for example, enemies and injured personnel can be extracted to mother base and players can recruit them from Diamond Dogs (the player's personal army). Although surviving the process is not guaranteed, killing enemies counts towards a players 'heroism' score (the likelihood that enemies will be recruited), and the demon point score, which is a hidden morality system that was implemented in MGS 5 in order to judge the player for their actions.

This hidden system is one of the most unique tools that casts a shadow of morality and ethics on the actions of the player. For example, if the gamer kills an animal they collect twenty DP, if they critically wound an enemy sixty DP, and it keeps building up, depending on how serious the offense is. This forces players to ethically reflect on their actions.

Furthermore, players who accumulate a certain threshold of points see changes in Venom Snake's appearance. When reaching 50,000 DPs, Venom gets drenched in blood that cannot be washed away and can be seen as Venom's complete submission to the Big Boss persona. This effect can of course be mitigated through morally righteous actions, such as disposing of nuclear weapons, and extracting animals from combat zones etc.

The following are research results which examined the different decisions players made:

In the martial group, only seventeen out of thirty-one individuals stated they were aware of the DPS, with fifty-three percent demonstrating changes in their behavior. On the other hand, twenty-one out of thirty-one non-martial individuals admitted being aware of the DPS, leading to forty-eight percent of them changing their behavior.

As for the boss fight with The End, both groups turned out quite similar. In fact, most players used non-lethal ways to defeat The End. Although a popular method was to execute him on Graninyi Gorki dock, the rest of the players were mostly divided between a traditional sniper showdown and employing lethal means to kill at a closer range or letting him die of old age.

Regarding The Boss, the players are not offered many options, either they do it or they don't (and making the scene indefinite in consequence). But that does not mean that the participants failed to provide interesting responses. To start with, forty-three percent of the martial group and thirty-nine percent of the non-martial group provided similar statements about expressing negative emotions after pulling the trigger. Some martial individuals expressed how the moral dilemma made them feel uncomfortable or sad, while others described it as an 'ethical crime,' interpreting it as a necessity or a soldier's duty.

One participant even reported waiting for thirty minutes before pulling the trigger. Another participant of this experiment perfectly described the implicated moral dilemma as follows: "Morally it was wrong to kill [your] own master; but in the sense of duty, it was the thing to do." One might argue that, given their experiences in real life, the martial players did not bother waiting to see if they could avoid executing The Boss because they ultimately knew that allowing her to survive was simply not an option available to them.

Conclusion

After exploring these different video games, the reader should be better acquainted with how games essentially can act as cultural artifacts.

They bear a strong potential of shaping players' perspectives and acting as powerful critics to social ills and challenges. The characteristic format of the medium enables them to add substantial weight to the different sacrifices the player is asked to act out on the screen. As such, video games can be estimated to have proved itself as a strong and influential contemporary learning tool, and as a format of expression that needs to be considered as greater than its initial value of entertainment and providing fun for the sake of it. Of course, there has been much criticism concerning video games for a very long time with some theorists arguing that the video games' violence can cause players to actually mimic these types of behaviors. However, some findings do indeed demonstrate that the player is placed in a moral dilemma linked to carrying out a particular action (for instance, the execution of your own master) in the game space even though these virtual actions have no real-world consequences. As a result, it can be argued that game narratives can provide instances of moral discomfort. This can act as fuel for the free will debate. Yet, the players are compelled to make a moral decision outside their conventional comfort, thus realizing that their in-game free will is, in truth, limited. Furthermore, being responsible for the murder of a virtual character the player has become familiar with after playing for multiple hours -even though the act of killing is for the greater good in the game space- is something distinctive to video games. Since as a popular form of media, it is accepted that video game players have interactive command at their fingertips (even though the game narratives are predetermined) in comparison with book readers and film audiences, game developers have taken advantage of this unique medium and will no doubt continue to do so by expanding game narratives that explore other avenues inclusive of the cultural and the social. Perhaps, video game developers confront the same type of moral dilemmas that artists in other types of media also confront when deciding what exactly to include in their works under the ethical decisions umbrella. In this framework, the relationship takes a more delicate turn as a balance must be sought; a balance that satisfactorily enjoins customer preferences, marketability, artistic expression as well as keeping an eye on the possible impact the game itself may have on the players. Since, as form of media and expression, video games are classified as a more recent media, the power to affect those who play them are still viewed as an area open to ethical debate.

Bibliography

Bogost, Ian. 2009. "The Rhetoric of Video Games." In *The ecology of video games: connecting youth, games, and learning*, edited by Katie Salen, 117–140 (Cambridge: MIT Press, 2008).

Bolea, Stefan. "The persona and the shadow in analytic psychology and existentialist philosophy." *Philobiblon* 21, No. 1 (2016): 84–94.

Brusseaux, Denis, Courcier, Nicolas, and El-Kanafi, Mehdi. 2019. *Metal Gear Solid: Hideo Kojima's Magnum Opus.* Toulouse: Third Editions.

Detmer, David. 2008. *Sartre Explained. From Bad Faith to Authenticity.* Chicago: Open Court.

Did You Know Gaming?. "Hideo Kojima: From Metal Gear to Death Stranding - Did You Know Gaming? Feat.

Furst." *YouTube*. Accessed April 9, 2023, https://www.youtube.com/watch?v=LDqvzhPOSqA.

Gowans, Christopher W. ed. 1987. *Moral Dilemmas*. New York: Oxford University Press.

Gregory, Derek, and Walford, Rex. 1989. *Horizons in Human Geography.* London: Barnes and Noble.

Kuznetsova, Evgeniya Kuznetsova. "Trauma in Games: Narrativizing Denied Agency, Ludonarrative Dissonance and Empathy Play." Master Thesis, University of Alberta, 2017, doi:10.7939/R30Z7196H.

Miller, Alan. 2018. Order by Accident: The Origins and Consequences of Group Conformity in Contemporary Japan. New York: Routledge.

Pohl, Kirsten. "Ethical reflection and emotional involvement in computer games." In Conference proceedings of The Philosophy of Computer Games 2008, edited by Stephan Günzel, Michael Liebe, Dieter Mersch, 92–107 (Potsdam: Universitätsverlag Potsdam, 2008).

Rauch, Peter Edward. "Playing with good and evil: Videogames and moral philosophy." Dissertation, Massachusetts Institute of Technology, 2007.

Reynolds, Ren, "Playing a "Good" Game: A Philosophical Approach to Understanding the Morality ofGames," International Game Developers Association, 2002, 1–12.

Ruti, Mari. 2012. *The Singularity of Being: Lacan and the Immortal Within.* New York: Fordham University Press.

Schulzke, Markus. "Defending the morality of violent video games." *Ethics and Information Technology* 12 (2010): 127–138.

Seraphine, Frederic. "The Rhetoric of Undertale. Ludonarrative Dissonance and Symbolism." *Proceedings of the 8th Conference of the Digital Games Research Association Japan 2018.*

Chapter Nine
Pseudo-Individualization? An analysis of the incorporation of subcultures into commodified aesthetics on Tik Tok

Martin A. M. Gansinger, Kinda Al-Aridi

Introduction

In a tale as old as time, the yearning for a cogent identity and communal belonging has dictated human behavior in society. However, despite said yearning, society continues to fail at being entirely inclusive. Through enforcing a 'one size fits all' methodology, certain societal norms and standards are set to maintain the current paradigm. Inevitably, such selective criteria were met with deviance in conformity that, in turn, marked the rise of subcultures.

Haenfler describes the phenomenon as "smaller pieces" of a larger culture or society, differing in some way from "mainstream culture."[1] These neo tribes essentially create an alternate mass identity as a result of varying factors. Whether it be a product of marginalization, resistance, or shared ideation, these "scenes" have managed to rise in popularity over the past decades.

In the wake of digitalization, these cultural movements have transformed into what is now known as aesthetics or 'cores'[2]. The latter range from "cottagecore" and "alt" to "kidcore" and "egirl" amongst countless others. While the subculture's style would be gate-kept

---

[1] Ross Haenfler, *Subcultures: The Basics* (New York: Routledge, 2014).

[2] Danai Dana, "How Subcultures Became "Aesthetics:" Menswear Has No Limits And It's All Gen Z's Fault," *mrporter.com,* July 26, 2022, https://www.mrporter.com/en-hk/journal/fashion/subculture-aesthetics-style-tiktok-gen-z-internet-trends-17519550.

within the community originally, social networking platforms such as TikTok have facilitated broader access to the ideas and signatures of these cultural groups.[2]

In a 2021 British Vogue article, English journalist Yomi Adegoke compares the latter to The Buggles' hit song 'Video Killed the Radio Star:' "If video killed the radio star, then it was the internet that killed subcultures."[2]

Similarly, Dana[2] brings forth trend turnover and aesthetic fluidity as relevant factors to take into consideration upon assessing the grand scheme of subculture's manifestation into commodified aesthetics. In employing inherent romanticism and saturated associations, this contemporary aesthetics have prompted users to link commodified tangibles with abstract cultures, in turn resulting in foundational patterns that re-occur across the curation of TikTok's aesthetic content.

Through conducting a content analysis of five TikTok aesthetics in particular, this study aims to examine the incorporation of such respective subcultures into their corresponding contemporary aesthetics. Furthermore, this chapter will assess the repercussions entailed by said incorporation while paying respect to TikTok's aesthetic vitality, trend cycle, and trend fluidity.

Purpose of the study

The purpose of this study is to understand the process through which cultural groups and their distinguishing characteristics have been translated into digitized aesthetics on the social media platform TikTok over the course of early October 2021 to late November 2022. Particularly, this chapter further investigates the re-occurring patterns that persist throughout the respective process and offers insight into the transformation of these neo tribes accordingly.

Research questions

Main Research Question

1. What are the incorporation patterns implemented on TikTok to facilitate the translation of subcultures into commodified aesthetics?

Sub Questions

1. Has this incorporation caused a diffusion in the essence of subcultures?
2. Has this incorporation provided subcultures with a temporary lifeline?
3. Has this incorporation made subcultures subject to displacement with their corresponding aesthetics' expiry?
4. Has this incorporation been tainted by cross pop cultural references?

Significance of the study

This study is meant to shed light on the power of social media in influencing identity and posing as a vessel for cultural phenomena respectively. It also aims to assess the means through which such effects are achieved.

Although the concept of commodification with respect to this matter is well researched, this study proposes an interesting angle in reference to the platform in which its focus research resides.

TikTok is a bustling social media platform that is worthy of examination as it engages a vast majority of the youth. With interesting advancements taking place on the interactive network day by day, it provides multifaceted output on the everchanging media ecology. Ultimately, this study's significance lies in the patterns associated with the incorporation process of subcultures into commodified aesthetics accordingly.

Limitations

It remains important to acknowledge, however, that this research was subject to a few limitations along its course respectively. First and foremost, these findings were facilitated through a purposive sampling technique; while the latter is not favorable, it sustains its relevance to this research as it (a) eliminated any parody videos on the "coquette" aesthetic in particular, and (b) curated a relevant selection of videos to better serve the purpose of this paper. Furthermore, another factor worth noting is the quantity of "indie" (2020-2021) and "indie sleaze" aesthetic videos analyzed, equating to a total of thirty videos all together. Since the revival of the "indie sleaze" aesthetic is relatively recent, the selection of videos discussing its re-emergence are rather limited respectively, hence the number of videos analyzed during this research.

Theoretical framework

The theoretical framework referenced throughout the course of this study is Postmodernism. This theory can, in essence, be summarized as the absence of a center. Essentially, it is Hutcheon's[3] work that is of particular interest to this research as it orients aesthetics, decentering, and narrative in its very foundation[3]. Hutcheon's premise suggests that a post-structuralist stance created by decentering moves can essentially suffice as an opportunity for ideological and social expansion, ultimately forging an appreciation to difference in the current social paradigm[3].

Furthermore, the concept of intertextuality also resonates with this research's direction of interest as a postmodern world is bound to acknowledge and embrace the overlap of media text respectively[4]. In

---

[3] Linda Hutcheon, *A poetics of postmodernism, history, theory, fiction* (New York: Routledge, 2003).

[4] Allen, Graham, "Intertextuality," n. d., https://www.litencyc.com/php/stopics.php?rec=true&UID=1229.

similar regard, Baudrillard's[5] simulacrum proves to be fundamental to the course of this research in its postulation; the abstraction essentially argues that in the void of absence, a representation of reality will suffice in its place, resulting in a hyperreality accordingly.

Literature review

Haenfler[6] discusses the dilemma of posers plaguing subcultures. He contemplates the impact of commercialization and commodification on the overall subcultural experience. In his discourse, Haenfler brings forth "subcultural capital," hence, artifacts, habits, or mindsets, as a measure for authenticity in these neo tribes.

This chapter aims to utilize the latter in its assessment of inspired DIY aesthetics created by users of TikTok and offer insight as to whether they too are mere posers in the grand scheme of these subversive cultures, ultimately contributing to Adorno's[7] pseudo individualization, hence, the consumption of formulaic, commodified popular culture under the impression to act under individual agency.

According to Lee et al.,[8] it is the algorithms that facilitate the latter. In this article, the authors analyzed twenty-four interviews with TikTok users to foster an understanding of how the algorithmic process aids in the personalization of said users' feeds, therefore informing their knowledge of identity and respective orientation towards others.

Drawing on the metaphor of crystals and their properties, the algorithmic crystal framework is analytic in the sense that it not only reflects multifaceted and dynamic user self-concepts, but it also orients

[5] Baudrillard, Jean. 1988. *Selected Writings*. Stanford, California: Stanford University. 166–184.

[6] Haenfler, "*Subcultures.*"

[7] Theodor Adorno, *The Culture Industry: Selected Essays on Mass Culture* (London and New York: Routledge, 2001).

[8] Angela Y. Lee, Hannah Mieczkowski, Nicole B. Ellison, and Jeffrey T. Hancock. "The Algorithmic Crystal: Conceptualizing the Self through Algorithmic Personalization on TikTok." *Proceedings of the ACM on Human-Computer Interaction, Vol. 6, No. CSCW2, Article No.: 543, 1–22.*

users to recognize both refracted and diffracted parts of themselves in ephemeral connections respectively[9]. The latter can be of good use to this research as it provides insight on the significant impact behind TikTok's algorithm on its users accordingly.

In similar regard, Wei Song[10] also aims to explore the mechanics behind TikTok's operation, through targeting her core research to assimilate an understanding of the youth's consumption habits in "Psychological Characteristics of Contemporary Young People from Tiktok Videos." In this article, Song narrows down user psychology to five specific aspects: (1) Users advocate external beauty, (2) Users are eager to express themselves, (3) Users strive for recognition, (4) Users embrace curiosity, and (5) Users seek a sense of belonging[11].

Particularly, eagerness of self-expression, curiosity, and a sought-after sense of belonging are what ultimately resonate with the course of this research. Song's findings will provide this analysis with an improved comprehensive foundation to base its understanding of users on.

Meanwhile, Goulding, Saren, and Canniford[12] orient their research on what they refer to as fragmented and multilayered postmodern subcultures. The authors describe a transitionary stance in which commodification and diffusion into mainstream consumer society takes its course. They specifically analyze the case of the goth subculture in their study to assess the process of this phenomenon accordingly. This work of research will suffice the analysis underway as it facilitates an understanding of the commodification process through which

---

[9] Lee et al., "The Algorithmic Crystal."

[10] Wei Song, "Psychological Characteristics of Contemporary Young People from Tiktok Videos," *Psychiatria Danubina* 33, No. 7 (2021): 76–78.

[11] Song, "Psychological Characteristics."

[12] Goulding, Christina, Saren, Mike and Canniford, Robin. "From Rebellion to Commodification: the Case of Goth." In *E - European Advances in Consumer Research Volume 7*, eds. Karin M. Ekstrom, and Helene Brembeck (Goteborg: Association for Consumer Research, 2005), 139–140.

subcultures may in turn transform into refashioned incarnations, or, in the case of this aesthetic study, romanticized aesthetics.

Dana[13] also explores the everchanging realm of said aesthetics, in respect to men's fashion. Dana brings forth standup comedian Pete Davidson's style as an ideal example to depict both the rotation and alternation between contemporary aesthetics inspired by subversive subcultures. The literature cited is of value to this research for it yields a discernment of how modern aesthetics differ from their successors, subversive subcultures, in an updated paradigm of renewed structure, or rather the lack of there is, and reestablished norms.

Common inferential ties between the makeup industry and subversive subcultures are overtly depicted in the work of Goldstein.[14] While the cosmetic industry goes hand in hand with both commodification and aestheticization without saying, it will be interesting to explore the utilization of said subcultures, now deemed aesthetics, to these commodified products; a specification frequented in all the analysis frames listed below drew inspiration from Goldstein's literary piece.

KhosraviShakib's[15] contribution proves to be of substance to this research as it poses reflective grounds on which a keener understanding of the postmodernist transformative conditions can be assessed furtherly.

Mishrell takes an alternate route to KhosraviShakib, as he assesses the aesthetics of Florida Death Metal and Norwegian Black Metal, claiming that the respective subculture is, in essence, threatening the social order as it challenges preexisting ideologies respectively[16]. Patterns (a) and (f) relate this history thesis to Haenfler, who investigates subcultural

---

[13] Dana, "How Subcultures Became 'Aesthetics.'"

[14] Judith Goldstein, "The Female Aesthetic Community," *Poetics Today* 14, No. 1. (1993): 143–145.

[15] Mohammad KhosraviShakib, "Marxist Feminism and Postmodernism," *Journal of Language and Culture* 1, No. 3 (2010): 28–30.

[16] Kirk Mishrell, *Rockin' The Tritone: Gender, Race & The Aesthetics of Aggressive Heavy Metal Subcultures* (Master Thesis, Georgia State University, 2012).

globalization, emplacement, and whether subcultures have ultimately gone virtual in the wake of prominent digitization.

Another phenomenon that has come about in the wake of said digitization is the personalized algorithm curating users' content selection and tailoring their consumption accordingly. In their study of the interplay between identity and algorithmic processes on TikTok, Karizat, Delmonaco, Eslami, and Andalibi conduct fifteen semi-structured interviews with TikTok users.[17]

It remains important to note that this study differs from Lee et al.[18] in the sense that it analyzes the algorithmic folk theories of the For You Page algorithm, using two inter-connected identity types for users, namely person and social identity. The authors contend against the selective means of TikTok's algorithm as it tends to be quite discriminative, oppressive, and exclusive to those that may inherently benefit from its specifications accordingly. This research aims to assess the latter considering the incorporation of subversive subcultures on TikTok respectively. In turn, inspiring patterns elaborated on in the discussion sector of this paper. Felski[19] shares mutual interest in the effects of modernity as Karizat et al., but in a rather alternate sense, as she proposes a multifaceted collection of essays which set forth nuanced perceptions of modernity.

Bloch and Ritter's[20] concept of synchronous non-synchronicity is of particular interest to this research. The primary argument in this context claims that not every individual experiences the same now, but rather proposes a mere figment of an external front can present accordingly,

---

17 Karizat, Nadia, Delmonaco, Daniel, Eslami, Motahhare, and Andalibi, Nazanin. "Algorithmic Folk Theories and Identity: How TikTok Users Co-Produce Knowledge of Identity and Engage in Algorithmic Resistance." *Proceedings of the ACM on human-computer interaction* 5, CSCW2 (2021), 1–44.

18 Lee et al., "The Algorithmic Crystal."

19 Rita Felski, *Doing Time: Feminist Theory and Postmodern Culture* (New York: NYU Press, 2000).

20 Ernst Bloch, and Mark Ritter, "Nonsynchronism and the obligation to its dialectics," *New German Critique* 11 (1977): 22–38.

therefore sufficing as the lone mutual factor. Through relating this line of theory to the incorporation of subcultures, this research aims to assess Bloch and Ritter's ideas as validating criteria to the origins of subcultures and their inevitable influence on current deviant behaviors in modern culture.

Watts[21] assesses globalism's stance between the macro and micro of culture with respect to the re-evaluation of postmodern geographics, global capitalism, and its locally mediated generation. Evidently, this literary work can aid this research in fostering an awareness of the local-global nexus made ubiquitous in the wake of digitization and commodification accordingly.

Jacobson[22] analyzes the internet subculture 'Vaporwave' through musician Daniel Lopatin's experimental electronic audiovisual "Memory Vague," which essentially repurposes "dead" or "archival" media by looping and redistributing visual artifacts.

Schielea and Venkatesh[23] take this a step further as they examine the process of subcultural commodification through employing a multi-method ethnographic approach to assess the particular process by which *Harajuku,* a Japanese consumer subculture, undergoes production, fragmentation, and incorporation respectively. Their work also explores how non-western subcultures cope with the repercussions of mainstream commodification and how they, ultimately, manage to reclaim their sense of identity, authenticity, and belonging accordingly.

---

[21] Michael J. Watts, "Mapping meaning, denoting difference, imagining identity: dialectical images and postmodern geographies," *Geografiska Annaler: Series B, Human Geography* 73, No.1 (1991): 7–16.

[22] Jordan J. Jacobson, "Fast Forwarding the Past (on Pause): Daniel Lopatin's *Memory Vague* and the Hauntological Aesthetic of Vaporwave," *The Velvet Light Trap* 90 (2022): 28–37.

[23] Kristen Schiele, and Alladi Venkatesh, "Regaining Control through Reclamation: How Consumption Subcultures Preserve Meaning and Group Identity After Commodification," *Consumption Markets & Culture* 19, No. 5: 427–443.

Dagalp and Hartmann[24] follow a similar route in their course of research as they argue two primary points. The authors seek to re-orient discourse from the aesthetic (the abstract product) through the process by which said aesthetic is rendered and, in turn, becomes part of a grander scheme of the deliberate consumer-cultural paradigm. In elaboration on this premise, by introducing three types of processes that demonstrate the influence of aestheticization on consumption, brands, and market mechanisms, the discourse in this article ultimately supports the primary research question of interest here, as it provides well researched insight on what processes these movements undergo to reach a state of aesthetic respectively. Furthermore, it appeals to a selection of the established patterns discussed further in the upcoming sectors of this discourse.

Methodology

This quantitative content analysis sampled a video selection of primary data collected through the social media platform TikTok and the following section further details the sampling methods and the data collection means employed throughout the course of this study. Furthermore, the particular frames and specifications directing the course of this study will also be elaborated on as follows.

Sampling methods and data collection

This research utilized a purposive sampling technique to curate a selection of relevant and appurtenant videos, each falling under the five following aesthetics: (a) The "Femme Fatale" Aesthetic, (b) The "Coquette" Aesthetic, (c) The "Hippie" Aesthetic, (d) The "Indie" Aesthetic (2020-2021), and (e) The "Indie Sleaze" Aesthetic. While the "Femme Fatale" embraces the persona of the mysterious seductress, the "Coquette" employs the elements of dainty femininity to create or mimic a sense of the cat and mouse; thereby the "coquette" is the

---

[24] Ileyha Dagalp, and Benjamin J. Hartmann, "From "Aesthetic" to Aestheticization: A Multi-layered Cultural Approach," *Consumption Markets & Culture* 25, No. 1 (2022): 1–20.

ultimate tease. The "Hippie," however, imbues the commercial sense of these saturated digital cultures with a sense of grounded-ness; the "hippie" is a natural, she is stripped back, and she is effortlessly cool.

Conversely, the "Indie" embraces an excessively saturated palette, decorative embellishments, and an almost chaotic sense of style; it remains important to acknowledge that modern day "Indie" is often misconstrued to be a repackaged incarnation of its near doppelgänger "kidcore"; despite their overlapping elements, the "indie" aesthetic often deviates toward influences of skater culture and alternate motifs respectively[25]. However, the "Indie Sleaze" dates to the original 2012-2014 Tumblr era; it employs soft grunge elements, neutrals, and partycore in its foundational elements; the "indie sleaze" is often described as the cool, nonchalant older sister of the listed aesthetics for its rejection of perfection respectively.

Category of TikTok	**Number of videos analyzed**
The "Femme Fatale" Aesthetic	40
The "Coquette" Aesthetic	40
The "Hippie" Aesthetic	40
The "Indie" Aesthetic (2020-2021)	15
The "Indie Sleaze" Aesthetic	15
Total:	150

Table 9-1: *Sampling methods*

[25] Malavika Pradeep, "What is kidcore? Here's everything you need to know about the latest internet aesthetic," *screenshot-media.com,* February 24, 2021, https://screenshot-media.com/culture/internet-culture/what-is-kidcore/.

Frame labels	Attributes and specifications
TikTok context	- Link accessed - User account - Date released - Duration - TikTok Caption - Views - Likes - Comments - Shares
Music and Audio	- Is an Alternative/Indie song used? - Is the word "siren" used? - Are the words "Femme Fatale" used? - Are the words "Dark Feminine" used? - Is the audio used a pop culture reference from film?
Legitimation	- Does the video fall under the lines of a certain community? - Does the video embrace a deviance from the mainstream? - Does the video aid in normalizing certain behaviors to a group or audience?
Commodification	- Was red lipstick featured in videos? - Were pearls/shells featured in videos? - Were candles featured in videos? - Were music records featured in videos? - Were makeup products featured in videos?
Aestheticization	- Does the video appeal to a certain niche? - Does the video make clear use of semiotics? - Does the video depict a lifestyle? - Does the video group certain commercial elements?

Table 9-2: *Theoretical framework–The "Femme Fatale" Aesthetic*

Frame labels	Attributes and specifications
TikTok Context	- Link accessed - User account - Date released - Duration - TikTok Caption - Views - Likes - Comments - Shares
Music and Audio	- Is an Indie Pop or Alternative Pop song used? - Are the words "coquette aesthetic" used? -Is the word "coquette" used? - Is the word "dollete" used? - Is the audio used a pop culture reference from film?
Legitimation	- Does the video fall under the lines of a certain community? - Does the video embrace a deviance from the mainstream? - Does the video aid in normalizing certain behaviors to a group or audience?
Commodification	- Were Chanel or Dior products featured in videos? - Were Betty Janes/loafers featured in videos? - Were lace, satin, or tulle articles of clothing featured in videos? - Were bows featured in videos? - Were knee-high socks or frilly socks featured in videos? - Were makeup products featured in videos?
Aestheticization	- Does the video appeal to a certain niche? - Does the video make clear use of semiotics? - Does the video depict a lifestyle? - Does the video group certain commercial elements?

Table 9-3: *Theoretical framework–The "Coquette" Aesthetic*

Frame Labels	Attributes and Specifications
TikTok Context	- Link accessed - User account - Date released - Duration - TikTok Caption - Views - Likes - Comments - Shares
Music and Audio	- Is any Rock subgenre song used? - Is the word "hippie" used? - Is the word "hippietok" used? - Are the words "hippie aesthetic" used? - Is the audio used a pop culture reference from film?
Legitimation	- Does the video fall under the lines of a certain community? - Does the video embrace a deviance from the mainstream? - Does the video aid in normalizing certain behaviors to a group or audience?
Commodification	- Were midiskirts or harem pants featured in videos? - Were crystal necklaces featured in videos? - Were hair accessories or embellishments featured in videos? - Were boho bags featured in videos? - Were peace signs featured in videos?
Aestheticization	- Does the video appeal to a certain niche? - Does the video make clear use of semiotics? - Does the video depict a lifestyle? - Does the video group certain commercial elements?

Table 9-4: *Theoretical framework–The "Hippie" Aesthetic*

Frame Labels	Attributes and Specifications
TikTok Context	- Link accessed - User account - Date released - Duration - TikTok Caption - Views - Likes - Comments - Shares
Music and Audio	- Is a parodical sound used? - Is the word "phase" used? - Are the words "worst" or "cringe" used? - Is the song "Roast Yourself" by Gabbie Hanna used? - Is the audio used a pop culture reference from film?
Delegitimization	- Does the video associate the Indie aesthetic with a particular time period? - Does the video use degrading language when describing the Indie aesthetic? - Does the video entail that the Indie aesthetic is outdated?
Humor Paradigm	- Was satire featured in videos? - Was exaggeration featured in videos? - Was parody featured in videos? - Was humor featured in videos through audio text? - Was humor featured in videos through written text?
Aestheticization	- Does the video appeal to a certain niche? - Does the video make clear use of semiotics? - Does the video depict a lifestyle? - Does the video group certain commercial elements?

Table 9-5: *Theoretical framework–The "Indie" Aesthetic (2020-2021)*

Frame Labels	Attributes and Specifications
TikTok Context	- Link accessed - User account - Date released - Duration - TikTok Caption - Views - Likes - Comments - Shares
Music and Audio	- Is an Indie Rock song used? - Is the song "Girlfriend" by Hemlocke Springs used? - Is the word "reappear" used? - Are words insinuating the comeback of the indie sleaze aesthetic used? - Is the word "Tumblr" used? - Is the audio used a pop culture reference from film?
Legitimation	- Does the video fall under the lines of a certain community? - Does the video use a researched analysis in its discourse? - Does the video reference articles in its discourse?
Commodification	- Were chunky black boots featured in videos? - Were silver accessories or chokers featured in videos? - Were distressed tights featured in videos? - Were leather/fur articles of clothing featured in videos? - Were messy makeup looks featured in videos?
Aestheticization	- Does the video appeal to a certain niche? - Does the video make clear use of semiotics? - Does the video depict a lifestyle? - Does the video group certain commercial elements?

Table 9-6: *Theoretical framework–The "Indie Sleaze" Aesthetic*

Discussion

The purpose of this research is to foster an understanding of the reoccurring patterns associated with the incorporation process of saturated subcultures into commodified aesthetics in the following respect: (a) watering down values, deeper meanings, and origins, (b) curating a selective representation of what is palatable or marketable to the public, (c) targeting a younger audience, (d) essentially serving as an assessment of human value, (e) presenting as packaged lifestyles, and (f) correlating or cross-networking with different media products.

Alternatively, the route of sustainability in this respect is also explored through the following means: (g) the aesthetic was short lived and reminiscent of a fad, and (h) the content analyzed was factual/nonfactual. Throughout the course of this research, one is able to establish that such incorporated aesthetics have, as a matter of fact, undergone diffusion at the expense of their respective origins and grander meanings to fit the mold of what is marketable and palatable to the youthful public. Essentially, in referencing patterns (d) and (e), such saturated aesthetics have developed commodified criteria through which users may be evaluated and in turn validated in light of their commitment and dedication to what ultimately is presented as a packaged lifestyle.

Haenfler[26] elaborates on the concept by referring to subcultural capital, a measure for authenticity. However, with the ongoing dilemma of "fakes" plaguing these cultural movements, we are pushed to question whether the upcoming flood of TikTok 'subculturists' are merely posers in the grander scheme of identity, a theory ultimately contributing to Adorno's pseudo individualization, a fabricated sense of individualism in which mere formulaic popular culture is consumed instead.

While the subcultural movement was originally created to formulate an alternate mass identity, it has now become subject to the very paradigm

---

26 Haenfler, "*Subcultures.*"

it was negating to begin with. Taking this a step further, this discourse aims to explore the possibility of whether we are not only mere fabrications of character, but rather a figment of grey space in a time of divide between postmodernity and modernity; is it possible to establish a middle ground between both eras?

Considering Haenfler's notion of a radical DIY aesthetic, Goulding, Saren, and Canniford[27] orient their research on the remodeled versions of these incorporated subcultures into what is now addressed as romanticized aesthetics, particularly resonating with patterns (a) and (b) the most. It is important to acknowledge, however, that this refashioning process has also been propelled by Kristeva's[28] intertextuality theory.

The latter not only validates the origins of the incorporated-subcultures-turned-commodified-aesthetics targeted in this research, but also further affirms pattern (b).

Similarly, other products of said theory are the cross-cultural references frequently noted during these videos, shifting the aesthetics' focal inspiration from the core subculture they were respectively derived from to the hyper-saturated incestuous mess of intertext derived from contemporary pop culture. The latter is evident in Dana's[29] proposition that stylistic identities are ultimately becoming a product of the rotation and alternation between contemporary aesthetics, or rather, their abstract intertextuality. This contributes to patterns (b) and (c) as this overlapping selection of cultural elements do appeal to TikTok's youthful audience and their respective niches on the digital platform[8].

Furthermore, it also aids in presenting a palatable conglomeration infused with experimentation and play, ratifying patterns (b) and (e) in

[27] Golding, Saren, and Canniford, "From Rebellion to Commodification."

[28] Julia Kristeva, "'Nous deux' or a (hi)story of intertextuality," *Romanic Review* 93, No.1/2 (2002): 7–13.

[29] Dana, "How Subcultures Became 'Aesthetics.'"

its due course. Murphy and O'Riordan[30] coin the term "intrinsic engine of change" to describe this phenomenon[17]; essentially, it is meant to serve as a collective manifestation of what the scholarly pair deems as deviations in our contemporary media. As evidenced by the vaster majority of patterns listed previously, this holds a particular magnitude of validity as content is tailored at sustaining traction, interaction, and ultimate "weight" in the grander scheme of digital algorithms[7].

Elaborating on the latter, TikTok's content is often characterized as "hot" and "trendy." Therefore, it is not farfetched to infer that the digital platform may have played an inherent role in propelling this phenomenon. Considering this modern phenomenon snowballing into a means of production as opposed to mere deviations, Dagalp and Hartmann[31] theorized two primary concepts: (a) the process by which aesthetics - in essence, abstract products - are rendered, ultimately melds them into part of the grander scheme of the deliberate consumer-cultural paradigm.

This particular point of analysis not only reaffirms all the discussed patterns in this paper, but also draws on the everchanging media ecology with respect to viewer consumption habits and content curation. (b) The elucidation of how aestheticization permeates consumption, brand, and market processes through theoretical and empirical implications is also another theorized concept that resonates strongly with the directional sense of this discourse as it yet again conveys the inherent repercussions entailed by the incorporation patterns discussed throughout the course of this research.

This may also trace back to Haenfler's poser dilemma, Bloch's mismatched sense of time, and, eminently, most patterns produced by this research. It remains important to acknowledge, however, that patterns (g) and (h) mostly appeal to the "indie" (2020-2021) and "indie

---

[30] Jill Murphy, and Nicholas O'Riordan, "Deviate!," *Alphaville: Journal of Film and Screen Media*, 9 (2015): 1–5.

[31] Dagalp, and Hartmann, "From 'Aesthetic' to Aestheticization."

sleaze" aesthetics as they are not only validated through the provided specifications and frames, but they also prove to sustain cogency on the grounds of digital interaction; the latter encompasses views, comments, likes, shares, and saves.

Considering the sample under study, the findings provided by this research evidently aid in establishing a sense of direction (see appendices IV and V for more information). As per the "indie" (2020-2021) content analyzed, a pattern of short-lived enthusiasm regarding the aesthetics' stylistic elements and distinct signatures became eminent. Not only was some mockery and humor employed in these videos, but both their text and audio correlated with themes of belittlement and nostalgia, ultimately classifying the wave as an ephemeral craze as opposed to a sustainable movement that attains longevity.

Notwithstanding, it proves essential to note that, due to intertextuality, the "indie" aesthetic under discussion is far from the original, sufficing as mere repackaged "kidcore." an aesthetic notorious for its overly saturated and vibrant color scheme;[32] the latter is supported by pattern (a) in its foundation. Considering such an establishment, we are then prompted to question whether subcultures will too be sentenced to an inevitable expiry in the wake of the digitized age.

As per the "indie sleaze" content finings, such a theory has proven disputable. Seemingly, the aesthetic at hand has a significant count of refashioned incarnations such as "Tumblr Girl" and "Tumblrcore" as its successors with sixty percent of users referencing the prime 2014 platform in their videos; its essence has actually been the subject of a resurgence now rebranded as "indie sleaze." Essentially, the stylistic elements and characteristic signatures of the cultural movement have persevered, yet its inspirational focus has remarkably shifted; instead of drawing stimulus or incentive from its time of origin, the movement

[32] Pradeep, "What is kidcore?."

now dwells on contemporary pop culture and novel fiction to establish renovated creative grounds, resonating with patterns (a) and (f).

Seeing as it has recently integrated itself into common digital discourse, it comes as no surprise that media analysts and fashion critics on the platform have come to assess the figurative space and time of the "indie sleaze" wave in respect to TikTok's everchanging trend cycle; as of recent developments, "indie sleaze" appears to fall somewhere between the end of the "It Girl" phase and the prime of the "Y2K" spell that has overtaken the platform by storm. In the numerical sense as opposed to that of the literary findings of this research set forth the following: with over eighty-six percent of creators using words insinuating the comeback or revival of the aesthetic, themes of legitimacy and validity found grounds of discussion in this respect accordingly.

Evidently, it is not only media outlets such as *Vogue* and *The Cut* that have sponsored this resurgence, sparking the interest of pattern (f), but it is rather the work of TikTok users including fashion analysts, pop culture critics, and "#fashiontok," the designated fashion niche on the platform, that have further facilitated this phenomenon. However, a theme that has held its ground since the very beginning of the aesthetic movement on TikTok proved sustainable with a hundred percent of videos falling under the lines of a particular community on the platform; essentially, it is that sense of a united front or shared mass identity that not only attracts users to these digitized movements, but it also simultaneously mimics the respective sense of semblance and "citizenry" present in subcultural phenomena.

Further legitimizing this revival, 66,6 percent of these videos referenced previous comprehensive research that depicts an inherent understanding and knowledge of the "indie sleaze" creative culture; pattern (h) addresses this development in its analysis respectively. Nonetheless, the latter has all been sustained and facilitated through the beacon of commodification with 73,3 percent of videos featuring silver accessories or chokers while another 93,3 percent showcased messy makeup looks to further appeal to the aesthetic and its respective audience, ultimately presenting in the pattern findings as (b) and (e).

Furthermore, patterns (c) and (d) are evidently supported by findings of a totality of users appealing to a particular digitized niche on TikTok through depicting "indie sleaze" as an immersive lifestyle as opposed to some temporary fad, optimizing its longevity and appeal in doing so. As for its not so fortunate successor, the "indie" aesthetic has assimilated fewer positive findings in its analysis. While 73,3 percent of videos use a parodical soundtrack in their reflection on the declining movement, 53,3 percent reference the term "phase" in their discussion of its prime reign over TikTok's trend cycle, ranging from early 2020 to late 2021; evidently, the latter holds true to pattern (g).

Despite such sardonic nostalgia targeting the abate aesthetic, all the analyzed videos maintain that the "indie" aesthetic has in fact appealed to a particular niche on the platform. Nonetheless, this finding must concede that (a) this sense of communal appeal may have preserved its influence from the aesthetics' prime, and (b) the context through which it has attained said appeal is no longer, in part, a positive association but rather a result of belittlement and mockery.

Furthermore, nichification central, TikTok, may in turn facilitate the digital space for haters of the aesthetic to forge their own respective community. Ultimately, this finding also seemingly dismisses internet trolls and their mechanisms in further platforming the aesthetic through humor-centered methodology. Nonetheless, another totality of videos analyzed depict the deteriorating aesthetic as a lifestyle of sorts yet eighty percent correlate it with a particular time frame, furthering the validity of patterns (d) and (e) in their due course.

Ultimately, 93,3 percent of videos entail the aesthetic is in fact outdated through their audio choice, in-video text, or even captions, optimally resurrecting pattern (g). Satire was a frequently noted facilitator of doing so with 93.3 percent of the videos utilizing its humorous means. Other eighty percent feature a significant deal of exaggeration to further accentuate their point and communicate a stark rejection of the days of the "indie" aesthetic subsequentially; both previously listed findings evidently appeal to pattern (g) yet again.

Conversely, the following findings have in fact shown that the days of the "hippie" aesthetic have successfully weathered the test of time since the late 1970s. Through 87,5 percent of the videos using the term "hippie" to establish a sense of mass identity, the aesthetic appeals to pattern (d). Likewise, in sixty percent of videos analyzed, the term "hippie aesthetic" was featured; the latter directs the movement in a more deviant direction of aestheticization and commodity, in turn appealing to patterns (a) and (b).

Through resurrecting patterns (c) and (d), all videos either embrace a sense of deviance from the mainstream or aid in normalizing particular behaviors to an audience through inherent romanticism respectively. Furthermore, regarding the commodification of the aesthetic, it is patterns (a) and (e) that are resonated with the most as eighty percent of videos feature midiskirts or harem pants while another 77,5 percent feature crystal necklaces in their content.

Ultimately, it is pattern (e) that is most targeted when addressing a curation of lifestyles or an employment of commercial elements, both equating to ninety-five percent each. The "coquette" aesthetic, however, is rather a fragmentation of intertextuality and cultural themes all together, embodying the lively manifestation of pattern (f). 72,5 percent of the videos under study used an Indie Pop or Alternative Pop song as their background music of choice; this too appeals to pattern (f). The use of the term "coquette" equated to a total eighty percent respectively, prompting patterns (b) and (e) into play.

As for its appeal to legitimacy themes, all videos fell within the borders of a particular community on TikTok while simultaneously normalizing certain behaviors in association with the aesthetic in an equal one hundred percent of others. Ultimately, the latter not only appeals to pattern (d), but it does so to pattern (b) as well for it ultimately curates a persona users can vicariously experiment and live through. Nonetheless, the reoccurring

theme of commodification proved prevalent in these "coquette" videos as 57,5 percent of videos featured lace, satin, or tulle articles of clothing in their composition.

Evidently, the marketing of a curated persona, pattern (b), and the assessment of essential human value, pattern (d), are prompted into question. On the likewise premise of commodified elements, another eighty percent of videos analyzed featured bows of all shapes and sizes, ranging from room décor and hair accessories to clothing embellishments and jewelry; essentially, it is pattern (e) that comes across the strongest here as the romanticized article in question serves as an extension of the ever-enchanting "coquette" and her dainty ways of life.

Regarding technical matters, the content under study employed a great deal of semiotics with 87.5 percent of videos featuring pastel pinks and powdery whites, the classic "coquette" colors, while others embraced a hyper-feminine red and untainted white instead, the signature color scheme of the fan-favorite "Americana." Finally, the "coquette" content analyzed featured abundant commercial elements that were frequently integrated, equating to ninety-five percent in total.

The previously listed findings optimally appeal to patterns (b) and (e) respectively as their subliminal associations adorn the aesthetic with palatable extensions of a romanticized and saturated lifestyle. The final digitized commercial movement that underwent analysis in this respective study happens to be the "femme fatale" aesthetic; picture red lipstick, black leather, and decorative pearls as a hyper-feminine manifestation clad in sex appeal. An approximate sixty-five percent of the videos employed the term "femme fatale" while other forty-five percent used "dark feminine" either in correlation with the latter, or as a substitute in its place.

The latter not only formulates a romanticized sense of mass identity, but it is also rather marketable to a younger impressionable audience as this inherent persona is essentially a seductress; she embodies power, mystery, and appeal simultaneously, presenting as patterns (b) and (c) in this study. In alignment with patterns (c) and (e), all the content featured encourages a deviance from the mainstream while 72,5 percent appeals to a particular community on the platform respectively.

Commodified elements such as candles, 30 percent, and makeup products, 82,5 percent, were also featured to further accentuate a romanticized image of the "femme fatale" accordingly; this ultimately calls patterns (b) and (e) into play as they both project a hyper-saturated lifestyle that users may immerse themselves in collectively. On the premise of lifestyles, it remains relevant to set forth that 97,5 percent of videos depicted the aesthetic as such; this not only appeals to pattern (e) for obvious reasons, but it also calls into question whether the "femme fatale" is a culturally appropriated pyramid scheme that furthers the objectification of women, or if it is simply a mere means of embracing sexuality, self-expression, and feminine energy through a vicarious persona, calling forth pattern (d).

Finally, seventy percent of the videos were classified into a particular niche, validating pattern (c) in their course. Cumulatively, as elaborated on in this discussion, this research has produced a foundation of frequented patterns that may be referenced as evaluative criteria upon assessing TikTok's aesthetic movement in respect to incorporated subcultures, aesthetic vitality, and trend fluidity; the data also provided may be of potential interest to future research. In essence, this research strives to serve greater academia and analytical discourse respectively.

Conclusion

Upon instigating a content analysis of TikTok aesthetic videos published within early October of 2021 to late November of 2022, this study establishes a foundation of patterns through the theoretical frames listed prior. Evidently, said patterns not only persist in terms of incorporation of subcultures, but they also facilitate their commodification into products of saturated and commercial properties respectively. The primary aesthetics of interest in this research are: (a) The "Femme Fatale" Aesthetic, (b) The "Coquette" Aesthetic, (c) The "Hippie" Aesthetic, (d) The "Indie" Aesthetic (2020-2021), and (e) The "Indie Sleaze" Aesthetic.

It remains important to acknowledge, however, that the respective findings of this study were facilitated through purposive sampling to curate a relevant selection of content that best serves the purpose of this research. On the premise of these findings, this study concludes that such inherent patterns bridge the path to digitization, revitalization, and delegitimization in some cases of these refashioned incarnations derived from subcultures respectively. Ultimately, this paper draws on TikTok's prominent cultural influence on the trajectory of contemporary pop culture.

Recommendations

When dabbling with matters of incorporated subcultures, it is recommended to study a broader selection of "indie" and "indie sleaze" aesthetic videos accordingly as the latter's revival is a relatively recent development in TikTok's digital discourse. Furthermore, a likewise foundation of reoccurring patterns may be established with respect to the music and audio sector of these TikTok videos.

Not only is a strong correlation eminent between certain music genres and their seemingly corresponding aesthetics, but the short span with which these videos depict their content selection can be elaborated on further with respect to viewer attention span, intensity, and speed as potential subthemes considering sound design. Another plausible pattern may be the frequent cross-referencing of pop culture snippets and soundtracks in these aesthetic videos; evidently, the latter can be subject to further research and required elaboration.

Bibliography

Adorno, Theodor. 2001. *The Culture Industry: Selected Essays on Mass Culture*. London and New York: Routledge.

Allen, Graham. "Intertextuality." n. d. https://www.litencyc.com/php/stopics.php?rec=true&UID=1229.

Bloch, Ernst, and Ritter, Mark. "Nonsynchronism and the obligation to its dialectics." *New German Critique* 11 (1977): 22–38. doi:10.2307/487802.

Dagalp, Ileyha and Hartmann, Benjamin J. "From 'Aesthetic' to Aestheticization: A Multi-layered Cultural Approach." *Consumption Markets & Culture* 25, No. 1 (2022): 1–20. doi:10.1080/10253866.2021.1935900.

Dana, Danai. "How Subcultures Became 'Aesthetics:' Menswear Has No Limits And It's All Gen Z's Fault." *mrporter.com*. July 26, 2022, https://www.mrporter.com/en-hk/journal/fashion/subculture-aesthetics-style-tiktok-gen-z-internet-trends-17519550.

Felski, Rita. 2000. *Doing Time: Feminist Theory and Postmodern Culture*. New York: NYU Press.

Goldstein, Judith. "The Female Aesthetic Community." *Poetics Today* 14, No. 1. (1993): 143–145, doi:10.2307/1773145.

Goulding, Christina, Saren, Mike and Canniford, Robin. "From Rebellion to Commodification: the Case of Goth." In *E - European Advances in Consumer Research Volume 7*, eds. Karin M. Ekstrom, and Helene Brembeck (Goteborg: Association for Consumer Research, 2005), 139–140.

Haenfler, Ross. 2014. *Subcultures: The Basics*. New York: Routledge

Hutcheon, Linda. 2003. *A poetics of postmodernism, history, theory, fiction*. New York: Routledge.

Jacobson, Jordan J. "Fast Forwarding the Past (on Pause): Daniel Lopatin's *Memory Vague* and the Hauntological

Aesthetic of Vaporwave." *The Velvet Light Trap* 90 (2022): 28–37, doi :10.7560/VLT9004.

Karizat, Nadia, Delmonaco, Daniel, Eslami, Motahhare, and Andalibi, Nazanin. "Algorithmic Folk Theories and Identity: How TikTok Users Co-Produce Knowledge of Identity and Engage in Algorithmic Resistance." *Proceedings of the ACM on human-computer interaction* 5, CSCW2 (2021), 1–44.

KhosraviShakib, Mohammad. "Marxist Feminism and Postmodernism." *Journal of Language and Culture* 1, No. 3 (2010): 28–30.

Kristeva, Julia. "'Nous deux' or a (hi)story of intertextuality." *Romanic Review* 93, No.1/2 (2002): 7–13.

Lee, Angela Y., Mieczkowski, Hannah, Ellison, Nicole B., and Hancock, Jeffrey T. "The Algorithmic Crystal: Conceptualizing the Self through Algorithmic Personalization on TikTok." *Proceedings of the ACM on Human-Computer Interaction, Vol. 6, No. CSCW2, Article No.: 543pp 1–22,* doi: 10.1145/3555601.

Mishrell, Kirk. 2012. Rockin' The Tritone: Gender, Race & The Aesthetics of Aggressive Heavy Metal Subcultures. Master Thesis, Georgia State University. doi:10.57709/2761634.

Murphy, Jill, and O'Riordan, Nicholas. "Deviate!." *Alphaville: Journal of Film and Screen Media,* 9 (2015): 1–5, doi:10.33178/alpha.9.00.

Pradeep, Malavika. "What is kidcore? Here's everything you need to know about the latest internet aesthetic." *screenshot-media.com.* February 24, 2021, https://screenshot-media.com/culture/internet-culture/what-is-kidcore/.

Schiele, Kristen, and Venkatesh, Alladi. "Regaining Control through Reclamation: How Consumption Subcultures Preserve Meaning and Group Identity After Commodification." *Consumption Markets & Culture* 19, No. 5: 427–443. doi:10.1080/10253866.2015.1135797.

Song, Wei. "Psychological Characteristics of Contemporary Young People from Tiktok Videos." *Psychiatria Danubina* 33, No. 7 (2021): 76–78.

Watts, Michael J. "Mapping meaning, denoting difference, imagining identity: dialectical images and postmodern geographies." *Geografiska Annaler: Series B, Human Geography* 73, No.1 (1991): 7–16, doi:10.1080/04353684.1991.11879612.

Contributors

Adebola Adewunmi Aderibigbe: College of Computing & Communication Studies, Bowen University, Iwo/Nigeria

Kinda Al Aridi: Communication and Information Studies/American University in Dubai

Ayodeji O. Awobamise: Associate Professor at Kampala International University, Uganda

Martin A. M. Gansinger: External Reader, Al Akhawayn University, Ifrane, Morocco, Taoist Health practitioner

Joel Isabirye: Assistant Professor at Kampala University, Uganda

Yosra Jarrar: Associate Professor at American University in Dubai

Tamara Khlefat: Graduated Student/Department of English Language and Literature/Faculty of Languages and Communication/American University of Madaba, Jordan

Ayman Kole: Assistant Professor at Onbeş Kasım Kıbrıs University, Cyprus. Director of Academic Research Institute

Gabriel E. Nweke: Head of Psychology Department at Girne American University, Cyprus.

Emre Daghan Tokgoz: graduated from Final International University, Cyprus, English Language Teaching program.

Shahla Ujayli: Associate Professor of Modern Arabic Literature & Cultural Studies/Department of Translation/Faculty of Languages and Communication/American University of Madaba, Jordan

www.ingramcontent.com/pod-product-compliance
Lightning Source LLC
LaVergne TN
LVHW101505200926
848483LV00001B/230